"Act the way you'd like to be, & soon you'll be the way you act."
— Geo W. Crane —

"All deception in the course of life is indeed nothing else but a lie reduced to practice, and falsehood passing from words to things."
— Robert Southey —

Rightness as Fairness

IBRAM Kendi

Stamped from the beginning

The definitive Hx / Racist Ideas in America

—Not Factual Based

Groups = but NIT Stating the same

= b/c human collection of imperfect individuals

"IF YOU ARE TOO CAREFUL, YOU ARE SO OCCUPIED [b'g so] that you ARE SURE to stumble OVER something."
— Gertrude Stein

"Double, double toil & trouble; Fire burn, and cauldron bubble."
— Wm Shakespeare

"The way to read a fairy tale is to throw yourself in."
W. H. Auden

"He that will NOT APPLY NEW REMEDIES MUST EXPECT NEW EVILS; for time is the greatest INNOVATOR."
— Francis Bacon

"MEASURE YOUR MIND'S height by the shade it CASTS!"
— Robert Browning

Rightness as Fairness

A Moral and Political Theory

Marcus Arvan
Assistant Professor, The University of Tampa, USA

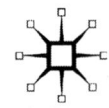

© Marcus Arvan 2016

All rights reserved. No reproduction, copy or transmission of this publication may be made without written permission.

No portion of this publication may be reproduced, copied or transmitted save with written permission or in accordance with the provisions of the Copyright, Designs and Patents Act 1988, or under the terms of any licence permitting limited copying issued by the Copyright Licensing Agency, Saffron House, 6–10 Kirby Street, London EC1N 8TS.

Any person who does any unauthorized act in relation to this publication may be liable to criminal prosecution and civil claims for damages.

The author has asserted his right to be identified as the author of this work in accordance with the Copyright, Designs and Patents Act 1988.

First published 2016 by
PALGRAVE MACMILLAN

Palgrave Macmillan in the UK is an imprint of Macmillan Publishers Limited, registered in England, company number 785998, of Houndmills, Basingstoke, Hampshire RG21 6XS.

Palgrave Macmillan in the US is a division of St Martin's Press LLC, 175 Fifth Avenue, New York, NY 10010.

Palgrave Macmillan is the global academic imprint of the above companies and has companies and representatives throughout the world.

Palgrave® and Macmillan® are registered trademarks in the United States, the United Kingdom, Europe and other countries.

ISBN: 978–1–137–54180–2

This book is printed on paper suitable for recycling and made from fully managed and sustained forest sources. Logging, pulping and manufacturing processes are expected to conform to the environmental regulations of the country of origin.

A catalogue record for this book is available from the British Library.

Library of Congress Cataloging-in-Publication Data

Names: Arvan, Marcus.

Title: Rightness as fairness : a moral and political theory / Marcus Arvan.

Description: New York : Palgrave Macmillan, 2016. | Includes bibliographical references and index.

Identifiers: LCCN 2015039323 | ISBN 9781137541802 (hardback)

Subjects: LCSH: Fairness. | Truth. | Ethics. | Political science—Philosophy.

Classification: LCC BJ1533.F2 A78 2016 | DDC 171/.2—dc23

LC record available at http://lccn.loc.gov/2015039323

For Maryana

"MORAL choices do not depend on personal preference & private decision but on right reason, + I would add, divine order."
— Basil Hume

diachronic — fixed + fluid, sensitive to process, development, evolution, + mutability.
synchronic — tries to "freeze" a given moment + describes what obtains at precisely that moment.

1N should, in every relevant XN:
aim to:
ACT ON i's that it is:
- INSTRUMENTALITY RATIONAL to act on (from a MOP stdpt)
- where or when your i's (vely, involty or semi-velty) are identical to those of any other b'g (human or non human)
- and where relevant XNS (defined recursively) are those it is I.R. to treat as such (from a MOP stdpt)

IN EVERY RELEVANT XN, one should aim to act ON i's (volty, involty or semi volty (that are instrumentally rational (from a MOP stdpt) which is the case when your i's are identical w/ those of any other b's (human or non-human)

and where relevant XNS are those from a MOP stdpoint that are I. Rational.

MOP replaces future selves — ones + others ???

Contents

Acknowledgments   xi

Introduction   1

1 **Ethics for the Twenty-First Century**   9
   1   Distinguishing truth from seeming truth   10
   2   Seven principles of theory selection   13
       2.1   Firm Foundations   14
       2.2   Internal Coherence   17
       2.3   External Coherence   18
       2.4   Explanatory Power   20
       2.5   Unity   21
       2.6   Parsimony   21
       2.7   Fruitfulness   23
   3   The case for instrumentalism   24
       3.1   The firmest foundation   24
       3.2   The promise of parsimony, unity, explanatory power, and fruitfulness   27
       3.3   Advantages over alternatives   30
            3.3.1   Advantages over intuitionism   30
            3.3.2   Advantages over reflective equilibrium   31
            3.3.3   Advantages over moral language analysis   32
            3.3.4   Advantages over constitutivism   33
            3.3.5   Advantages over second- and third-personalism   33
            3.3.6   Advantages over Sterba's dialecticalism   34
            3.3.7   Conclusion   35
   4   Disarming initial concerns   36
       4.1   The wrong kinds of reasons?   36
       4.2   Not a firm foundation?   36
       4.3   Unconvincing and artificial?   37
       4.4   Three promissory notes   38
            4.4.1   Not the wrong kinds of reasons?   38
            4.4.2   Firm foundations after all?   40
            4.4.3   Intuitive and convincing?   40
   5   Conclusion   41

2 The Problem of Possible Future Selves — 42
1 Our capacities to care about our past and future — 44
2 The problem of possible future selves — 47
   2.1 Possible futures — 51
   2.2 Possible psychologies — 53
   2.3 Possible choices — 56
   2.4 A very real problem — 64
3 Morality as the solution? — 65
4 Is the problem too contingent? — 67
5 Two nonsolutions — 71
   5.1 Nonsolution 1: probable futures — 71
   5.2 Nonsolution 2: diachronic motivational consistency — 72
6 Conclusion: an unsolved problem — 74

3 The Categorical-Instrumental Imperative — 75
1 Interests in diachronic cooperation — 79
2 Three types of interests — 85
   2.1 Involuntary interests — 86
   2.2 Semivoluntary interests — 88
   2.3 Voluntary interests — 90
3 The Categorical-Instrumental Imperative — 91
4 Just conscience? — 110
5 An intuitive solution to the problem of possible future selves? — 111
6 Conclusion — 115

4 Three Unified Formulations — 116
1 The Humanity and Sentience Formulation — 118
   1.1 Possible other-human-regarding interests — 121
   1.2 Possible nonhuman-animal-regarding interests — 124
   1.3 Possible sentient-being-regarding interests — 126
   1.4 Derivation of the Humanity and Sentience Formulation — 127
2 The Kingdom of Human and Sentient Ends Formulation — 128
3 Advantages over Kantian ethics — 130
   3.1 Firmer foundations — 131
   3.2 Greater internal coherence — 133
   3.3 Greater external coherence — 133
   3.4 Greater explanatory power, unity, and parsimony — 137
   3.5 Greater fruitfulness — 137
4 Conclusion — 138

5	**The Moral Original Position**		**140**
	1 Rawls' Original Position		141
	1.1 Rawls' Kantian rationale		142
	1.2 Rawls' reflective equilibrium rationale		143
	1.3 Rawls' public reason rationale		144
	2 Some common critiques		144
	2.1 Kantian critiques		144
	2.2 Reflective equilibrium critiques		145
	2.3 Public reason critiques		145
	3 The case for a Moral Original Position		146
	4 Corroborating the critiques		149
	4.1 Corroborating Kantian critiques		149
	4.2 Corroborating reflective equilibrium critiques		150
	4.3 Corroborating public reason critiques		151
	5 Conclusion		151
6	**Rightness as Fairness**		**153**
	1 Derivation of Four Principles of Fairness		155
	1.1 The Principle of Negative Fairness		155
	1.2 The Principle of Positive Fairness		166
	1.3 The Principle of Fair Negotiation		168
	1.4 The Principle of Virtues of Fairness		176
	2 Rightness as Fairness: a unified standard of right and wrong		178
	3 Rightness as Fairness in practice: principled fair negotiation		184
	3.1 Kant's four cases		186
	3.2 How numbers should count: trolleys, torture, and organ donors		188
	3.3 World poverty		194
	3.4 Distribution of scarce medical resources		196
	3.5 The ethical treatment of animals		198
	4 Conclusion		200
7	**Libertarian Egalitarian Communitarianism**		**202**
	1 Libertarianism, Egalitarianism, and Communitarianism		203
	1.1 Libertarianism: attractions and critiques		203
	1.2 Egalitarianism: attractions and critiques		204
	1.3 Communitarianism: attractions and critiques		205
	2 The case for Libertarian Egalitarian Communitarianism		206

3	Additional advantages	212
	3.1 (Qualified) fair negotiation over divisiveness	212
	3.2 Resolving the scope and requirements of justice	214
	3.3 Resolving the ideal-nonideal theory distinction	216
4	Conclusion	217

8 Evaluating Rightness as Fairness — 218
1. Firmer foundations — 218
2. Greater internal coherence — 220
3. Greater external coherence — 222
4. Greater explanatory power — 224
5. Greater unity — 226
6. Greater parsimony — 226
7. Greater fruitfulness — 227
8. Conclusion — 229

Notes — 230

Bibliography — 243

Index — 259

Acknowledgments

I thank Maryana Arvan, Robert Audi, Matt DeStefano, Steven Geisz, Dean Goorden, Rob Gressis, Moti Mizrahi, L.A. Paul, and several anonymous reviewers. I am also grateful to Brendan George, Esme Chapman, and the editorial team at Palgrave Macmillan for believing in the project, and for their support.

Introduction

There was a time when ancient Greek cosmologists disagreed profoundly about the fundamental nature of the physical world. Some argued that everything is ultimately made of fire, some that everything is air, others that everything is water, others that everything is made of indivisible 'atoms', still others that everything is 'the boundless,' and so on.[1] Fortunately, that time is past. Although physics is still incomplete, we now know that the visible matter of our universe is composed of subatomic particles such as quarks and electrons interacting via other force-carrying particles.[2]

Similarly, there was a time in the early-to-mid-twentieth century when psychologists disagreed profoundly about the nature of the human mind. Behaviorists argued that all behavior is the result of reward and punishment, Freudians that it is the result of subconscious drives interacting with the 'Ego' and 'Superego', Instinct Theorists that it is the result of hardwired instincts, Humanists that it is the result of a drive to 'self-actualize', and so on.[3] Fortunately, that time is past as well. Although empirical psychology is still very incomplete, there are now many well-known, established facts about psychology confirmed by rigorous scientific methods.

Finally, there was a time when philosophers disagreed profoundly about the nature of morality. Some argued that moral statements express beliefs that can be true or false; others denied it, claiming that moral statements merely express emotional attitudes.[4] Some argued that there are objective, 'mind-independent' moral facts.[5-6] Others argued that there are objective moral facts, but that they are mind-dependent – with some arguing that moral facts depend on reason alone,[7-11] and others arguing that moral facts depend critically on desire or emotion.[12] Still others argued that morality is not objective at all, but rather relative to individuals or cultures.[13-15] And, of course, others argued that there are no moral facts, holding that morality is little more than a myth.[16-17] Further, of those who held that morality is objective, some argued that there is a fundamental moral principle – with some defending a consequentialist principle that morality is a matter of producing optimal outcomes,[18-21] others a deontological, Kantian principle that morality is not a matter of producing outcomes but rather a matter of acting on universalizable principles[7, 23-24], still others a principle that morality is a matter of acting in ways that other people cannot 'reasonably reject,'[25] others that morality is a matter of acting as a morally virtuous person would,[26-27] and so on. Finally, others denied that there is any fundamental moral principle, with some arguing that morality consists of several competing values or principles[28-29], and others that morality is objective but cannot be reduced to any general principles.[30]

Unfortunately, this time is not yet past. It is the present. Moral philosophers not only disagree profoundly over morality's nature, but also over the very methods we should use to investigate it. Whereas some argue that moral philosophy should be based on our 'considered moral beliefs,'[31-34] others hold it should be based on 'self-evident' moral truths,[35-36] others still that it should be based on the 'face-value' of our moral language, experience, or practices,[5-6, 37-39] still others that it should be based on a theory of normativity,[7-9, 41] or practical deliberation,[7-10, 23-24, 41-42] and so on.

This book aims to help moral philosophy do better. Chapter 1 argues that moral philosophy currently lacks any reliable method for distinguishing what is actually true about morality from what merely 'seems true' to some investigators but not to others, and that seven principles of theory selection adapted from the sciences comprise the best available method for reliably distinguishing these things. Chapters 2–8 then use these principles to defend a new moral theory, Rightness as Fairness – a theory that I argue is not only based on firmer evidential foundations than predominant moral theories, but also reconciles a variety of traditionally opposed moral frameworks (consequentialism, deontology, contractualism, and virtue ethics) and normative political frameworks (libertarianism, egalitarianism, and communitarianism). I further argue that this theory provides a fruitful new method of 'principled fair negotiation' for resolving applied moral questions, and that it coheres with and explains a variety of empirical findings related to moral deliberation and responsibility. Indeed, as we will see, this book's argument for Rightness as Fairness is based on a very specific type of interest regarding our future that virtually all of us possess – interests that have been empirically demonstrated to prompt improvements in human moral and prudential behavior when made salient.[43-46]

Chapter 1, 'Ethics for the Twenty-First Century,' argues that moral philosophy needs a method for reliably distinguishing what is actually true about morality from what merely 'seems true' to some investigators but not others, and then defends the following seven principles of theory selection as the best available method for doing so:

Seven principles of theory selection

1. *Firm Foundations*: theories based on common human observation – or observations that are taken to be obvious, incontrovertible fact by all or almost all observers – should be preferred over theories based on controversial observations that may seem true to some investigators but not to others.
2. *Internal Coherence:* all things being equal, and subject to Firm Foundations, theories with fewer or no internal contradictions should be preferred over theories with more.
3. *External Coherence*: all things being equal, and subject to Firm Foundations, theories cohering with more known facts and observations should be preferred over theories cohering with fewer.
4. *Explanatory Power*: all things being equal, and subject to Firm Foundations, theories explaining more facts and observations should be preferred over theories explaining fewer.
5. *Unity*: all things being equal, and subject to Firm Foundations, theories unifying disparate phenomena, showing how they have a common explanation, should be preferred over theories providing more fragmentary explanations.
6. *Parsimony*: all things being equal, and subject to Firm Foundations, theories that successfully explain phenomena with fewer facts or entities should be preferred over theories explaining the same phenomena with more.
7. *Fruitfulness*: all things being equal, and subject to Firm Foundations, theories solving more existing theoretical or practical problems should be preferred over theories solving fewer.

Finally, Chapter 1 argues that these principles strongly support founding moral philosophy on a simple theory of normative rationality universally recognized in everyday life and the history of moral philosophy:

> **Instrumentalism:** if one's motivational interests would be best satisfied by ϕ-ing, then it is instrumentally rational for one to ϕ – that is, one instrumentally ought to ϕ.

Rather than presupposing that instrumentalism is the one true theory of normativity, I argue that insofar as it is the most widely accepted theory of normative rationality available – one commonly recognized both in everyday life and in the history of moral philosophy – it is the only *starting point* for moral philosophy that satisfies Firm Foundations and promises maximal explanatory power, unity, and parsimony.

Chapter 2, 'The Problem of Possible Future Selves', argues that when instrumentalism is combined with several other known facts – facts about how we can care about their future and past – the result is an oft-encountered problem for which there is no known solution: the problem of possible future selves. In brief, the problem of possible future selves is that, all too often – when we are uncertain about what to do, or we are tempted to violate moral norms – we want to *know* the interests of our future selves. Further, when the future comes, our future selves often wish our past selves had known their future interests. We often find ourselves regretting our actions precisely because, when the future unexpectedly turns out ways we do not want, our present and future selves both wish our present selves could know their future. Yet, Chapter 2 argues, there currently exists no adequate solution to this problem. It can neither be solved by probabilistic decision-theory, nor by invoking a non-instrumental requirement of rationality that one's selves have consistent motivational interests across time.[47]

Chapter 3, 'The Categorical-Instrumental Imperative', then argues that because our present and future selves can have three different types of interests – 'involuntary' interests that just happen to them, 'semivoluntary' interests that they can experience themselves as having some control over, and 'voluntary' interests that they experience themselves as having full voluntary control over – the problem of possible future selves can be solved if, and only if, our present and future selves voluntarily cooperate with one another to act on the following principle:

The Categorical-Instrumental Imperative: voluntarily aim for its own sake, in every relevant action, to best satisfy the motivational interests it is instrumentally rational for one's present and every possible future self to universally agree upon given their voluntary, involuntary, and semivoluntary interests and co-recognition of the problem of possible future selves, where relevant actions are determined recursively as actions it is instrumentally rational for one's present and possible future selves to universally agree upon as such when confronted by the problem – and then, when the future comes, voluntarily choose your having acted as such.

Although this is an admittedly complicated principle, I show through several examples that it embodies a commonsense idea that many of us already attempt to approximate in real-life: the aim of being fair to ourselves, advancing our present interests while 'not putting our future in jeopardy.'

Chapter 4, 'Three Unified Formulations', shows that the Categorical-Instrumental Imperative is a distinctly moral principle: one requiring us to seek a universal agreement with our future selves on the supposition that our interests could be identical to those of any possible human being or nonhuman sentient creature. I show this by explicating the Categorical-Instrumental Imperative's central notion of one's 'possible future selves,' arguing that although it may be unlikely that one's future self may identify their interests with the interests of other human or nonhuman beings, the mere possibility that one will makes it rational to interpret the Categorical-Instrumental Imperative as follows:

> **The Humanity and Sentience Formulation:** voluntarily aim for its own sake, in every relevant action, to best satisfy the motivational interests it is instrumentally rational for one's present and every possible future self to universally agree upon given co-recognition that one's voluntary, involuntary, and semivoluntary interests could be identical to those of any possible human or sentient being(s), where relevant actions are determined recursively as actions it is instrumentally rational for one's present and possible future selves to universally agree upon as such in cases where one's present self wants to know and advance their future interests – and then, when the future comes, voluntarily choose your having acted as such.

Next, I show that when this formulation is combined with the first, we get the following, third formulation:

> **The Kingdom of Human and Sentient Ends Formulation:** voluntarily aim for its own sake, in every relevant action, to abstract away from the interests (or ends) of particular human or nonhuman sentient being(s), acting instead on interests (or ends) it is instrumentally rational for all human and nonhuman sentient beings to universally agree to share given their different voluntary, involuntary, and semivoluntary interests, where relevant actions are determined recursively as actions it is instrumentally rational for one's present and possible future selves to universally agree upon as such in

cases where one's present self wants to know and advance their future interests – and then, when the future comes, voluntarily choose your having acted as such.

Finally, Chapter 4 notes some broad similarities between these principles and Immanuel Kant's three formulations of his moral principle, the categorical imperative[48], but argues that my Categorical-Instrumental Imperative's three formulations are preferable to Kant's theory on all seven principles of theory selection defended in Chapter 1.

Chapter 5, 'The Moral Original Position', argues that the Categorical-Instrumental Imperative's truth-conditions – and therefore, what it requires of us – can be modeled by a hypothetical thought-experiment similar to the 'original position' that John Rawls famously defends as a method for deriving principles of justice[49]: a *Moral Original Position* where one deliberates a behind a 'veil of ignorance' that requires one to deliberate as if one's interests could turn out to be identical to any possible human or nonhuman sentient being.

Chapter 6, 'Rightness as Fairness,' then derives the following Four Principles of Fairness from the Moral Original Position:

The Principle of Negative Fairness: all of our morally relevant actions should have as a guiding ideal, setting all costs aside, avoiding and minimizing coercion in all its forms (coercion resulting from intentional acts, natural forces, false beliefs, and so on), for all human and nonhuman sentient beings, for its own sake.

The Principle of Positive Fairness: all of our morally relevant actions should have as a guiding ideal, setting all costs aside, assisting all human and non-sentient beings in achieving interests they cannot best achieve on their own and want assistance in achieving, for its own sake.

The Principle of Fair Negotiation: whether an action is morally relevant, and how the Principles of Negative and Positive Fairness and Virtues of Fairness (see below) should be applied factoring in costs, should be settled through an actual process of fair negotiation guided by the Principles of Negative Fairness, Positive Fairness, and Virtues of Fairness, where all human and nonhuman sentient beings affected by the action are afforded equal bargaining power to the extent that such a process can be approximated, and to the extent that cannot be, through a hypothetical process approximating the same, for its own sake.

The Principle of Virtues of Fairness: all of our morally relevant actions should aim to develop and express stable character traits to act in accordance with the first three principles of fairness, for its own sake.

These principles are then combined into the following single analysis of moral rightness:

Rightness as Fairness: an action is morally right if and only if it satisfies the Four Principles of Fairness, that is, if and only if it is (A) is morally relevant, (B) has coercion-avoidance and minimization, assisting human and nonhuman sentient beings to achieve interests they cannot best achieve on their own and want assistance in achieving, and the development and expression of settled dispositions to have these ends, as at least tacit ideals, and (C) is in conformity with the outcome of an actual process of fair negotiation approximating all human and sentient beings affected by the action being motivated by the above ideals and having equal bargaining power over how those ideals should be applied factoring in costs, or, if such a process is impossible, the outcome of a hypothetical process approximating the same, where moral relevance is determined recursively, by applying (B) and (C) to the question of whether the action is morally relevant.

Other deontic notions – moral wrongness, permissibility, indeterminacy, and the supererogatory – are then defined in a similar way. Chapter 6 also argues that these principles not only reconcile a variety of traditionally opposed moral frameworks – consequentialism, deontology, contractualism, and virtue ethics – but also entail a compelling, transformative theory of applied moral reasoning: a method of *principled fair negotiation* according to which answers to applied moral issues cannot be soundly arrived at by merely 'thinking through' or debating issues, as in a classroom or journal article, but must instead be created through fair, real-world negotiation based on the ideals of negative and positive fairness, and weighing them against costs and conflicts. Chapter 6 illustrates the plausibility and fruitfulness of this analysis by briefly applying Rightness as Fairness to Kant's famous four cases from *Groundwork of the Metaphysics of Morals*, as well as to trolley cases, torture, organ transplants and the distribution of scarce medical resources, world poverty, and the ethical treatment of animals.

Chapter 7, 'Libertarian Egalitarian Communitarianism,' then argues that Rightness as Fairness also reconciles several traditionally opposed political theories – libertarianism, egalitarianism, and communitarianism – into a coherent whole. Specifically, Rightness as Fairness is shown to entail that libertarianism, egalitarianism, and communitarianism all involve legitimate moral ideals, but take these ideals too far, holding them as non-negotiable requirements. According to Rightness as Fairness, justice is a matter of negotiating the proper balance between these opposing ideals on an ongoing basis, in light of real-world facts and contexts. As such, Chapter 7 argues, Rightness as Fairness also entails a compelling, transformative analysis of political debate: political debate requires *negotiation* between people committed to liberty, equality, and other values, rather than divisive 'standing on principle.'

Finally, Chapter 8, 'Evaluating Rightness as Fairness', argues that Rightness as Fairness fares better than its rivals across all seven of the principles of theory selection defended in Chapter 1. It is based on firmer foundations, and has greater internal and external coherence, explanatory power, unity, parsimony, and fruitfulness, than other predominant moral theories.

This book does not purport to be the final word on morality. As with all theories, problems are sure to remain, and mistakes sure to be made. Yet, despite this, I will argue that it is a worthwhile new word on the subject – indeed, one that succeeds substantially where other theories founder.

1
Ethics for the Twenty-First Century

This book argues that a new moral theory, Rightness as Fairness, is superior to existing theories. However, in order to argue this effectively, we need standards for theory comparison. When should we judge one moral theory to be superior to another?

Section 1 of this chapter argues that moral philosophy currently lacks any method for reliably distinguishing what is true about morality from what merely 'seems true' to some investigators but not to others. Section 2 then argues that the following seven principles of theory selection adapted from the hard sciences are the best method available for reliably accomplishing this, and thus, for comparing moral theories:

Seven Principles of Theory Selection

1. *Firm Foundations*: theories based on common human observation – or observations that are taken to be obvious, incontrovertible fact by all or almost all observers – should be preferred over theories based on controversial observations that may seem true to some investigators but not to others.
2. *Internal Coherence:* all things being equal, and subject to Firm Foundations, theories with fewer or no internal contradictions should be preferred over theories with more.
3. *External Coherence*: all things being equal, and subject to Firm Foundations, theories cohering with more known facts and observations should be preferred over theories cohering with fewer.
4. *Explanatory Power*: all things being equal, and subject to Firm Foundations, theories explaining more facts and observations should be preferred over theories explaining fewer.

5. *Unity*: all things being equal, and subject to Firm Foundations, theories unifying disparate phenomena, showing how they have a common explanation, should be preferred over theories providing more fragmentary explanations.
6. *Parsimony*: all things being equal, and subject to Firm Foundations, theories that successfully explain phenomena with fewer facts or entities should be preferred over theories explaining the same phenomena with more.
7. *Fruitfulness*: all things being equal, and subject to Firm Foundations, theories solving more existing theoretical or practical problems should be preferred over theories solving fewer.

Next, Section 3 argues that these principles strongly support founding moral philosophy on the following instrumental conception of normative rationality:

Instrumentalism: if one's motivational interests would be best satisfied by φ-ing, then it is instrumentally rational for one to do φ – that is, one instrumentally ought to φ.

Section 3.1 shows that instrumentalism enjoys virtually universal acceptance in everyday life and the history of philosophy, thus satisfying Firm Foundations. Section 3.2 shows that an instrumentalist moral philosophy also promises, all things being equal, to better satisfy the other principles of theory selection than alternatives. Section 3.3 then systematically compares instrumentalism to prominent alternatives, showing that an instrumentalist moral philosophy promises to best satisfy all seven principles of theory selection.

Finally, Section 4 defuses several possible concerns. Section 4.1 addresses the concern that instrumentalism can at best explain that it is prudent to obey moral norms, not their status *as* moral norms; Section 4.2 then responds to the concern that instrumentalism is not obviously true; and Section 4.3 addresses the concern that instrumental arguments for moral behavior cannot succeed given clear conflicts between morality and prudence.

1 Distinguishing truth from seeming truth

This book's introduction referenced several episodes from the history of science. First, I gave the case of ancient Greek cosmology, where some theorists argued that everything in the world is made of air, others that everything is made of fire, others that everything is made of water, and so on. Second, I discussed early-to-mid-twentieth century psychology, where some psychologists (Behaviorists) argued that all human behavior is the result of reward and punishment, others (Instinct Theorists) argued that all human behavior is the result of instincts, others (Freudians) that all human behavior is the result of interactions between subconscious drives, and so on.

Although some of these theories have been found to contain element(s) of truth,[1-2] we nevertheless look back at them mostly with bemusement. After all, instead of deriving the theories in question from careful observation and experiment – as mature sciences now do – the above theories were based on little more than what 'seemed true' to particular investigators. It seemed to Thales that everything must be made of water because water can change, to Anaximander that everything must be the 'boundless' because the universe can have no end, to Anaximenes that everything must be air, as in his view only air could explain things like fire, and so on.[3] Similarly, it seemed to Behaviorists that all behavior must be the result of reward and punishment, to Instinct Theorists that it must be the result of instincts, to Freudians as though it must be the result of subconscious sexual drives, and so on.

However, this is plainly no way for an epistemically responsible discipline to function. For what 'seems true' and what actually is true can be, and often have turned out to be, very different things. For instance, it seems true (and was believed for millennia) that the sun revolves around the earth. Similarly, it seems true, and was widely believed by Newtonian scientists, that space and time must be absolute, rather than relative to observers. And it even seems true to some people today that human beings could not have evolved from primates. Yet all of these 'seemings' are false. The sun does not revolve around the earth; space and time have been empirically demonstrated to be relative to observers;[4-7] evolution is highly confirmed, and so on.

Because what 'seems true' and what is actually true can be very different things, mature sciences have insisted that their practitioners obey rigorous evidential standards: standards that reliably distinguish truth from 'seeming truth.' The most basic of these standards is that of *common observation*. The sciences insist that theories not be based merely on what 'seems true,' but rather on the basis of observations and experiments that anyone can verify/replicate.[8] Anyone can, in principle, run experiments on gravity, biological cell functions, and so on, to test whether existing theories make true predictions. Or consider cholesterol-lowering drugs. It does not merely 'seem' as though these drugs lower cholesterol. Their cholesterol-lowering properties have been demonstrated repeatedly in rigorous, controlled experiments and observational studies.

Moral philosophy, however, does not obey the standard of common observation. Rather than insisting that moral theories be based on facts that virtually everyone recognizes to be true, moral philosophers commonly base arguments and theories on premises that 'seem true' to some but not all. For example, utilitarians tend to argue that happiness is the only thing of intrinsic value,[9] yet many others doubt utilitarian premises. Kantians argue that it is not happiness but our *humanity* or 'rational nature' that has intrinsic, unconditional value.[10-16] Yet Kantian premises do not seem true to others—among others, those who question Kantian analyses of practical rationality and moral psychology,[17-21] as well as moral pluralists, to whom it seems that there is no sole thing of intrinsic value, but rather many different things.[22-23] Still others have attempted to base moral philosophy on 'self-evident' moral judgments or intuitions.[25-28] For instance, following Moore, Bambrough writes,

> My proof that we have moral knowledge consists essentially in saying, 'We know that this child, who is about to undergo what would otherwise be painful surgery, should be given an anaesthetic before the operation. Therefore we know at least one moral proposition to be true.'[29]

Unfortunately, these types of claims do not seem obviously true to everyone, either. Moral skeptics[30-32] and anti-realists[33] think morality is far from self-evident. Nor, apparently, does morality seem self-evident to the would-be child-torturer, who might think there is no reason at all why a child undergoing an operation should be given anesthetic. Further, as we see as far back as Plato's dialogues (where many characters repeatedly express skeptical doubts about morality[34-35]) and in recent studies indicating that people commonly express less 'objectivity' to moral claims than nonmoral claims,[36] moral skepticism of varying degrees is common.

Similar problems plague other approaches to moral philosophy. Some theorists argue that moral philosophy should respect the 'face value' of moral language, moral experience, or moral practices.[37-41] Yet many others deny this. For one, moral anti-realists often argue that whatever the face value of moral language or practice may be, moral facts do not exist.[33] Indeed, 'non-cognitivists' such as expressivists[42] and quasi-realists[43] hold that while the face value of moral language may appear realist, these appearances are illusory: moral language merely expresses emotional or evaluative attitudes. Finally, other theorists contend that moral philosophy should be based on none of the above, but should simply draw 'our settled beliefs and convictions' about morality into greater coherence.[44-47] Yet the problem with coherence-based approaches to philosophy are well known: settled beliefs and convictions, no matter how coherent they may be, may be systematically mistaken.[48] People once had settled beliefs and convictions that the world is flat, that Earth is the center of the Solar System, and so on – and yet all of these settled beliefs and convictions turned out false.

Now again, individual theorists sometimes claim that they have finally discovered a reliable method for distinguishing genuine truth from 'seeming truth.' G.E. Moore famously argued that moral philosophy must be based on our moral intuitions 'to possibly pretend to be scientific,'[49] Kant argued morality must be derived from pure practical reason,[11] and so on. Yet, in every case, the methods these theorists defend for distinguishing truth from seeming truth are considered by other theorists or nonphilosophers to not be obviously true.

This is an unfortunate situation. It is bad epistemically because there is no clear, established, known-to-be-reliable method for distinguishing when moral philosophy is getting at genuine truth, as opposed to what merely 'seems true' to this or that theorist. It is bad practically because, to the extent we lack such a method, it is difficult to make a compelling case to the public – to our students, friends, and other nonphilosophers – that moral philosophers actually understand morality. Why should the public trust moral philosophers when we defend such a wide variety of views about morality without any known-to-be-reliable method for distinguishing which view is correct?

Some might suggest that this is just the nature of philosophy – that unlike the sciences, which are based on commonly observable facts, predictions, and experiments, all we have to go on in moral philosophy are how things 'seem' to us (and, of course, arguments based how things seem). Perhaps. But I will now argue that we can do better.

2 Seven principles of theory selection

Moral philosophy clearly cannot be based on precisely the same methods as the physical sciences. The sciences test descriptive hypotheses – about gravity, cell growth, and so on – against measurable observations. Moral philosophy cannot, however, be tested against predictions of how the world behaves – for moral philosophy is not concerned with describing the world, but with what *ought* to be: with how people ought to behave. Sciences, in a word, are descriptive, moral philosophy normative. Yet although moral philosophy deals with a different kind of phenomena than the sciences, the sciences utilize several reliable methods for distinguishing truth from 'seeming truth' that can, and should, be extended to moral philosophy.

2.1 Firm Foundations

Let us begin by thinking about what distinguishes epistemically respectable sciences from 'pseudoscience.' As we saw earlier, modern science insists, above all else, that theories be based on common observation: on *observational facts* that virtually everyone recognizes as such. Physics and chemistry are founded on common observation of ordinary objects and substances. We all see tables, chairs, people, water, and air – and modern physics and chemistry make predictions about how these things behave. It is not merely this or that investigator who can remove a small piece of skin from a person, put it under a microscope, and test modern biology's hypotheses about how skin cells function. Anyone can look through a microscope and observe whether the predictions the theory makes are correct. Similarly, it is not merely the physicist who can observe clocks flown at immense speeds to test whether Einstein's predictions about the relativity of time are correct. Anyone who looks at such a clock can see whether it has slowed down relative to clocks on Earth, as Einstein's theories predict.[50]

Modern sciences are epistemically respectable for this reason. Although the nature of truth is notoriously contentious,[51] it is by insisting that theories be based on common observation – on observations that virtually all observers take to be incontrovertible fact – that the sciences are built upon 'verifiable facts': facts we can all see, hear, touch, or taste. As Kuhn put it: 'First, a theory should be accurate: within its domain...consequences deducible from a theory should be in *demonstrated agreement* with the results of existing experiments and observations.'[52] Now, of course, there are even more stringent possible epistemic standards than this. Descartes famously argued that because even our senses may be mistaken, we should base philosophy and science on premises that are beyond all possible doubt.[53] Yet this Cartesian standard appears impractical, calling into question all knowledge of the external world.[54] Consequently, the sciences are not built on Cartesian standards, but on the standard of common observation. We say that physics, chemistry, biology, and psychology get at the truth – rather than mere seeming truth – because they make predictions that

Ethics for the Twenty-First Century 15

anyone can verify or falsify.[9,55] In contrast, astrology, creationism, and parapsychology are pseudosciences precisely because they fail to respect the norm of common observation and are instead based merely on how things 'seem' to a given investigator.[56]

It is precisely by insisting upon this standard that, after scuffling around in interminable debates – debates in ancient Greek cosmology and early-to-mid-twentieth century psychology – the sciences have finally made demonstrable progress. Although there are of course still science denialists, the public today generally trusts the sciences because of its reliance on common observation. Physics is no longer this or that theorist's opinion about how things 'seem.' Physicists can show us how things work: they can show us that clocks slow down when flown in a fast airplane, how GPS satellites require the truth of Einstein's theories of relativity to work, and so on.[4-7] Similarly, psychologists no longer merely claim that all human behavior is explained by reward or punishment, or instincts, and so on: they can show us through experiments and data collection the extent to which human behavior is influenced by reward, punishment, instincts, subconscious drives, and so on.

This is no accident. The truth is not what 'seems true' to this or that investigator. Setting aside skeptical arguments on whether we can know anything about the external world (which we need not examine here), our standard for truth in everyday life and the sciences is what people in general can verify through common observation. When we say it is true that there is a stop sign on the corner of such-and-such street, we mean that anyone can see it there. When we say it is true that human, animal, and plant bodies are composed of cells, we mean that anyone who looks under a microscope at human, animal, or plant tissue can see the outlines of cells right before their own eyes. And again, there is a good epistemic purpose to this standard. Insisting that theories be based on facts verifiable by common observation – facts that all people recognize to be facts – precludes bias. It prevents the theory from being based merely on how things seem to this or that investigator, tying the theory to facts commonly observable by anyone.

Consequently, if we want moral philosophy to have a reliable standard for distinguishing genuine truth from 'seeming truth' – and for the reasons given above, we clearly should – we should insist upon the same standard. We should insist, above all else, that moral philosophy conform to the following principle:

1. *Firm Foundations*: theories based on common human observation – or observations that are taken to be obvious, incontrovertible fact

16 Rightness as Fairness

by all or almost all observers – should be preferred over theories based on controversial observations that may seem true to some investigators but not to others.

Some readers may have concerns about the notion of 'facts recognized by common observation.' First, might different investigators be likely to interpret different things as such? Consider technical debates over 'observation' in the philosophy of science, in which some philosophers argue that we observe things through microscopes and others deny it.[57–58] Second, some might wonder whether any observations are recognized as incontrovertible facts by virtually all observers. For consider once again skepticism about the external world, which holds that none of our beliefs about the external world are obvious, incontrovertible facts.

Can Firm Foundations be formulated in a precise, adequate manner? My reply is that we have compelling epistemic and practical grounds for interpreting the principle intuitively, in a manner as close as possible to its interpretation in the hard sciences. For, setting aside skepticism and theoretical questions about the nature of observation, the sciences are based on an intuitive, comparative understanding of 'common observation' according to which the more widely an observation is shared, the more appropriate it is to take it as a genuine observation. Since, setting skeptical concerns aside, we all see ordinary macrophysical objects – such as tables and chairs – and anyone can see the linings of cell walls in microscopes and the like, the sciences take these *as* observations. By a similar token, I submit that Firm Foundations should be understood in the same way in moral philosophy: as requiring moral philosophy to be based on premises that virtually everyone is apt to accept as obviously true. Now, some philosophers might doubt whether there are any such premises to be found. This book will argue, however, that there are such premises.

Before proceeding, let us summarize the epistemic and practical advantages of Firm Foundations, thus understood.

First, the general epistemic problem we face in moral philosophy is this: we lack any clear, known-to-be-reliable method for distinguishing actual truth from 'seeming truth.' There are a variety of conflicting moral theories and arguments based on conflicting premises – theories that 'seem based in truth' (or likely truth) to their proponents, but which do not seem that way to their critics. Firm Foundations promises a clear, reliable method for resolving this problem. It requires basing moral philosophy not on how things 'seem' to individual investigators, but on facts recognized as such by common human observation. It is only by respecting Firm Foundations – by basing moral philosophy on facts attested to by virtually all observers – that we can reliably ensure that moral philosophy is based on truth rather than 'seeming truth.'

Second, Firm Foundations has practical advantages. Broadly speaking, the general public pays attention to and respects the sciences. Although there are science skeptics, ordinary people rely heavily on science, recognizing its value. We commonly recognize computers, medications, airplanes, and other things we depend upon to be made possible by scientific inquiry. Further, scientific results are often touted and widely distributed in the media (including social media), shared publicly as discoveries of new facts. Moral philosophy, on the other hand – as any instructor of moral philosophy can tell you – appears to exist mostly outside of the general public's awareness. Unlike physics, which can show the public, 'Here are the particles physical things are made of,' or biology, which can show the public, 'Here is the stuff that cells are made of,' moral philosophers cannot do the same. There just is not enough consensus in moral philosophy for philosophers to be able to point to a particular theory and say, 'Here it is: a clear demonstration of what morality is and why you, the general public, should care.' Unless and until moral philosophy is based on Firm Foundations – unless and until we found moral philosophy on observations that anyone is apt to accept as true – this will likely continue to be our fate. Firm Foundations is necessary for arriving, as the sciences have, at a scholarly consensus about facts that can be presented to the public as such.

2.2 Internal Coherence

It is widely accepted in philosophy and science that, all things being equal, theories should be internally consistent, not involving contradictions.[59-60] Contradictions, after all, cannot be true – at least not according to commonsense and standard logic.[61] Thus, it seems, true theories should not involve any. However, freedom from internal contradiction is not always epistemically advantageous. Sometimes theories with internal contradictions can be more accurate on the whole – explaining more observations, accounting for more truths – than theories without any. Consider Newtonian physics and the two theories that supplanted it: quantum mechanics and Einstein's Theory of Relativity. Although Newtonian physics is internally consistent, it fails to cohere with a variety of observations predicted by quantum mechanics[62] and relativity.[4-7] Yet although quantum mechanics and relativity are universally recognized as our best theories of fundamental physics for these reasons, there is also no known way to render them jointly consistent.[63] Consequently, our 'single best theory of physics' at present – the conjunction of quantum mechanics and relativity – arguably contains internal contradictions. While this is admittedly regarded as a problem – one that physicists are attempting to solve – quantum mechanics and relativity are still superior, on the whole, to Newtonian theory, despite their possible inconsistency.

Accordingly, when comparing theories, internal consistency should not be taken as an absolute end in itself. It should be weighed against other epistemically relevant features of theories, such as the other principles this chapter defends.

As such, the following principle of theory selection should be applied to moral philosophy:

2. *Internal Coherence:* all things being equal, and subject to Firm Foundations, theories with fewer or no internal contradictions should be preferred over theories with more.

2.3 External Coherence

Philosophers and scientists alike also commonly recognize the epistemic importance of external coherence, or coherence of theory with known facts and observations.[44,59–60,64] The epistemic reasons to prize external coherence are obvious: the more a theory fits with known facts and other observations, the more it coheres with our overall body of evidence. Consider the theory of evolution, which coheres with geological, fossil, radioactive, DNA, and other evidence. The fact that the theory coheres with many other things we know provides many lines of independent support for the theory. Similarly, consider Einstein's Theory of Relativity. Whereas Newton's theory of motion successfully coheres with a wide variety of known facts and observations – observations of the behavior of ordinary objects here on Earth – it fails to cohere with other known facts, such as Mercury's orbit[5], observations of the bending of light from distant stars[65], the slowing of clocks on a fast-moving object[50], and so on. It is precisely because it coheres with all of these independent facts and observations that Einstein's theory is accepted over Newton's.

Yet, although external coherence is epistemically important, it is also, like internal coherence, only qualifiedly so. Indeed, there is a critical difference between how empirical scientists understand the value of external coherence and the way that philosophers have traditionally understood it. Empirical scientists insist that external coherence be subsumed under Firm Foundations. One is not allowed in science to say that a theory has external coherence simply because it coheres with how the facts and evidence 'seem.' To see how, consider 'Young Earth Creation Science' – the doctrine which aims to fit observed facts (about fossils and the like) into the theory that the universe is only a few thousand years old (instead of the 13.8 billion years attested to by scientific observation). 'Young Earth Creation Scientists' hold that their theory coheres with the evidence as they see it: namely, the fact that the Bible seems true to them, and implies that the world is only a few thousand years old.[66] Yet this kind of 'external coherence' lacks epistemic value, for it assumes 'facts' (namely, that the Bible is true) that cannot be demonstrated through common observation. The sciences insist that external coherence is valuable only insofar as theories cohere with *observed* facts. Similarly, we should not want moral philosophy to externally cohere with how things 'seem' to us about morality, for as we have already seen, how things 'seem' can end up being false. Moral philosophy should not be in the business of cohering with preconceptions about morality any more than science should be about cohering with preconceptions about space and time or Biblical truth. The job of a good theory is to cohere with observed facts, not mere preconceptions. Thus, like science, moral philosophy should utilize the following principle:

3. *External Coherence*: all things being equal, and subject to Firm Foundations, theories cohering with more known facts and observations should be preferred over theories cohering with fewer.

One critical thing about this principle, as stated, is that – by indexing external coherence to Firm Foundations – it enables us to use facts to *reject* mere preconceptions. Two prime examples here are quantum mechanics and Einstein's Theory of Relativity. Both theories contradict things we 'thought we knew' about the world. Quantum mechanics tells us, contrary to 'commonsense,' that particles can be in two places at once, affect each other instantaneously at immense distances, and so on. Similarly, Einstein's theory tells us, contrary to 'commonsense,' that space and time are not absolute, but can shrink and stretch depending on gravity, one's frame of reference, and so on. These theories are now accepted as our best theories of physics because, although they contradicted things 'we thought we knew,' they are both supported by observational facts. Thus, although External Coherence is important – subject to the constraint of Firm Foundations – it is otherwise a defeasible principle: one which allows us to use observational facts to reject preconceptions about how space and time, or morality, 'seem.'

2.4 Explanatory Power

Scientists and philosophers of science also widely recognize the epistemic value of explanatory power, or how much a theory successfully explains.[44,59,64,67–69] Consider once again contemporary physics. Physicists currently recognize four known forces of nature: electromagnetism, weak nuclear force, strong nuclear force, and gravity. The Standard Model of particle physics (a branch of quantum mechanics) currently explains the first three of these forces through an exquisitely well-verified model of particle interactions.[70] However, the Standard Model fails to explain gravity, as well as observations suggesting the existence of 'dark matter' and 'dark energy.'[70] Currently, our most well-verified model of gravity is Einstein's General Theory of Relativity[4–7] – yet it too fails to explain dark matter or dark energy. Consequently, physicists today hold that the Standard Model and General Relativity together are the best physical theories we have. Yet, because both theories fail to explain some observations, physicists are also looking for theories that have greater explanatory power: a 'theory of everything' that explains the four known forces of nature as well as dark matter and dark energy. After all, the more observations a given theory successfully explains, the more observed truths the theory accounts for.

Accordingly, provided a moral theory conforms to Firm Foundations, Internal Coherence, and External Coherence, there are compelling epistemic grounds for moral philosophy to also conform to:

4. *Explanatory Power*: all things being equal, and subject to Firm Foundations, theories explaining more facts and observations should be preferred over theories explaining fewer.

Critically, this principle is also subsumed under Firm Foundations. We should not be looking for a theory that 'seems' to explain the moral domain, or one that explains 'our considered beliefs and convictions' about morality, as moral philosophers often do[44–46] – for again, how things 'seem,' and what 'our considered beliefs and convictions' are, may have no relation to truth. We should seek a moral theory that explains known facts and observations: namely, those that satisfy Firm Foundations. This restriction will prove crucial as we move forward. For just as scientific theories – such as Einstein's Theory of Relativity – sometimes overthrow dogmas about how things 'seem' to some people (Einstein's theory famously disproved the common belief that space and time must be absolute), so too will this book argue, on the basis of Firm Foundations, that we should reject some dogmas in moral philosophy: specifically, the view accepted by some[11,71] but not all[72-73] that morality must be 'categorical,' applying to all possible rational agents regardless of their motivational interests.

2.5 Unity

Scientists also widely recognize the importance of theoretical unification.[59,64,74-77] The reasons to prize unity are related to but not identical to those of explanatory power. Two theories may appear to successfully explain two separate classes of phenomena, yet a further theory unifying the two theories or phenomena would have even greater explanatory power, showing how they have deeper, single explanation.

Consider physics once again. On the one hand, the Standard Model of particle physics explains electromagnetism, the strong nuclear force, and the weak nuclear force.[70] On the other hand, relativity explains gravitation.[4] Yet, because these two theories are independent (and not clearly consistent), physicists are looking for a more unified theory – a theory of quantum gravity – to unify particle physics with the Theory of Relativity. Such a theory would have more explanatory power than the ones we currently have precisely by providing a unified, single explanation instead of the two separate explanations we currently have.

Similar considerations apply to moral philosophy. Suppose we had two separate theories – a theory of prudence and theory of morality – each of which seemed explanatorily successful in its own domain: one theory, that is, that explains prudence and another explaining morality. These might be good theories. Now suppose that there were a more unified explanation, one showing that prudence and morality both derive from a single normative source. This would show something new and important: namely, how morality and prudence can be unified. It would provide a deeper explanation of each. Thus, although it is in a sense an instance or corollary of Explanatory Power, we have compelling epistemic grounds to also utilize the following principle:

5. *Unity*: all things being equal, and subject to Firm Foundations, theories unifying disparate phenomena, showing how they have a common explanation, should be preferred over theories that provide more fragmentary explanations.

2.6 Parsimony

It is also widely recognized in philosophy and science that theories should aim to be ontologically parsimonious, utilizing the fewest number

22 Rightness as Fairness

of entities and properties necessary for successfully explaining the relevant target phenomena.[64,75,78] To see why, consider that it was once believed that a special life force – *élan vital* – was necessary to explain life. Today, biologists recognize no need to invoke such a mysterious force, as we can explain living systems in terms of observable phenomena: DNA, proteins, mitochondria, cell bodies, and so on. Given that we can explain life-processes without *élan vital*, we have no good reason to believe that such a strange force exists. Similarly, while it was once believed that a special substance – 'phlogiston' – was necessary to explain fire, we can now explain fire in terms of ordinary molecular interactions, without having to posit such a strange substance.

Thus, there are good epistemological and practical reasons to hold moral philosophy to the same standard, namely:

> **6. *Parsimony***: all things being equal, and subject to Firm Foundations, theories that successfully explain phenomena with fewer facts or entities should be preferred over theories explaining the same phenomena with more.

Indeed, one thing that concerns many moral philosophers today (myself included) is the willingness of some theorists to invoke entities and properties that are not clearly necessary to explain morality. For instance, hard-core moral realists argue that morality somehow consists of 'objective, mind-independent moral facts': facts that somehow exist in the world independently of any of us or our values.[37–38] Although realists argue we should believe in such facts, moral skeptics and anti-realists argue (correctly in my view) that such facts are not necessary to explain our moral beliefs, behavior, or practices.[31,79] And indeed, as Mackie famously argued, 'mind-independent moral facts' seem hopelessly 'queer': it is unclear how there could be such strange entities in the world.[80] 'Mind-independent moral facts' seemed to Mackie (as to me) hopelessly mysterious, and in much the same way as *élan vital* and phlogiston. If, on the contrary, we could explain all of morality in terms of well-known and established entities and properties – say, in terms of motivational goals and a concept of normative rationality – then, epistemically, we should prefer that theory over less parsimonious ones. A theory that fully explains phenomena in terms of widely observed and known entities and properties is clearly epistemically preferable to a theory that attempts to explain the same phenomena with additional, controversial entities and properties.

2.7 Fruitfulness

Finally, it is widely recognized in philosophy and science that good theories solve theoretical and practical problems.[44,59,81] Theories that run into theoretical and practical problems do so, generally speaking, because they fail to cohere with or explain observations. Theories that then solve those problems do so, generally speaking, because they uncover some unexpected truth(s). To see how, consider again a few instances from scientific history.

Ancient Ptolemaic astronomy – which held that the sun and other planets revolve around Earth – ran into notorious theoretical and practical problems. Ptolemaic astronomy could not explain certain properties of observed planetary motion without theorists having to draw in 'epicycles' for different planets: little orbits around their main orbits. These epicycles lacked any clear explanation – that is, until Copernicus and Kepler came along and showed that we can explain planetary orbits by simply reconceptualizing Earth and other planets as revolving around the sun. This not only resolved the theoretical problem of explaining the observed motions of heavenly bodies (no epicycles were necessary); it also resolved practical problems. Before Copernican astronomy, observers of celestial bodies had to draw in epicycles for each planet on the basis of painstaking observation. After the Copernican revolution, this problem simply went away. One could plot, and predict, a planet's future motion from its past behavior combined with the assumption it revolves around the sun in an ellipse.

Similarly, consider the many theoretical and practical problems solved by Einstein's Theory of Relativity. Newtonian theory made incorrect predictions about Mercury's orbit around the sun, presupposed a mysterious substance ('aether') pervading all of space, and so on. In contrast, Einstein's theory not only predicted Mercury's orbit, the bending of starlight around the sun, the slowing of clocks in fast-moving objects, and so on; it has also proved necessary for solving practical problems, such as synchronizing the precision clocks that modern-day GPS devices (including smart phones) require to function properly.[4-7]

Good theories solve theoretical and practical problems, in other words, because they get closer to the truth – predicting and explaining phenomena that were previously not well understood. Thus, epistemic and practical considerations favor applying the following principle to moral philosophy as well:

7. *Fruitfulness*: all things being equal, and subject to Firm Foundations, theories solving more existing theoretical or practical problems should be preferred over theories solving fewer.

As we will see throughout this book, moral philosophy faces a vast variety of theoretical and practical problems. The more of those problems a moral theory solves, provided it satisfies Firm Foundations, the better the theory.

3 The case for instrumentalism

Moral philosophers have investigated the nature of morality from countless perspectives. Some have attempted to found moral philosophy on the meaning of moral language,[82] the nature of reasons,[83–84] practical deliberation,[11–13,85–88] normativity,[12,88] moral sentiments,[89–91] and so on. Others have advocated broadly coherentist approaches, arguing that moral philosophy should not 'justify' morality but rather systematize and revise 'our considered moral beliefs.'[44–47] And again, others still have attempted to argue that morality is self-evident.[24–29] Yet, while many of these approaches are illuminating, we have already seen that they face a common problem. They are based on how things 'seem' to particular theorists, rather than facts established by common observation, as Firm Foundations requires. If moral philosophy is to reliably distinguish truth from 'seeming truth,' we should insist on Firm Foundations. But are there any such foundations? I will now argue that there are.

3.1 The firmest foundation

Moral philosophy is concerned with norms, that is, with how people ought to behave. Traditional moral norms tell us that people generally ought not to tell lies, steal, or kill for their own benefit – and that, at best, there may be exceptions to these rules. Consequently, if moral philosophy is to conform to Firm Foundations, it must be based on an analysis of norms that enjoys universal (or virtually universal) assent. Is there any such analysis? The answer is yes. When we look at everyday human life and the history of moral philosophy, we see that virtually everyone – ordinary adults, children, criminals, philosophers, and even the most hardened sociopath – accepts the following instrumental conception of normative rationality:

> **Instrumentalism:** if one's motivational interests would be best satisfied by ϕ-ing, then it is instrumentally rational for one to do ϕ – that is, one instrumentally ought to ϕ.

Consider to begin with ordinary, everyday conversations. Suppose you and I are in line at a restaurant attempting to decide what to eat. You know I am motivated to lose weight – that I have a motivational interest in losing weight. Suppose then that I were to ask you, 'What should I eat?' How would you answer? In ordinary conversation, the answer is unequivocal: you would speak to my interests. You might say, 'Given that you want to lose weight, you should probably get the salad. It is low in calories.' And if I were serious about losing weight, the right thing for me to say in reply is obviously, 'Of course, you're right. I should get the salad.' If, on the other hand, I told you that I was no longer interested in losing weight – but that I just wanted something delicious – you would be apt to respond differently, as in, 'In that case you should really get the burger. It's fantastic, and I know you like burgers.'

Instrumentalism is not only commonly appealed to in ordinary conversation: its verdicts are recognized by ordinary speakers as expressing normative truths. No competent speaker of language would say that if you want to win at the game of tennis, it is 'just a matter of opinion' whether you ought to hit the ball over the net onto the other side of the court. Everyone knows it is obviously true that you ought to hit the ball over the net – and for the simple reason that doing so is necessary for accomplishing what you want (winning the game). Similarly, no competent speaker would say that if you want to stay alive, it is just a matter of opinion that you should not jump off a high cliff without a parachute. We all recognize that it is obviously true that if you want to stay alive, you should do no such thing. And so on.

Indeed, we can see just how widely accepted the instrumental theory is by looking at children, criminals, and even psychopaths. I remember, as a young (eight-year-old) child learning to play baseball, my father teaching me that I should grip the ball with only my thumb and two fingers. At first, I did not understand why. It seemed to me that more fingers on the ball would impart more force to it. Still, he said to me, 'You should throw it this way. It will go farther.' I tried it, and I saw he was right. I wanted to throw the ball far, and gripping it with two fingers made it do exactly that. I saw right then and there why I should throw it with only two fingers. Throwing it that way was a better instrument for achieving what I wanted than throwing it with all of them. Similarly, consider the criminal. Suppose you were to ask the con man what you should do if you want to con people. The con man would presumably say something like the following, 'That's easy. If you want to con people, you should firstly gain the other person's confidence. Once they trust you, you can manipulate them to get just anything you want.' Or, indeed, consider a psychopathic serial killer. Suppose you were to ask them what you should do if you want to kill an innocent person and hide the body without getting caught. They would almost certainly say something like, 'The hiding the body is the easy part. You should buy a plastic tarp to prevent blood splatter evidence, utilize a bone saw to cut up the person into little pieces, use acid to dissolve flesh, and scatter the remains in a remote location that no one ever visits. Killing a person without a getting caught it is bit more difficult. But, if you really want to do it, you should...'

Instrumentalism is not only commonly recognized in everyday life. It has been repeatedly invoked by philosophers throughout history. First, the dominant theory of normative rationality even today – decision theory – understands rational action in purely instrumental terms: in terms of desirable outcomes.[92] Second, moral philosophers have attempted, time and again, to show that morality is in our interest, and for precisely this reason: we all share an instrumental conception of normative rationality. For example, if we look back at Plato's great dialogues, we see characters repeatedly asking Socrates to show them that obeying moral norms is in their interest. In Books I and II of Plato's *The Republic*, several characters – Thrasymachus, Glaucon, and Adeimantus – systematically question whether they should obey conventional moral norms, given that such norms often appear to be against our interests. Indeed, Thrasymachus famously maintains that true 'justice' is not conforming to conventional moral norms at all, but is simply whatever is actually in the interests of the stronger; and Glaucon and Adeimantus repeatedly press Socrates to show that justice is more advantageous than injustice.[34] We see similar questions in Plato's *Gorgias*, where Polus and Callicles both argue that power – not morality – is the good, because power is in a person's interest.[35] Importantly, instead of trying to change the subject to some other account of normativity, Socrates simply accepts his interlocutors' instrumental way of framing these questions – presumably because he recognized that he and his interlocutors shared the same instrumental conception of rational behavior. And Plato is far from alone. Aristotle founded his theory of morality on the notion that moral virtue is a necessary, constitutive means for realizing our highest end (or interest), *eudaimonia* ('happiness' or 'personal flourishing').[93] Several centuries later, Thomas Hobbes took instrumentalism as foundational in his great work *Leviathan*, arguing that it is plain that we call the objects of our motivations 'good' and objects of our aversion 'bad.'[94] Contemporary contractarians such as Gregory Kavka and David Gauthier have done the same.[95-96] Finally, even people who are skeptical about morality – even con men and psychopaths, not to

Ethics for the Twenty-First Century   27

mention many skeptical moral philosophers – recognize instrumental normative rationality.[71]

Here, then, is what we have. Ordinary adults commonly invoke instrumentalism in everyday conversation. Children do as well. So do criminals and psychopaths. And so do philosophers. In short, human observers in general – at least before doing any moral philosophy (more on this later) – accept instrumental norms as obvious truths. Indeed, although (as we will see in Section 4) some philosophers have attempted to cast some doubt on instrumental normativity, this book aims to show that we can explain these very doubts in instrumental terms – thus verifying the instrumental theory we all find attractive to begin, and undermining all philosophical considerations against it.

As such, I propose that instrumentalism – provided we can explain away doubts some philosophers may have about it (more on this later) – is the firmest foundation for moral philosophy. If we could show, on the basis of observed facts, that we have instrumental grounds for obeying moral norms, then, and only then, would we have a moral philosophy based on Firm Foundations that everyone (ordinary people, criminals, philosophers, and even psychopaths) could recognize to be grounded in fact. While I recognize and will turn to obvious worries about this approach in Section 3, the point for now is simply this: instrumentalism is clearly the most widely accepted conception of normativity available. Therefore, if philosophy could be derived from purely instrumental foundations, that would be a much firmer foundation than any other alternative.

Before proceeding, I want clarify that I am not claiming that instrumentalism is the one true theory of normativity. Perhaps there are other kinds of normativity: categorical normativity[12–16], teleological normativity[97], and so on. All I am arguing is that instrumentalism is the safest place – the firmest foundation – to begin moral philosophy from, as it is a conception of normative rationality that is universally recognized.

3.2 The promise of parsimony, unity, explanatory power, and fruitfulness

In addition to satisfying Firm Foundations, instrumentalism promises a parsimonious, unified, fruitful, explanatorily powerful foundation for moral philosophy.

Instrumentalism promises maximal parsimony in two respects. First, because it aims to reduce all of morality to prudence – analyzing what people (morally) ought to do purely in terms of instruments for achieving their motivational goals – instrumentalism posits only one

28 Rightness as Fairness

kind of normativity, and only one class of normative entities: instrumental normative facts. As we will see in later chapters, this is in stark contrast to most moral theories, which effectively divide the normative into two separate domains: the moral and the prudent. Instead of having to assert two fundamentally types of normativity and normative entities – prudential normativity and moral normativity – instrumentalism promises a parsimonious, unified analysis of normative rationality. Although we will return in Section 4 to concerns that instrumentalism cannot account for moral normativity adequately, the point for now is simply that if (as this book argues) it *can*, then such an account is favored on grounds of parsimony and unity. Second, in addition to affirming only one kind of fundamental normativity, instrumentalism can (I believe) *reduce* to widely recognized non-normative facts, thus achieving even greater parsimony. Allow me to explain.

Recently, some philosophers have argued that all normativity in some sense must be a 'queer,' primitive part of reality.[98] I believe this to be a mistake, and that our concept of instrumental normativity can be used reduce instrumental normativity to non-normative facts in a compelling fashion (I am, as such, proposing a 'Humean reduction' of the normative to non-normative[99–100]). Here is how. Consider what a person playing tennis is asking for when they say 'Why should I swing the racket that way?' According to the instrumental conception of normativity, all they are asking for is an explanation of how swinging the racket in a certain way is an optimal instrument for achieving their motivational interests. If you show them this – by, for instance, showing them that it enables them to hit the ball more accurately – they will say, 'Oh, now I see why I ought to swing that way.' There is a simpler way to put this. Our instrumental concept of normative rationality contains certain *satisfaction conditions*. That is, we say any sentence, 'X ought to do ϕ' is true in an instrumental sense when and only when ϕ is, at a purely descriptive, factual level, the optimal means for X to achieve their motivational goals. In other words, our instrumental concept of normativity identifies prudential normativity with certain purely natural, non-normative facts about the world: relationships between motivational interests and instruments for satisfying them. Instrumentalism, as such, enables us to avoid introducing primitive normative properties in our ontology. It bridges the famous 'is/ought-gap,' which holds that no 'ought' can ever be validly inferred from an 'is.'[101] On the semantic analysis just presented – according to which the satisfaction conditions for sentences involving the instrumental 'ought' concept identify 'oughts' with purely natural facts – to say that someone instrumentally ought to do ϕ just is to say that φ is (descriptively) the best means for them to achieve their interests. While some theorists may raise objections to this sort of reductive proposal – arguing that it 'eliminates' genuine normativity altogether, positing nothing more than descriptive facts about optimal means for achieving goals[102–103] – I have two replies to this concern. First, although I do not have room to defend the above reductive semantics in detail, others have done so,[104] arguing persuasively in my view that such a reduction does not eliminate normativity but rather reduces it to natural facts (as, on such a reduction, there are *true propositions* of the form 'X ought to φ'; it is just that the *truthmakers* for those propositions are natural facts about motivations and means). Second, and perhaps more importantly, little of substance in this book depends upon the success of such a reduction. All that my moral theory presupposes is that instrumentalism itself – whether it ultimately invokes primitive normative facts or ones reducible to natural phenomena – is a firm foundation: a conception of normative rationality that virtually everyone shares (which I have argued to be the case). At the end of the day, if this book showed nothing more than that morality is in our interests, that alone would (I think) be a finding of importance, regardless of the ontological status of instrumental normativity.

Further, instrumentalism promises maximal unity and explanatory power. Moral philosophy, broadly speaking, is inspired by several questions:

(A) What is morality?
(B) Why should we care about morality, obeying its norms?
(C) How are morality and prudence related?

Many approaches to moral philosophy answer (A) and (B) by severing any essential connection between morality and prudence, holding that morality is one thing and prudence another.[10–16,22–29,37–38] An instrumental derivation of morality – particularly the kind of derivation I will provide – bridges this gap, providing a unified answer to all three of the above questions. It promises to explain all of morality (qua A), and why we should obey morality's norms (qua B), in terms of prudence (qua C).

Finally – in ways we will begin to see in Chapter 2 and beyond – instrumentalism promises unique theoretical and practical fruitfulness: by founding moral philosophy on observable human motivations, it will enable us to merge moral philosophy with the empirical sciences of human behavior, explaining and predicting recent empirical results, including results strongly linking moral behavior to motivational concern for one's future.[105–108]

3.3 Advantages over alternatives

Although we cannot compare instrumentalism to all possible alternatives, allow me to explicate its presumptive advantages over prominent alternatives.

3.3.1 Advantages over intuitionism

Many moral philosophers maintain that moral philosophy should one way or another be based on 'commonsense' moral intuitions. Some of these theorists argue that certain moral intuitions – such as the wrongness of torture – are 'self-evident.'[25–29] Others argue merely that our moral intuitions provide *prima facie* evidence of moral requirements.[23] And so on. Yet however attractive moral intuitionism may seem to some, such an approach fares poorly in comparison to instrumentalism on the principles of theory selection this chapter has defended.

First, moral intuitionism does not satisfy Firm Foundations. For although many people share the kinds of moral intuitions that inform intuitionistic accounts, there are significant classes of people who appear not to. Criminals, terrorists, and psychopaths do not appear to 'see anything wrong' with lying, cheating, stealing, or killing. Further, as we see in Plato's dialogues, in introductory moral philosophy classes (in which a surprising number of students deny moral objectivity, in my experience), and in empirical surveys, many ordinary people do not appear to share intuitions that morality is objective (in one recent of nonphilosophers, participants rated moral statements as 'objectively true' only 47% of the time[36]).

While intuitionists can attempt to argue that people who do not share common moral intuitions are 'psychologically deficient' – lacking 'appropriate' moral sensitivity – this too does not respect Firm Foundations. For while those with common moral intuitions may think that people who lack them are psychologically deficient, people who lack common moral intuitions do not see things the same way: they think it is those of us with moral intuitions who have been 'snookered' by the 'myth of morality.' For example, in Book I of Plato's *The Republic*, Thrasymachus argues that moral norms are merely a tool created by those in power to control people, and that real justice is simply the 'interest of the stronger.'[109] And indeed, many philosophers since have argued similar things: that our moral intuitions are a kind of illusion, making it seem to those of us who have them that morality is objective when, as a matter of fact, our moral intuitions are the result of Judeo-Christian cultural indoctrination[17,110] or evolution.[111] In contrast, as we have seen, virtually everyone – children, ordinary adults, criminals, even psychopaths – understands and accepts the instrumental theory of normative rationality. Thus, a moral philosophy based on moral intuitions does not satisfy Firm Foundations, whereas one based on instrumentalism does.

Second, instrumentalism also promises greater explanatory power, unity, parsimony, and fruitfulness than moral intuitionism. Moral intuitionism splits the normative in two: into prudential norms and moral norms. Instrumentalism promises greater unity, as it promises to explain morality in *terms* of prudence. Instrumentalism thus also has greater explanatory power and parsimony. For whereas intuitionism must assert the existence of an entire domain of facts distinct from those of prudence – namely, objective moral facts – an instrumentalist moral philosophy, if successful, will explain moral facts in terms of ordinary observable facts: our motivational interests, concept of instrumental normative rationality, and facts about the best means for satisfying our interests. Finally, instrumentalism promises greater fruitfulness, as it promises to explain things – among other things, how morality is in our interest – that intuitionism does not.

3.3.2 Advantages over reflective equilibrium

Similar considerations speak to the superiority of instrumentalism over a reflective equilibrium approach to moral philosophy. In contrast to moral intuitionism, which is broadly foundationalist in nature[112] – taking our moral intuitions as directly, or noninferentially justified – reflective equilibrium approaches are broadly coherentist, aiming to arrive at 'an acceptable coherence'[44–47] among 'our moral beliefs.' Yet, as we saw earlier, such an approach faces a well-known epistemic problem: a set of beliefs can be coherent and yet have no relation to truth.[48] 'Our moral beliefs' may seem true to many of us, and even form a coherent whole – and yet, moral skeptics and anti-realists argue, our moral beliefs may be false.

Accordingly, reflective equilibrium-based approaches to moral philosophy do not satisfy Firm Foundations. Such approaches merely aim to render our moral beliefs consistent, when – as we have seen – it is not obvious to many people that any of our moral beliefs are actually true. Firm Foundations holds that an epistemically sound inquiry must be based on observations that all or almost observers recognize as obvious, incontrovertible fact. Yet there are not only many ordinary people – criminals, psychopaths, and ordinary 'immoralists' (such as Plato's Thrasymachus) – who do not share 'our moral beliefs.' There are also many philosophers – moral anti-realists and skeptics – who have systematically called those beliefs into question.

In contrast, as we have seen, instrumentalism does satisfy Firm Foundations. It also offers greater explanatory power, unity, parsimony, and fruitfulness than reflective equilibrium. Reflective equilibrium, in taking coherence of 'our moral beliefs' as its method, merely systematizes our moral beliefs rather than explaining them, and their truth, in anything more fundamental. In contrast, an instrumentalist moral philosophy promises to give a unified, parsimonious explanation of the rationality of specific moral norms, and why we should obey them.

3.3.3 Advantages over moral language analysis

As we have already seen, many philosophers have in one way or another attempted to extract substantive moral claims from semantic analyses of moral language. Many moral realists argue that moral philosophy should respect moral language's 'face value,' which they argue is realist in nature, asserting things as objectively right, wrong, good, or bad.[37-41] Others, however, have questioned both whether the face value of moral language and practice is realist in nature, and whether the face value of moral language and practice should even be respected.[113] Indeed, many anti-realists have argued that whatever the face value of moral language and practice may be, the reality is that moral facts do not exist[31-32,42-43], perhaps because moral language is primarily expressive, not actually asserting propositions or referring to moral facts at all.[114-17] Similarly, whereas Judith Thomson argues that normative terms such as 'good' are attributive adjectives – involving mind-dependent evaluations of various kinds of things[118] – others deny this, arguing that 'good' has nonattributive uses.[119]

Consequently, moral language analysis approaches to moral philosophy do not respect Firm Foundations. Firm Foundations requires us to base theory on facts of common observation – facts that are commonly regarded as obviously, incontrovertibly true. Yet, as the above debates indicate, the meaning of moral language seems different to different investigators: moral language seems realist to realists, anti-realist to anti-realists, attributive to attributivists, and so on. In contrast, as we have seen, virtually everyone shares our (nonmoral) concept of instrumental normative rationality. Instrumentalism is thus a firmer foundation. Finally, if this book is successful, instrumentalism can provide a single, unified explanation of our moral language, explaining in purely instrumental terms how sentences involving moral terms are true or false.

3.3.4 Advantages over constitutivism

Another popular approach to moral philosophy – constitutivism – aims to derive morality from the nature of practical reason or deliberation. Constitutivism's most famous proponent, Immanuel Kant, argued that in making choices, we impose practical laws upon ourselves – laws which must therefore conform to a supreme moral principle, the categorical imperative, in order to be true.[120–121] Somewhat similarly, Christine Korsgaard argues that the constitutive purpose of human action is to realize unified agency, making us 'whole persons' rather than beings whose lives are merely an array of disconnected goals – which, she argues, requires acting on moral laws.[86] Similarly, Barbara Herman has argued that the constitutive purpose of deliberation is to seek unconditional goodness.[87] Another type of constitutivism – Nietzschean constitutivism – argues that agency constitutes a will to power that has very different moral implications.[85]

However, constitutivist approaches to moral philosophy do not satisfy Firm Foundations, either. For as we have just seen, 'the constitutive features' of agency or deliberation seem different to different people. Kant's analysis of agency has been widely questioned,[17–21,110,122] as has Korsgaard's conception,[123–124] Herman's conception,[125–127] and so on. Constitutivist approaches to moral philosophy, in other words, are based on controversial claims about the nature of practical reason or deliberation that not everyone recognizes as true.[128] Instrumentalism is a far firmer foundation, one promising to provide a unified explanation of moral normativity not in contentious features of practical reason or deliberation, but rather in purely instrumental terms that everyone recognizes to be a component of deliberation.

3.3.5 Advantages over second- and third-personalism

Other philosophers have attempted to found morality in second-personal and third-personal perspectives. Stephen Darwall has attempted to found morality in the 'second-personal standpoint,' or the way in which we require others to justify their treatment of us.[129] To take one of Darwall's examples, if I step on your foot causing you pain, you will demand that I stop doing it, thereby giving me moral reasons not to do it.[130] Other philosophers, such as David Hume and Thomas Nagel, have attempted to explain morality third-personally, in terms of judgments or sentiments regarding our own and other' behaviors from an impartial standpoint.[131-132] And other theorists, such as P.F. Strawson, have attempted to ground moral responsibility in our reactive attitudes more generally.[133]

Such approaches do not satisfy Firm Foundations, however. For although some of us may recognize the normative force of second- and third-personal standpoints, many human observers do not. The con man or psychopath may say, 'You may think my stepping on your foot gives me a reason to stop. I happen to disagree. I see no reason to take my foot off yours at all.' Con men, psychopaths, and ordinary 'immoralists' – people who do not feel the force of their so-called moral obligations or reasons – simply do not recognize the normative validity of second- and third-personal perspectives. They say things like, 'I certainly see why you think I shouldn't kill you. But I see no reason to agree.' This, in brief, is why many moral theorists have argued that moral philosophy must fundamentally address the *first-personal perspective*.[134-137] Instrumentalism, on the other hand, addresses the first-personal perspective – and, if a compelling instrumental case can be made for morality, it is one that can be understood and appreciated from second- and third-personal perspectives as well. As such, instrumentalism not only is a firmer foundation than second and third-personal approaches; it promises greater explanatory power, unity, and fruitfulness.

3.3.6 Advantages over Sterba's dialecticalism

Finally, James Sterba has argued that morality can be derived from dialectical requirements on argumentation, that is, from a conception of reasonableness in argument.[138] According to Sterba, we can all recognize the argumentative illegitimacy of begging philosophical questions, or simply assuming what we intend to prove or justify. Next, Sterba argues that the most influential challenge to morality comes from the rational egoist: the individual who believes that each person only ought to act in their own interests, rather than the interests of others. However, Sterba argues the rational egoist cannot provide a non-question-begging argument for egoism over altruism. Whatever grounds the egoist gives for prioritizing self-interest over altruism will be rejected by the altruist, and conversely, whatever grounds the altruist gives for prioritizing altruism will be rejected by the egoist. Thus, Sterba contends, the only non-question-begging argument either side can give is one that accepts the *prima facie* force of both self-interested and altruistic reasons for action, and requires compromise when those reasons conflict. Reasonability in argument, Sterba concludes, entails a doctrine of 'morality as compromise.'

Unfortunately, Sterba's approach does not respect Firm Foundations, either. First, as critics have pointed out, his argument assumes something that true egoists reject: namely, that altruistic considerations provide *prima facie* reasons for acting.[139-142] Second, if my arguments in this chapter are correct, there appear to be strong, non-question-begging grounds – based on Firm Foundations – for rational egoism over altruism or compromise. We have seen that virtually everyone recognizes the truth of instrumentalism. Yet instrumentalism indexes normative rationality to a person's motivational interests, and many people – psychopaths and immoralists, as well as ordinary people in contexts where they are motivated to behave egoistically without guilt or remorse – appear to *only* have self-interested motives. Consider the thief who is motivated to steal with no remorse, or the student who simply wants to do well on exam, even if they need to cheat to do it. These individuals, by all appearances, only have self-interested motives concerning the actions in question – in which case instrumentalism entails they rationally ought to act purely egoistically. Thus, instrumentalism and human motivation appear to entail a strong, non-question-begging argument for rational egoism (at least in contexts where people have purely self-interested motives).

3.3.7 Conclusion

We have not examined every possible alternative to instrumentalism. However, we have considered several popular alternatives, and found that none of them satisfy the principle of Firm Foundations as well as instrumentalism. Moreover, we have seen that instrumentalism has compelling advantages over many alternatives on other principles of theory selection as well, principally Explanatory Power, Unity, Parsimony, and Fruitfulness. As such, although we have not considered every possible alternative to instrumentalism, I believe it should be clear by now that instrumentalism is the firmest foundation for moral philosophy. There is simply no theory of normative rationality that is as widely accepted among ordinary individuals and philosophers as instrumentalism. Virtually everyone – children, normal adults, con men, and psychopaths – recognizes the truth of instrumental norms. We all routinely make instrumental normative claims, such as 'If you want to lose weight, you should eat fewer calories,' and take ourselves to be obviously speaking the truth. Although some readers may doubt whether morality can be derived from instrumental foundations, the rest of this book will not only that argue that it can – but also that the particular moral theory derived from it, Rightness as Fairness, fares better on all seven principles of theory selection than alternatives.

36 Rightness as Fairness

4 Disarming initial concerns

Although we have just seen that instrumentalism satisfies Firm Foundations better than other prominent approaches to moral philosophy, there are several concerns about it that I would like to dispel before proceeding further. These concerns are that instrumental normativity is (Section 4.1.) fundamentally the wrong kind of normativity for moral philosophy, (Section 4.2) not as obviously true as I am suggesting, and (Section 4.3) carries no realistic possibility for success, given clear conflicts between morality and self-interest.

4.1 The wrong kinds of reasons?

One common concern about instrumental approaches to moral philosophy is that even if a compelling instrumental argument can be provided for obeying moral norms, instrumentalism necessarily fails to give the right kinds of reasons for obeying those norms – that it cannot provide a theory of morality per se, but rather merely a theory of why morality is prudent, or in our interests.

This concern has been raised in a couple of different guises. First, it is often suggested that instrumentalism provides the wrong kinds of *normative* reasons for action: norms contingent upon our interests, whereas genuinely moral norms must be 'categorical,' or absolutely binding upon us regardless of our interests.[11–16,26,143] As such, the objection goes, it is mistake to try to explain morality in purely instrumental terms, for that is not a theory of morality at all: it is at most a theory of why morality is prudent. A second common concern is that an instrumental explanation of morality does not even generate normative reasons, but rather merely 'motivational reasons.' As H.A. Prichard once put it, once you show a person why it is prudent to keep their engagements, it will not 'convince us that we ought to keep our engagements; even if successful on its own lines, it only makes us *want* to keep them.'[144] As such, Prichard complains that instrumental arguments for moral behavior are not even genuinely normative, but rather purely motivational.

4.2 Not a firm foundation?

A second possible concern with using instrumentalism as a foundation for moral theorizing is that instrumentalism – as I have formulated it, as an analysis of 'ought-statements' – is not as obviously true as I have made it out to be. For instance, Matt Bedke[145] and Judith Thomson[146] have both raised the following concern: the instrumental analysis of 'ought'-statements entails that if one wants to kill someone, and poisoning their drink would be best means to doing so, then one ought to poison their drink. But, Bedke and Thomson argue, this is false: even if poisoning B's drink would best advance one's interests, there is no sense in which one ought to do it, since poisoning him would be morally wrong. As Thomson writes,

> Suppose Ann intends to kill Bert. Suppose also that the only means she has of killing Bert is poisoning his coffee. Then it is true that her poisoning Bert's coffee is practically necessary as a means to her attaining something she intends to attain... Does it follow that the words, 'Ann ought to poison Bert's coffee' have a meaning under which you would be speaking truly if you said them? Intuitively, she ought not poison Bert's coffee. Period. Intuitively, anyone who says, 'She ought to' either misuses the words he says or speaks falsely.[147]

Interestingly, neither Bedke nor Thomson denies that there may be an instrumental sense in it is rational to poison someone's coffee. They just deny that, following **instrumentalism** (as I formulated it), one can validly derive from its instrumental rationality that one *ought* to do it. As such, one might worry, attempting to found moral philosophy on instrumentalism is once again a mistake.

4.3 Unconvincing and artificial?

A final concern about attempting to found morality on instrumentalism is that history and commonsense strongly suggest that no such attempt can ever succeed. As Prichard once implied, attempts to demonstrate that morality is in our interests always come off as unconvincing and artificial, as there seem to be obvious cases where morality requires sacrificing one's interests for the sake of others.[148] For instance, when Aristotelian virtue ethicists argue that moral virtue is the best means for living a flourishing life,[149] many of us balk. For while a variety of empirical studies admittedly indicate significant links between morality and personal well-being – indicating that altruistic behavior has statistically positive relationships to physical and mental health[150-153] – these are merely statistical results. They do not show that moral virtue or moral behavior improves every person's well-being, something that everyday life strongly suggests to be false. Just as Polus famously gives the example of Archelus in Plato's *Gorgias* – a man who gained great wealth and power and appeared happy despite achieving these things through profoundly immoral means (including murder)[154] – so too do many of us know morally bad people who seem to flourish, and morally good people who suffer. And so, the worry goes, instrumental derivations of morality will always fail to be convincing. No matter how hard we may try, instrumental derivations of morality run up against the commonsense fact that immoral actions can benefit people.

A second concern about instrumental normativity echoes the concerns raised in Section 4.1 – namely, that no matter how successful an instrumental derivation of morality may be, it will necessarily fail to provide the kind of answer we are looking for: an explanation of why we categorically ought to obey moral norms. Instrumental justifications, the thought is, can only account for 'hypothetical' imperatives ('If you want to be happy, you ought to tell the truth'). Moral propositions, however, are 'categorical' imperatives, requiring us to act for their own sake ('You ought to tell the truth') because they are inherently right.

4.4 Three promissory notes

My reply to all three concerns come in the form of promissory notes: promises, that is, that the rest of this book will disarm each of them. Allow me to explain.

4.4.1 Not the wrong kinds of reasons?

The wrong kind of reasons concern, as we saw above, comes in roughly two guises. The first is that an instrumental derivation of morality will provide the wrong kinds of normative reasons – explaining why it is prudent to obey moral norms, whereas morality is intuitively a matter of categorically binding reasons. The second is that instrumental arguments do not even provide normative reasons, only motivating ones.

My reply to the normative concern comes in several parts. First, given the principle of Firm Foundations, it is not the legitimate place of moral theorists to decide – by fiat – what 'the right kinds of reasons' for moral behavior are, any more than it is the legitimate place of physicists to decide by fiat what the right kind of analysis of physical things are. Prior to Einstein's Theory of Relativity, it was believed by Newtonian philosophers and scientists that space and time 'must be absolute.'[155–156] The problem, of course, is that observation showed this to be false. The Theory of Relativity's predictions that space-time is relative to reference-frames have been spectacularly well confirmed by observations and experiments. By a similar token, since, as we saw above, not everyone shares the intuition that morality 'must be categorical,' this should not be taken as an absolute requirement that a compelling moral theory must conform to. And indeed, although the theory this book defends has instrumental foundations, we will see in future chapters that we can in

Ethics for the Twenty-First Century   39

fact derive impartial, quasi-categorical moral reasons for action – reasons that require us to categorically 'justify' our actions to all other human and nonhuman sentient beings, regardless of our own contingent interests – from instrumental foundations, thus explaining (in purely instrumental terms) why many of us have the intuition that 'morality must be impartial and/or categorical.' In short, my reply to the 'wrong kind of normative reasons' is a promissory note: namely, that this book will show we can derive 'categorical enough' normative grounds for moral behavior from instrumental rationality alone.

My reply to the concern that an instrumental derivation of morality merely gives motivating reasons also comes in several parts. First, Prichard's argument that instrumental arguments merely motivate us, rather than providing normative reasons – his argument that instrumental 'oughts' evaporate once we are convinced an actions advances our interests – does not cohere well with ordinary linguistic practice or action. First, it not as though, the moment someone provides us with a cogent instrumental argument that some action will enable us to achieve our aims, we are automatically motivated to act. Sometimes we have weakness of will. We say, 'You're right. Given that I want to lose weight, I should have the low-calorie salad. But I'm just so tempted by the burger.' Sometimes we are motivated to eat the burger against our better judgment, thinking afterwards, 'I really shouldn't have done that.' Second, we do not treat instrumental 'oughts' the way Prichard claims – our 'oughts' do not simply evaporate the moment we are convinced that an action is in our interests. On the contrary, we typically say things like, 'You're right. Given that I want to lose weight, I should order the salad.'

Finally, there is something a bit odd about the Prichard-type concern that an instrumental derivation of morality will 'merely' motivate people to act (as though actually motivating people would be bad thing!). One of the main concerns that many people have about moral philosophy (a concern that I have long shared) is that moral philosophy – precisely insofar as it fails to found morality in our interests – fails to motivate people to change their behavior. Recent studies not only indicate that moral philosophers behave no morally better than other people[157]; further, to my knowledge, there is no empirical evidence that moral philosophy, as it has so far been developed, actually motivates anyone to behave better. This is disappointing, to say the least. I believe that moral philosophy has failed in this regard precisely by abandoning instrumentalism in favor of 'impartial moral reasons,' reasons which – insofar as they are impartial – predictably fail to motivate people (again, see the attitudes of various characters in Plato's dialogues: Thrasymachus, Gorgias, Polus, and so on – all of whom care about their own interests as opposed to the interests of others). I believe we should want a moral theory capable of actually motivating people. We should want this not only on theoretical grounds – as a theory that unifies motivating and normative reasons in a single framework (as instrumentalism does) has greater explanatory power than theories that fragment them into different domains. We also have practical grounds to want moral philosophy to be motivating. As Karl Marx famously wrote, 'philosophers have only interpreted the world in different ways; the point is to change it.'[158] What could be better than a moral theory which, by engaging with people's interests – showing them how moral behavior is instrumentally rational – would be able to actually motivate people to behave morally? As we will see throughout this book, I believe that Rightness as Fairness achieves precisely this. We will see that, insofar as we typically care about our own future, the only rational way to behave – the only way to effectively pursue our own interests – is to treat ourselves and others fairly.

4.4.2 Firm foundations after all?

My reply to the Bedke and Thomson-type concern about instrumentalism is even more straightforward. This book argues that instrumental rationality requires treating others fairly, and that since poisoning someone's drink involves unfairness (with perhaps some extreme exceptions, such as poisoning a murderous criminal if necessary prevent them from carrying out an atrocity), an instrumental analysis of 'ought-statements' entails that one ought not to poison someone's drink – just as Bedke and Thomson claim. Thus, or so I shall argue, instrumentalism satisfies Firm Foundations after all. It is a conception of normative rationality that (A) virtually everyone accepts, and which (B) properly understood, explains the very case Bedke and Thomson use to raise concerns about it as an analysis of ought-statements.

4.4.3 Intuitive and convincing?

Finally, my reply to the concern that instrumental arguments for moral behavior are 'artificial and unconvincing' is also a promissory note. When it comes to existing instrumentalist moral theories (such as those of Hobbes, Gauthier, and *eudaimonistic* virtue ethics), I agree with this charge. Like many, I have never been convinced that Hobbesian contractarians have a good answer to the 'immoralist' (see Joyce for a brief summary of common concerns[159]). Similarly, like L.W. Sumner,[160]

I have never been convinced by virtue-theoretic arguments that morality is constitutive of, or an optimal means to, personal happiness or flourishing – in part because empirical studies linking altruism to mental and physical well-being are merely statistical in nature, and in larger part because there seem to be too many cases of bad people appearing to flourish in life. My hope, at any rate, is that this book will do better: that it will show, in convincing and intuitive terms, why being fair to ourselves and others is the only instrumentally rational way to act given our ignorance of the future.

5 Conclusion

This chapter argued that moral philosophy needs, but has until now lacked, a reliable method for distinguishing what merely 'seems true' from what actually is true. It then argued that seven principles of theory selection adapted from the sciences comprise just such a method. Finally, it argued that a simple instrumental theory of normative rationality – the theory which analyzes how we ought to behave in terms of optimal means for achieving our motivational goals – satisfies the first and most important of these principles, Firm Foundations, better than prominent alternatives, while also promising to satisfy other compelling principles of theory selection, as well. The rest of this book will use this firm foundation to derive a new moral theory – Rightness as Fairness – that I argue satisfies all seven principles of theory selection better than existing theories.

2
The Problem of Possible Future Selves

Chapter 1 argued that moral philosophy should be based on Firm Foundations – on truths commonly recognized by human observers – and that the following instrumental conception of normative rationality is the firmest such foundation:

> **Instrumentalism:** if one's motivational interests would be best satisfied by ϕ-ing, then it is instrumentally rational for one to ϕ – that is, one instrumentally ought to ϕ.

The present chapter argues that when instrumentalism is combined with other known facts, the result is a problem for which there is presently no adequate solution: the problem of possible future selves.
Section 1 argues that we – typical adult human beings – are capable of caring about our future and past: of having forward-looking (or prospective) interests about how we want our future to go, but also backward-looking (or retrospective) interests regarding how we wish our past had gone. Further, Section 1 argues, we sometimes have interests regarding the very interests of our past or future selves: we want our past selves to have wanted particular things, and our future selves to want particular things.
Section 2 then argues that we face a systematic problem in life. We typically care about our future, including about the interests of our future selves. Indeed, we typically want our future selves to be happy – or at least satisfied – with our decisions. Further, in some cases, we do not merely want our future selves to probably be satisfied with our decisions: we want to know whether they *will* be satisfied with them.

However, we also want to be happy in the present. Thus, it turns out, in at least some cases, that we have interests in:

(A) Knowing our future interests,
(B) Knowing how to order our future interests with our present ones, and
(C) Acting in ways sure to satisfy both sets of interests, without merely 'betting' on probable futures.

But, Section 2 argues, it seems – thanks to the unpredictability of (Section 2.1) future events, (Section 2.2) our future psychology, and (Section 2.3) our future choices – that we cannot accomplish these things. This is the problem of possible future selves: we sometimes want to know which 'future self' we will be, so that we can ensure that *that* specific self is satisfied with our decisions. However, since the future has not yet happened, we cannot know which self that is. Finally, Section 2 argues, this is a genuine problem we often encounter in life – one that, to the extent that we fail to solve it, sometimes results in disastrous, heartbreaking futures.

Next, Section 3 argues that there are *prima facie* reasons to believe that morality is the solution to this problem. We teach our children, and ourselves, not to 'bet' on likely outcomes in moral cases precisely because such bets could turn out badly, resulting in unlikely outcomes our future selves may regret. Further, we urge people to make decisions that are 'fair to themselves,' taking into account the possible things their future selves might care about, including the interests of other human beings and nonhuman creatures.

Section 4 then argues that although the problem of possible future selves is contingent upon us at least sometimes wanting to know our future interests, being ignorant of them, and wanting not to 'bet' on probable outcomes, there are several related reasons to believe that morality's normative force may indeed be contingent on these things. This is, obviously, contrary to the claim made by some philosophers that morality's normative force must be 'categorical,' applying to 'all rational agents' regardless of their interests.[1-2] However, on the basis of the principle of Firm Foundations, I argue that moral philosophers are not epistemically entitled to assume that morality is categorical, and that whether it is categorical is something that should be determined utilizing the seven principles of theory selection defended in Chapter 1. Further, I argue that actual and possible agents who lack the interests and ignorance that give rise to the problem of possible future selves – namely, children, psychopaths, and science fiction possibilities – appear to fail to experience morality's normative force, thus calling into question its supposed categorical force.

Finally, Section 5 argues against two potential answers to the problem of possible future selves. Section 5.1 shows that it cannot be adequately solved by probabilistic reasoning. Section 5.2 then shows that another possible proposal – Michael Smith's recent proposal that rationality requires motivational consistency across time[3] – cannot be straightforwardly justified on the kinds of instrumental grounds that Chapter 1 argued should be moral philosophy's foundation.

1 Our capacities to care about our past and future

We, typical adult human beings, often – and perhaps always – care about our past, present, and future. We obviously tend to care about our present, having motivational interests in what happens to us now (I care very much, right now, about the pain in my back). We also often care about the past, wishing we hadn't experienced the bad day we just had, or wishing we had said something different in a conversation. Finally, we often – if not always – care about the future, wanting certain things to happen. I want today's writing to go well, for instance, and, several months from now, to have published a good book. In short, we often have prospective (or forward-looking) interests about how our future will go, as well as retrospective (or backward-looking) interests about how our past went[4-6] – interests that become clear to us when we engage in 'mental time travel,' recalling past events or imagining possible future events.[7] Indeed, when we recall past events sometimes we rejoice over them, wishing them to have gone exactly as they actually did. Other times, however, we wish the past had gone differently: that different things had happened, or that our past selves had behaved differently. Similarly, when we think of the future, we think of ways our lives could go, daydreaming about how happy it might make us to win the lottery, write a good book, and so on. Finally, we often have interests regarding the interests of our past and future selves. We may want our past self to not have wanted the things they did. If, for instance, one wastes years working on a failed project, one may wish that one had never wanted to begin the project to begin with. Similarly, we often have interests in our future interests: we want our future selves to want particular things. For instance, I want my future self to be glad that I decided to write this book: I want him to want me to have written it, not wish in retrospect that I hadn't.

Some readers might suggest that we always have some such interests – that is, that in some sense, we always care, at least implicitly, about our past and future. And to a certain extent this seems plausible. In some sense, it seems, I always care about my past. There are always things about my past that I am happy occurred, as well as things I wish hadn't occurred. Similarly, it seems plausible that we always care, at least in some implicit sense, about our future: that there is no decision we make in our lives that does not in some way express concern for our future. For instance, one might suggest that even if I rather thoughtlessly fetch a glass of water from the refrigerator, not explicitly thinking of the future, there is still a sense in which I care about it: I care about a future in which I drink some water. Still, as plausible as this seems, we should not assume it. As Chapter 1 argued, this book aims to respect Firm Foundations: the principle which states that theories should be based on obviously true observations. Consequently, since there are at least some cases in which it seems unclear whether we care about the future – in some instances, after all, we appear to merely 'act in the moment' on instinct or whatever inclinations strike us – we should not assume that we always care about the past or future. The fact that we sometimes do care will suffice for our purposes.

Notice, next, that we do not need to beg any controversial metaphysical questions about personal identity – about whether we are identical to our past or present selves – to establish that we are capable of caring about 'our' past and future in ways relevant to this book's project: providing an instrumental argument for obeying moral norms. For instrumentalism merely concerns our interests, analyzing what we ought to do in terms of what we care about. Since, whatever the truth about personal identity may or may not be, our present 'selves' care about their past and future 'selves,' we have all the material we need to make instrumental arguments. For, whatever the truth about personal identity may be, this 'self' – my present one – has interests regarding 'his' past and future 'selves.' My present 'self' cares about other person-stages as though they are stages of 'me.' Accordingly, if we can show that morality is instrumentally rational for this 'person-stage,' given his interests about the past, present, and future, then, whatever the truth about personal identity is or is not, we will have shown that it is instrumentally rational, at any given point, for 'person-stages' to obey moral norms (Michael Smith has previously made a similar point elsewhere[8]).

As such, whenever I write of past, present, or future 'selves,' this is how I should be understood: as referring to entities (or 'person-stages') we can care about.

Before proceeding further using these safe assumptions – the assumptions that we, typical adult human beings, often (if not always) care about our past, present, and future – it may be worthwhile to note some interesting relationships between the above capacities and moral responsibility. First, typical adult human beings – the kinds of beings we identify in law and everyday life as paradigmatic moral agents (or beings with full-fledged moral responsibility) – appear to have motivational interests and capacities for 'mental time travel' that other beings do not. Consider first paradigmatic nonmoral agents – creatures who we do not regard in law or everyday life as having real capacities for moral responsibility: namely, nonhuman animals. Although many nonhuman animals (including primates) have capacities to expect future events and modify their behavior on the basis of past events, there appear to be compelling behavioral and neurobiological grounds for believing that mental time travel per se – the ability to *imagine* the past or future – is unique to humans.[9] Next, consider 'questionable moral agents' – creatures whose capacities for moral responsibility we consider in law and everyday life to be compromised or ill-formed. First, consider children and teenagers. We typically do not hold children or teenagers to the same standards of moral responsibility as normal adults because, or so we often say, they are unable to 'appreciate the consequences' of their actions. Interestingly, the brains of children and teenagers are underdeveloped in areas of the brain thought to be responsible for mental time travel.[10–12] Further, adolescent impulsivity has been directly linked to the inability of adolescents to think through the future consequences of their actions.[13] Children and teenagers appear, in other words, to be 'unable to appreciate the consequences of their actions' because they have impoverished abilities to imagine their future: they focus, much more than adults do, on their present. Finally, consider psychopaths: a class of human beings who appear incapable of experiencing the normative force of moral claims, and who some philosophers and legal theorists therefore believe should not be treated as morally responsible agents.[14–16] Like children and nonhuman animals, psychopaths have a pronounced tendency to act impulsively, without much (if any) concern for their past actions (failing to feel guilt or remorse for things they have done)[17] or concern for future consequences.[17–18] Further, psychopaths have dysfunctional development of, and activity in, the same general brain centers thought to be responsible for mental time travel that are underdeveloped in children and teenagers.[7,19-22] Finally, recent empirical research has linked improved moral and prudential behavior to future-directed mental time travel. First, people save more money[23-25] and display lessened inclinations to cheat or buy stolen property[26] the more prompted they are to think about, imagine, or interact with a virtual-reality depiction of their future selves. Second, the 'tendency to live in the here and now...and failure to think through the delayed consequences of behavior' is known to be one of the strongest individual-level predictors of criminally delinquent activity.[27,28-30]

These facts will prove to be prescient. For as we saw in Chapter 1, two things that a good moral theory should do is cohere with known facts (external coherence) and provide unified explanations of things that lack good explanations (explanatory power, unity, and fruitfulness). As we will see in this and future chapters, this book will provide a unified explanation of precisely why nonhuman animals, children, teenagers, and psychopaths fail to appreciate the normative force of moral norms. They fail to appreciate the normative force of moral norms because, in lacking our robust abilities to care about their past and future, such beings lack the kinds of interests that give rise to the problem of possible future selves: the problem for which morality (or so I will argue) is an instrumentally rational solution.

2 The problem of possible future selves

We all repeatedly face a particular problem in life: each and every one of us tends to care about our future, yet we lack knowledge of what the future holds. There is no denying this. You care, for instance, about what will happen to you later today. You want your day to go well rather than poorly. And you care not just about today. You care about the rest of the year, too: you want your year to go well. And of course you want the rest of your life to go well, too. You do not, I presume, want to die miserable and alone. You want, moving forward, to be happy – or at least content – with how your life unfolds. But it is precisely here that we all face a problem. We want our futures to go well, but we do not know how they will go. This is not merely an academic problem, nor, as we will see, a trivial one. In some cases, it is simply a bit annoying: I want my day to go well today, but I cannot ensure that it will (yesterday, for instance, was full of frustrations and obstacles, despite my best efforts!). In other cases, however, our inability to know the future literally keeps us up at night. Indeed, when it comes to important, potentially 'life-changing' decisions – such as whether to buy a new home, or take a new job, and so on – our desire to know the future can lead to agony. We want to *know whether* buying the home will be a good investment, *whether* we will be happy or miserable in a different job, and so on. We want to know our future, in these cases, for an obvious reason: we care deeply about what happens to us, and we recognize there are different possible ways our lives could go. In one possible future, we imagine our decision to buy a new home going well. We imagine living there, enjoying its beautiful kitchen, enjoying happy 'family nights' in the living room, and so on. But then we imagine what could go wrong: the housing market could crash, leaving us owing far more than the home is worth; there could be a problem with the home's foundation, requiring enormously expensive repairs, and so on – all futures that could lead us to regret the decision of buying the home. Finally, of course, one may worry about what might happen if one doesn't buy the home ('What if we never find a home we like as much?,' one might fret). Similarly, consider the soon-to-be-newlywed with 'cold feet': a person who is unsure whether they should get married. Such a person may find themselves petrified, recognizing that there are different possible ways their life could go (they could get married and be happy, get married and be unhappy, choose not to get married and be happy, or choose not to get married and be miserable), and wishing desperately to know which decision will lead to the best future.

We often encounter this problem in 'moral' cases. Consider a student who is tempted to cheat on an exam. Suppose they know many other students have cheated successfully, and because they have not studied for their exam, they imagine how nice it would be to get away with it, too – doing well on their exam with little effort. Although some students might cheat impulsively in such a situation with little forethought, oftentimes when we encounter temptations like these – temptations to cheat or lie, or the like – it is all too natural to worry about the possibilities. For instance, the student might worry about the off-chance that they will get caught. 'If I get caught, I might fail the class,' they might think. Or they may worry about feeling guilty, or about how not studying for this exam might lead them to lack knowledge they need for future exams and assignments – which they might then also have to cheat on to do well (thus having to risk getting caught several more times). And so on. And, of course, as we all know when we have worries like these, one natural experience is to *want to know what will happen*. One wants to know not merely whether one is likely to get caught, or feel guilty, and so on. One wants to know whether one *will* get caught, feel guilty, and the like. One finds oneself desperately wanting to know the future because, if one could know it, one could know which risks are 'worth taking.'

Now, one natural thing to say here is that although it might be nice if we could know the future, we clearly cannot. However, this is to put the proverbial cart before the horse. Our task for now, following instrumentalism, is to focus simply on what our interests *are*. Instrumentalism, after all, defines normative rationality in terms of things we are actually motivated to want – and, as we see in the above cases (and know all too well from living), we sometimes do want to know the future. We want to know it, again, because we are worried. Indeed, we want to know it precisely because we recognize that 'betting' on likely outcomes – on what our future interests are likely to be – may not be 'good enough' for the future selves we care about. Allow me to explain.

Part of what makes the problem just introduced so vexing is that, although we care about the future and seemingly have to place 'bets' on how the future is likely to turn out – one has to either buy a home, leaving one's fate open to the possibility that the housing market will crash, or not – whether a bet is a 'good one in retrospect' seems to depend on how the future turns out. For instance, suppose all indications right now are that the housing market is strong, and so it seems likely, given one's current evidence, that buying a new home is a good investment. Then suppose the future turns out precisely how one expects. One's future self may be happy their earlier self took the 'calculated risk' of buying the home. Now suppose, however, that things turn out disastrously: that the housing market crashes, one's home enters foreclosure, one loses a ton of money, and the stress on one's marriage leads to a miserable divorce. As rational of a risk as buying the home might have appeared to one's earlier self, one's future self may wish for all the world that one had never taken it. They might wish they could 'go back in time' to change what one did.

This seems to be why, in many of these cases, we worry so much. When we are unsure of whether to buy a new home, or experience 'cold feet' before marriage, or are tempted to cheat on an exam, we sometimes do not want to 'place bets' on how the future is likely to turn out – and for the simple reason that we recognize that the bet can turn out badly, in ways we may never be able to undo. Consequently, sometimes what we really want is to know the future. We want to know whether our future self will be happy with the 'risk' we took. The soon-to-be-newlywed with cold feet wants to know whether her future self will be happy taking the 'risk' of marriage or not. She wants to know, in advance, whether the 'risk' will be worthwhile, so that it won't in fact be a risk at all. She wants to know not merely whether she is likely to be happy married. She wants to know, above all, whether she *will* be happy married.

This is the problem of possible future selves. In many cases in life, our concerns about possible – even if unlikely – outcomes (the mere possibility of our home getting foreclosed on, the possibility that we will get caught cheating on an exam, and so on), lead us to desperately want to know the future, so that we do not 'have to put our future in jeopardy.' We want to know whether buying the home will make our future selves happy, so that we do not have to risk them being miserable. We want to know whether, if we cheat on an exam, we will get away with it scot-free, without guilt, so that we do not have to risk the possibilities of disaster (getting caught and punished, feeling remorse, and so on). Yet, although we want to know these things, it seems we cannot. We want to know which of our 'possible future selves' we will be, but because the future has not yet happened, we cannot know which future self we will be.

The troubles we face here are compounded by the fact that, although we care about our future interests (we want our future to go well for our future selves), we also want things to go well for our present selves. We typically want things to go well for us now *and* in the future. This gives rise to another problem: our present and future interests can turn out to be at odds. My present self, for instance, may like to take risks (perhaps he has never suffered from any truly disastrous decisions yet). Yet, if I take a risk and the housing market collapses, my future self may become risk averse, wishing my present self not to take the risks he is about to take. We thus face a further problem: whose interests – the interests of one's present self or the interests of one's future self – should take priority? The answer, it seems, depends on whose interests are stronger. If my present self might benefit a little from a risk (feeling momentary pride, for instance, for taking a chance on buying a home and becoming a new homeowner), but my future self will suffer immensely (as a result of disastrous long-term consequences), then, presumably, my future self's interest should take priority. After all, I care now about both selves, and if a risk now will be more harmful than the advantages I will gain from it – taking both selves into account – then, instrumentally speaking, I would be better off not taking the risk. Conversely, however, if my present interests in taking risks are strong (I gain immense satisfaction from taking risks), but my present self turns out to be only mildly annoyed at the risks I take (as is sometimes the case – we are sometimes annoyed later on at choices our earlier selves made that made our earlier selves really happy at the time), then it is not so clear whether one should prioritize the interests of one's later self above those of one's earlier self. After all, in the case just described, one's present interest in risk-taking seems stronger than one's later interest in risk-aversion. Thus, the problem of possible future selves is compounded. We not only desperately want to know our future interests in some cases, so that we do not have to take potentially (even if only unlikely) disastrous risks: we also want to know, in many such cases, how to *order* our present and future interests. For instance, the soon-to-be-newlywed with cold feet might think to herself, 'Okay, I may not be quite sure about marrying this person, but I think I am willing to take the risk – well, at least right now. I wish I knew whether I will think the same thing later!').

In summation, although we may or may not always care about our future, and there may be cases where we are perfectly content to 'bet' on likely outcomes – when I grab a glass of water for instance, I do not 'stress' about the possibility that the water could be contaminated – there are clearly significant numbers of cases in our lives where we have strong, indeed overwhelming, interests in:

A. Knowing our future interests (that is, whether we will be happy with our decisions),
B. Knowing how to order our present and future interests, and
C. Acting in ways sure to *satisfy* those interests, without merely 'betting' on our probable future interests (since the whole point of these cases is that we do not want to 'bet': we want to *know*).

But can we satisfy these interests? Is there any possible way to know what we will want in the future, order our present interests with our future ones, and *satisfy* them in ways that do not involve 'betting'? The most obvious answer, again, is that we cannot: that these interests are in vain. However, as we will now begin to see, investigating precisely why they seem to be in vain can lead us to a solution: a way to satisfy at least some of them.

2.1 Possible futures

The most obvious difficulty we have knowing our future interests results from the uncertain nature of future events.

First, as we have seen, we sometimes have interests in knowing our interests in the near future, but those interests depend on how future events unfold. Consider again a student considering cheating on an exam. Such a student may think it is likely that they can cheat undetected, yet they may worry – wanting to *know* whether they will get caught. For their interests in the future may depend on that very fact. If they are not caught, they may be happy they cheated; but, if they are caught, they may wish they hadn't.

Similarly, sometimes our interests in knowing our future interests extend beyond the short term to the medium or long term. For instance, a couple may want to know whether they will be happy ten years from now with their decision to purchase a new home – yet whether they turn out to be happy depends at least in part on future events over which they have no control: housing markets, their employment situations, and so on. Or consider a putative 'moral' case. Suppose a husband has difficulty balancing his family and career interests. He wants to be successful in his career, yet the kind of focus he finds necessary for career success leads him to neglect his spouse and children. And so he begins to worry. He thinks to himself, 'I wish I knew what the right thing to do is. If I keep focusing on my career, I might be really successful, which I want. At the same time, if I keep focusing on it so intently, I might jeopardize my family: my children might become resentful, and my spouse might even want a divorce – none of which I want, either. Yet, if I focus less on my career, giving my spouse and children more attention, I might jeopardize my career success – which I do not want either. I wish I knew what will happen, and what I would be most happy with in the future.' Here again, however, it seems impossible for him to know the interests he wants to know: for the interests he will have in the future (the ones he wants to know now) depend in large part on future events – on whether he enjoys career success, whether his spouse or children feel resentment, and so on.

Now again, one might argue that in cases like these the most we can rationally do is focus on likely outcomes: on which risks are worth taking given what we do know. Yet there are two problems with this. First, in the cases in question, one does not want to bet on likely outcomes. One wants to know one's future interests for the express purpose of avoiding such risks – particularly the risks of unlikely outcomes (as in, 'I wish I knew whether the housing market would crash. Then I would know the right decision to make!'). For it is when we think about unlikely outcomes that those possible outcomes may appear unacceptable to us ('What if the improbable happens and the market tanks? We will be *miserable*'). In cases where we want to know our future interests, we typically want to know them precisely because we do not want to 'bet' on likely outcomes. Instead, we wish there were a better option – one that did not leave our fate open to the vicissitudes of future events, but which could give us certainty about what our future interests will be. Second, as we will see in Chapter 3 and beyond, such a better option exists: it is morality itself. Morality enables us to achieve a kind of certainty, in these cases, that we desire.

In order to appreciate the full extent of the problem I am presenting – and see the way to solve it – we need to look beyond our ignorance of future events and look at particular ways that we can be ignorant of our future psychological states, beginning with our psychological reactions to events.

2.2 Possible psychologies

As we have just seen, we often want to know our future interests, and how to order them with our present ones. However, our ignorance of future events – of housing markets, whether we will be caught cheating on an exam, and so on – stands in the way of our knowing them. This problem points to a more specific problem. It is not just (or even primarily) our ignorance of future events that causes us to be ignorant of our future interests: it is our ignorance of our future psychology that does so. Specifically, in order to know our future interests, and how to order them with our present ones, we need to know who we will *be* in the future. But, or so it seems, we cannot know that. We have already seen some instances of this. A couple considering purchasing a home does not merely want to know whether the housing market will turn out a certain way: they want to know, specifically, whether their future selves will be happy with their decision to buy the house. Similarly, a student considering cheating on an exam may not merely want to know whether they will get caught: they may want to know whether they will feel guilty having cheated, or whether, if they get caught, they will regret having cheated or simply shrug off their punishment with no remorse. Or indeed, as I sit here now, there are certain things I want to know about my future. I want to know not simply whether I will have written a good book: I worry, more specifically, about whether I will be happy in the future having written this book. I wish I could know these future psychological facts about me – I want to know whether I will be happy or miserable having written this book – because, from my present perspective, it personally matters to me a great deal.

But of course the problem here is the same as before. As much as we might want to know our future selves' psychological states – such as whether they will be happy or miserable with our decisions – there are numerous reasons why we cannot. Indeed, as we will now see, human beings are systematically poor at estimating their future psychological states.

First, empirical psychology indicates that human beings often experience *preference reversals*, wanting one thing at one time but the opposite thing at a later time, often in ways that involve contradictory forward-looking and backward-looking motivations concerning risk-taking.[31-34] For instance, I may want a promotion at work at one time, but then, once I get it, wish that I had not gotten it (perhaps because of the added stresses). Similarly, I may want to risk cheating on an exam before getting caught, but wish I had not taken that same risk after getting caught.

Second, one major reason why we undergo preference reversals is that human beings are surprisingly poor at *affective forecasting* – at estimating how our future selves will respond to various outcomes.[35-38] For instance, people tend to think they will enjoy long-term gains in subjective well-being by winning the lottery – yet data consistently show the opposite: winning the lottery only tends to lead to a short-term spike in subjective well-being, not long-term gains.[39-41] Or again, consider the case of a promotion at work. Before one gets a promotion, the money and increased social status may 'look great.' It is only after one gets the promotion that one experiences a variety of costs that might make the money and increased status no longer appear 'worth it,' such as longer work-hours, greater stress, and so on.

Third, as we saw earlier, all too often preference reversals are of a very specific sort, involving one's future self having backward-looking (or retrospective) preferences that one had never had an earlier, forward-looking preference to begin with. For instance, suppose I want to be a lawyer at time t, and decide to attend law school. However, once in law school, I find I do not enjoy it. Consequently, I may wish at this later time, t_n, not merely not to become a lawyer (contrary to my earlier preference to become one); I may wish that my earlier self had never wanted to become a lawyer to begin with. Indeed, as Daniel Kahneman points out, empirical psychology increasingly indicates that, in a very real sense, we often have two 'selves': a forward-looking self (with prospective preferences about how we want our future to go), and a backward-looking self (with retrospective preferences about how we wish our past had gone)[4,42-44]: selves who can have interests in each *other* having different interests.

Fourth, life arguably contains *transformative experiences* that make it impossible for us to reliably estimate our future interests. As L.A. Paul argues, some life-experiences appear so profound that they fundamentally change who we are – our deepest values and motivational interests – in ways that we cannot possibly anticipate.[45] Paul focuses on giving birth to a child. One may have one set of values or preferences before the experience – for instance, a desire to have a child and valuing having a family – and yet develop completely different, unexpectable, new values or preferences afterwards. For instance, a person may not feel ready to have a child or want one prior to giving birth (say, due to an unexpected pregnancy), but then find themselves transformed by the very act of giving birth: by a flood of never-before-experienced hormones and the experience of attachment to the child that one never expected. Conversely, for some people, the experience of having a child of one's own may be a transformative experience in the opposite direction. One may initially desire a child of one's own and 'feel ready' for one – but after actually having the child (perhaps as a result of a difficult pregnancy or difficult child) wish one hadn't. And indeed, there are many online support groups for parents who experience such unexpected transformations.[46–47]

Although research on transformative experience is still in its infancy, a great deal of life is arguably transformative in the way Paul describes. For instance, one may begin college with certain beliefs, preferences, and expectations about oneself – such as the expectation that one wants to become a medical practitioner – only to find oneself unexpectedly 'transformed' by a great course or teacher in another field. One may enter into a relationship expecting it to be a casual romance, only to find oneself transformed by falling in love. And so on.

One particular kind of (arguably) transformative experience that happens to many of us from time to time – though not all of us (such as, apparently, psychopaths) – is transformative empathy.[48] Sometimes we experience ourselves feeling for others, identifying our interests with theirs, in completely unexpected ways. I myself have had a variety of these experiences. Last summer, I went on a fishing trip to celebrate a friend's birthday. An hour or so into the trip, I caught a fish. There it was, staring back at me, and in a way that I did not expect – indeed, never would have expected, given that I had fished before – I felt terrible. For a brief moment, I felt what it would be like to be in the fish's position, staring back at me, gasping for air on a hook, wanting nothing more than to live. Similarly, consider a person who neglects his spouse for years or decades. This person may be 'coldhearted,' never appreciating his spouse's frustrations during all that time, only to finally feel his spouse's frustration during an argument, seeing himself from her perspective for the first time, and in a way that leads him to profoundly, and unexpectedly, regret the years of neglect – leaving him to wish now (say, in the midst of a divorce) that he could undo what he did.

Indeed, simply getting older is arguably transformative as well. While one may know through testimony and experience that older people tend to desire more career and family stability than younger individuals, younger individuals may be incapable of properly appreciating the significance of these facts precisely because they are young and have not yet gone through the transformative experience of becoming older. Such experiences appear to be quite common. It is quite common for people, later in life, to look back at the decisions of their younger selves and say, 'What was I thinking?' We may wish we had studied harder, instead of spending so much time socializing; we may wish we had invested earlier, instead of treating money so casually; and so on. And yet, it seems, it is precisely because our earlier selves were young and unable to experience life from the perspective of a 40-year-old future self that they behaved as they did. If only our younger selves were better able to appreciate the perspectives of our older selves, our decisions might be very different. Indeed, in a series of fascinating studies, researchers have shown that individuals who are presented with aged images of themselves – their future 'selves' – save more money for retirement and are less likely to engage in 'delinquent' behavior (such as cheating).[23-26]

And so we face the aforementioned problem yet again. We sometimes find ourselves wanting to know our future interests, and how to order them with our present interests, and yet, it seems – because of our inability to predict our psychological future or empathize with our future selves (rare experimental interventions aside) – we cannot know them. We may be able to predict our future interests with some amount of accuracy (though, as we have just seen, psychological science shows we can predict them with far less accuracy than we might naively expect). But it still seems that we cannot know our future interests, for the simple reason that our psychological future is, from our standpoint in the present, uncertain.

2.3 Possible choices

Thus far I have been focusing on things that 'happen' to us in the future: future events, as well as future psychological reactions (such as unexpected preference reversals, experiences of empathy, and so on). Yet we face an even deeper problem. In cases where we want to know our future interests, we experience many (if not all) of our dominant motivational interests – the interests we actually act upon – as being undetermined until we make them. Indeed, it seems impossible to know our future interests in advance because, from a first-personal point of view, our dominant motivational interests in the future do not seem to exist until our future selves make the choices they do.

Here is why the choices made by our future selves are important. Consider again the case where you buy a house and things turn out badly: the housing market crashes, your mortgage goes underwater, and you experience financial distress, leading to frustration and hardship between you and your spouse. Although you cannot control housing markets, nor (fully, at least) how you feel – you may experience anxiety or emotional difficulty against your will – you nevertheless experience some of your motivational interests as being controlled by your choices: among others, how much you choose to dwell on the past, fixate on your current anxieties, or simply 'put the past behind you,' taking active steps to improve your current financial situation and choosing to focus more on the future than the past. These are precisely the types of future choices – which will affect your future interests – that you cannot predict in advance. Because these kinds of voluntary decisions are so critical to arguments in future chapters, I would like to discuss them at length.

Notice first that I did not make an ontological point here, asserting that there is no fact of the matter about what our future choices (and so, dominant motivational interests) will be prior to our acting. Such facts may well be settled in advance, if determinism is true and all of our future actions are determined by causal laws.[49] My claim is merely an epistemic one concerning our ability to *know* our future choices. For whatever the ultimate metaphysical nature of free will may be – perhaps our choices are determined in advance, perhaps not – the simple fact is this: we experience our choices, now and in the future, as though they are undetermined before we make them. I cannot know what my future selves' motivational interests will be, in large part, because I regard their future choices as ones I have not yet made.

Now again, whether this is merely a contingent epistemic problem – one that we might be able surmount someday (if, for instance, determinism is true) – is a question we cannot yet answer. Although I have argued elsewhere that a primitive, utterly unpredictable form of libertarian free will is consistent with all known physics, and that certain types of scientific tests might provide strong evidence for or against the existence of such freedom[50], whether or not such freedom exists is an open question. Consequently, it is an open question of whether we could, in principle, know our future choices before we make them. We will come back to the contingent nature of our ignorance in Section 5.

Because our first-personal experience of choice – the sense in which we experience our dominant motivational interests as decided by us at the time we act – is critical to the argument I will give in future chapters, I would like to dwell in more detail on how we experience it. For, as we will now see, our experience of first-personal deliberation appears ambiguous between two competing accounts: two accounts which, if our inquiry is to respect Firm Foundations, we should work with simultaneously.

Let us begin by examining how we often explain our intentional actions as second- or third-personal observers, including when reflecting upon our past actions. Suppose Jones intentionally cheats on an exam. How will we (i.e. outside observers) explain his behavior? One natural way to explain it is in terms of *belief-desire pairs*, or combinations of representational states (beliefs) and motivational states (desires). For instance, we will say, 'Jones wanted to do well on the exam and believed he would do well by cheating – so he cheated.' And indeed, if you were to ask Jones why he cheated, he might give something like the same answer ('I wanted to do well and believed I would do well by cheating'). Let us call this the Humean Model of first-personal deliberation, as it conforms to the so-called 'Humean theory of motivation': the theory that understands intentional action as the result of belief-desire pairs.[51]

This book is not concerned with whether the Humean Model is correct as a theory of the causal basis of intentional action. For all this book shows, it may well be. Perhaps all of our actions are caused by combinations of motivational and representational states, just as the Humean Model states. I am less interested in the causal basis of action, however, than I am in the first-personal experience of deliberation. For whatever the causal truth about our actions may be, it is from within the first-personal perspective that we experience ourselves as making choices, including 'moral choices.' Let us examine, then, whether the Humean Model adequately models our first-personal experience of deliberation: that is, whether we experience our actions as resulting from mere belief-desire pairs of the sort mentioned above.

Interestingly, there are reasons to think the Humean Model may be broadly accurate as a model of first-personal deliberation for two types of beings: nonhuman animals and human psychopaths. Although it is difficult to know for sure 'how animals experience their own action' given our current evidence, one of the reasons why animal behavior is often so amusing is that animals appear to be 'pushed around the world' by their beliefs and desires. For instance, if Fido wants to go outside and believes that standing next to the door will get him outside, he will stand by the door. But, if the moment Fido gets outside, he wants to come back inside, he will stand by the door waiting to come inside. There does not seem to be any further first-personal question that comes into Fido's mind, such as, '*Should* I want to go back inside given that I just wanted to come outside a second ago?' Fido, for the most part, does not seem capable of entertaining first-personal questions like this (though one might wonder whether, in some cases, Fido does think about what he should do, such as when Fido 'knows he should not jump on the couch').

Similarly, human psychopaths often appear to find themselves impelled by their beliefs and desires – as 'not having a choice' of how to act. We see this in the following kinds of very striking reported statements of psychopathic serial killers:

> Jeffrey Dahmer: 'I...wanted him to stay with me so I strangled him.'[52]
>
> Edmund Kemper: 'I just wanted to see how it would feel to shoot grandma.'[53]
>
> Tommy Lynn Sells: 'I just knew I wanted to go in there, and hurt someone.'[53]
>
> Arthur Shawcross: 'She was giving me oral sex, and she got carried away...So I choked her.'[54]
>
> Gary Ridgeway: '[A]t a very young age, he stabbed a little boy, and when asked why he stabbed that little boy, he said he wanted to see and feel what it was like to kill somebody and see somebody die.'[55]

The striking thing about these statements is what they lack. Instead of asking (and answering) the kind of question that the rest of us would presumably raise in our own minds if (Heaven forbid) we were to be tempted to commit a heinous crime – namely, the question, 'Should I act on these desires?' – the individuals above give no indication of ever encountering this first-personal question. Rather than asking how they should behave, they appear to simply *behave*, acting on whatever belief-desire pairs they have at the time.

Nonhuman animals and psychopaths, in other words, appear to first-personally experience many – if not all – of their actions as conforming to the Humean Model. The rest of us, however, experience our decisions very differently. We do not experience all of our actions as caused by beliefs and desires that are out of our control. We experience some, if not all, of our actions as resulting from choices we make on the basis of first-personal normative judgments about how we should act.

Consider a simple case that should be very familiar to most readers: the choice of whether to get out of bed in the morning. Sometimes, getting out of bed is easy (well, for some people, at least). Sometimes you wake up excited to meet the day and just want to get out of bed. Other days, however, are very different. Sometimes getting out of bed can be a real chore, and you can find yourself lying in bed not wanting to get up. It is nice and warm in bed, perhaps, and you do not want to face the cold air and floors by getting up. Or, alternatively, perhaps it is a work day and you just do not feel like going to work, etc.

How do you experience this situation? First-personally, you do not (ordinarily, at any rate) experience your desires as 'pushing you around the world' against your will. Instead, you experience yourself as having the ability to choose what you do. But now how, first-personally, do you experience such choices? Imagine yourself lying in bed not wanting to get up. How do you experience your action? Arguably, as follows: First, at some implicit level, you consider your options. You may think about what might happen to you if you are late to work (viz. 'Will I get in trouble?'). You may think to yourself, 'Do I have another five minutes to waste?' And so on. All kinds of conscious thoughts may go through your mind, and you may well feel torn about what to do. At some point, though, you make a decision – and how will you do it? Arguably, like this: you will come to a judgment about what you ought to do ('I ought to get out of bed now'), and then, if you have strength of will, you will follow through on what you think you ought to do.

Here, for instance, is what usually happens to me. I am not a morning person, and typically do not want to get out of bed. But then it occurs to me consciously: 'I ought to get up now. I am going to be late for work if I do not get up, and I do not want to be late for work.' Indeed, sometimes I even say these things to myself out loud to motivate myself ('I really ought to get out of bed now'). Finally, if I have strength of will, I experience myself as though I will myself out of bed (I tell myself, 'Getting up now!,' and experience myself as making it so). Of course, things do not always go so nicely. Sometimes, when I am feeling particularly lazy, I might come to a very different judgment – for instance, the judgment that I ought to hit the snooze bar on my alarm clock a few times and sleep in. Other times, I think I ought to get out of bed, but then I lack the will to do so: I choose to stay in bed even though I think I ought to get up.

We can illustrate the same points with other cases. Suppose I go to the fridge to get a beer. First-personally, even if I desire a beer, I do not experience my desires as impelling me to get one against my will. Instead, I experience myself as having the capacity to choose whether to have a beer. And how do I choose? I do not experience myself as walking over the fridge against my will. Whatever I do – whether I get a beer or not – I arguably do so against the background of some first-personal judgment about what I ought to do. I just got a beer because I thought I ought to have one – as simple as that. If I thought I ought not to have a beer – because, say, it would render me too drunk to write – then I might have willed myself not to have a beer. Similarly, consider your decision to read this book. You made this choice. But how? Arguably, as follows: you judged for yourself – if only tacitly – that you ought to read it. You sat there, saw it on your bookshelf, and thought to yourself, 'Why not? I guess I ought to read it now,' thereby choosing to read it. Of course, these are not the only ways things can go. Sometimes we act against our own first-personal normative judgments. Sometimes I think to myself, 'I really should not have any ice cream – I'm putting on weight,' but then I go ahead and choose to have an ice cream anyway.

Let us call this the Kantian Model of first-personal deliberation. Although it is not obviously Kant's own view, it actually sits very well with many things Kant wrote – for instance, 'All human beings think of themselves as having free will. From this come all judgments upon actions as being such that they ought to have been done even though they were not done,'[56] and, '...for this "ought" is strictly speaking a "will" that holds for every rational being...'[57] In these passages, Kant seems to be suggesting what I am arguing – that we arguably experience our all of our choices first-personally along the following lines:

- *Component 1 (beliefs and desires):* We experience ourselves having wants/desires and beliefs, including instrumental beliefs about how to best satisfy our wants/desires (example: I want to stay in bed, but I also want to be successful, and believe that if I want to be successful, I ought to get out of bed).
- *Component 2 (explicit or tacit first-personal 'ought'-judgment):* We experience ourselves as having an explicit or tacit first-personal normative judgment about how we ought to act ('I ought to get out of bed now').
- *Component 3 (choice):* We experience ourselves as choosing whether to act on our ought-judgment ('I will get out of bed now') or to act against it ('I know I ought to get out of bed, but I will not').
- *Component 4 (action):* We experience ourselves actually acting.

Notice that I have not actually asserted that this how we deliberate first-personally. In presenting it, I have repeatedly invoked the qualifying phrase, 'arguably.' This is by design, for as we will see shortly, our experience of first-personal deliberation appears ambiguous between two competing models: the Kantian Model just presented, and a 'Hybrid Model' that combines elements of the Humean and Kantian Models. Before we see how this is the case, however, a bit more discussion of the Kantian Model is necessary.

First, as I mentioned earlier, I am not suggesting the Kantian Model of first-personal deliberation as a causal competitor to the Humean Model of intentional action. For all this book shows, it may turn out, scientifically, that the Humean Model is correct as a causal theory of action: that all of our actions may stem from belief-desire pairs. Nor am I claiming, by expounding the Kantian Model of first-personal deliberation, that we in fact have some special capacity to intervene in the physical-causal order to act against our brain's pre-existing motivations (something which Kant notoriously claims in arguing that we have 'transcendental freedom')[58–60]. Rather, my aim is merely to argue that the Kantian Model coheres better with how we typically experience our decisions than the Humean Model does. And this, by and large – with a few qualifications (to be examined shortly) – is certainly the case. We do not experience most, if any, of our actions as caused by belief-desire pairs that are out of our control. We experience ourselves as being in control of our actions: as deciding what we ought to do, and (at least ordinarily) having the capacity to choose whether we act as we judge we ought to – just as the Kantian Model claims.

Now, one possible concern with the Kantian Model is that it presupposes that all of our choices, first-personally, involve some kind of explicit or tacit 'ought'-judgment. For although we may indeed make some such judgments first-personally, at least at a highly tacit level, it is at least arguable that in some cases we do not do this at all. We seem to perform a good number of actions on 'autopilot,' without coming to a clear judgment about what we ought to do or engaging in any apparent act of willing. Sometimes, for instance, one just finds oneself getting out of bed in the morning: you desire to get out of bed, and you just do. Other times, one just finds oneself going to the fridge to get ice cream: you desire ice cream and get it without deliberating. Oftentimes, it is only once the following question enters your mind – 'Should I really be doing this?' – that we engage in a kind of Kantian deliberation. One may ask oneself, 'Should I really go to work today?,' or 'Should I really be eating more ice cream?,' and only then conceive oneself as making a decision. Furthermore, it oftentimes seems as though the cause of this question is conscience (one may think to oneself, 'Should I really lash out in anger? I might regret it later'). Let us call this alternative model – one in which we experience some of our everyday actions as simply following from belief-desire pairs (in accordance with the Humean Model), and other actions, those we deliberate about, as based on first-personal ought-judgments (in accordance with the Kantian Model) – the 'Hybrid Model' of first-personal deliberation (since, in essence, it combines the first two models).

I hold that we are not currently in an adequate position to know, empirically, which of these two conceptions of first-personal deliberation – the Kantian Model or Hybrid Model – is more accurate (again, not as a causal model, but merely as a model of how we experience our actions). There may be some tentative grounds for favoring the Hybrid Model, as it is a consensus view in empirical neuroscience that our habitual behavior and capacities for self-regulation are comprised by two different – and independent – brain-circuits that, in some but *not* all cases, interact with one another: a 'habit circuit' in the limbic system and 'self-regulation' system in the prefrontal cortex.[61] Further, it is deficits in and between precisely these circuits that, at least in part, appear to account for the impulsive behavior of psychopaths: that is, their simply acting on whichever beliefs and desires strike them, rather than their deliberating about which desires they should have or act upon.[62–64] Insofar as our 'habit' and 'self-regulation' circuits appear to be distinct, and it is their interaction that appears to lead nonpsychopathic adults to engage in first-personal normative deliberation, it appears plausible that only some of our actions may involve first-personal normative judgments: namely, actions where our 'self-regulation' circuits are engaged – which would seem to support the Hybrid Model over the Kantian Model. However, since the science here is still unsettled, and, as Kant and contemporary philosophers of mind have argued, our ability to reliably introspect the contents of our own minds is profoundly imperfect,[65–66] I would like to proceed on the supposition that either the Kantian Model or Hybrid Model is correct as a model of first-personal deliberation. I believe this is an entirely safe assumption, as it is clearly the case that we either experience some or all of our actions as involving first-personal normative judgments and the capacity to choose whether to act on those judgments. We may or may not always experience ourselves as making first-personal judgments about how we ought to act, or as first-personally having the choice of whether to act on those judgments – but we clearly experience ourselves this way at least sometimes. And this is all we need to proceed, as my argument for morality's rationality merely depends on us at least sometimes experiencing ourselves first-personally as having such capacities.

For now, the most relevant point is that both of the aforementioned models – the Kantian and Hybrid Models – make the problems we face about not knowing our future interests altogether worse than before. For now we see that it is not merely our inability to know in advance how future events will play out (will the housing market crash?) or our inability to know our future psychological reactions (will we be happy purchasing the house?) that comprise the problem. The problem, when we want to know our future interests and order them with our present ones, seems much worse in the following respect: insofar as we experience some, if not all, of our actions (as up to us) to choose at the time of action (as not determined by pre-existing belief-desire pairs, but as decided by us 'on the fly,' on the basis of first-personal normative judgments, *qua* the Kantian and Hybrid Models), we encounter our lives as though our dominant motivational interests (the interests we will act upon in the future) are unsettled – as interests *we ourselves have to choose in the future.*

Now, whether this is a merely contingent epistemic problem – one that we could in principle overcome – depends on metaphysical facts about the nature of free will. If we live in a deterministic world, our current ignorance of our future choices could, in principle, be overcome. On the other hand, if we live in libertarian world – one in which our choices are undetermined before they are made – then our ignorance of our future choices would be insurmountable. We will return to this in Section 5. The point for now is simply that it *is* a problem for us here and now as we live our lives. In cases where we want to know our future interests, it seems that we cannot know them because we have not made the relevant 'choices' yet.

2.4 A very real problem

The problem of possible future selves laid out above is not merely an 'academic' problem. It is one that sometimes quite literally keeps us up at night. When we have momentous decisions to make (about buying a home, or changing careers, or telling a dangerous lie), we often find ourselves wanting to know the future: wanting to know what our future interests will be – whether we will be happy with the decisions we made, want us to have made different decisions, and so on. Should we buy that house? We often want to know *now* what the right answer is: what will in fact make our future selves happy or satisfied. But the problem is that life is uncertain: it seems we cannot possibly know what we want to know. And so we find ourselves frustrated, fearful even, feeling like we have to take risks we do not want to take (as when we say in a resigned fashion, 'I wish I knew what the right thing to do is – but I have to make a decision. I hope it is the right one').

At this point, two possibilities present themselves. The first possibility is that this problem has no real solution – that no matter how much we might want to know the future, we cannot help but take risks, preferably calculated ones, based on probabilities of expected interests and outcomes. Another possibility, however, is that there are things about our future selves that we can know in advance, thus solving the problem either in whole or in part. Might it be possible to know our future interests in advance? We will now see how the answer to this question may indeed be 'yes,' and that morality may be the solution.

3 Morality as the solution?

Sometimes even the best among us are tempted to do things that violate moral norms. Some people are tempted to cheat on their spouses, others are tempted to cheat on tests, and so on – and of course, sometimes they give into those temptations. But let us think about why people don't give into them, when they don't. On the one hand, sometimes we do not give into temptation simply because we think doing so is wrong. We think to ourselves, 'It is wrong to cheat.' Oftentimes, however, this is not enough to motivate us. We begin to think about how we might benefit by acting against that judgment – that is, how doing something wrong might satisfy our interests. We think to ourselves how it might benefit us to cheat: how we might enjoy it, not get caught, not feel guilty, and so on. It is often at this point that we set aside our judgment that the action is wrong and focus – as the instrumental theory of normative rationality says we should do – on our interests. We begin to think, in particular, of future consequences. We imagine getting away with cheating, and how nice it might feel to cheat successfully. Then, however, we think about what it might be like to get caught: of how painful it might be to be caught cheating on a test, or caught cheating by one's spouse. Further, we might think about the possibility of not getting caught, but feeling guilty later on, and perhaps simply worrying about getting caught. In short, we think about potential outcomes, and how well those outcomes would satisfy our present and future interests ('Will I regret the choice to cheat?').

Notice what is going on here. Once we set whatever 'moral' judgment we have aside (such as 'cheating would be wrong') – as we sometimes do, thanks to temptation – we encounter the decision of whether to cheat as a struggle to predict the future, including our future motivational interests, and how to weigh them against our present interests. But this is just the problem of possible future selves. We want to know whether the tempting thing will benefit us in the future, and yet we do not know what the future holds. And how we solve, or do not solve, this problem is what leads us to our eventual action. If we judge it instrumentally rational to 'bet' on cheating – if we think we are likely to get away with it, not feel guilt, and so on – then we are apt to cheat. If, on the other hand, we judge it to be against our interests to bet on cheating (perhaps because we worry about getting caught, or feeling guilt, and so on), then we are apt not to cheat. As 'calculating' as this may seem, I trust we all recognize that this is more or less the kind of process people go through when they struggle with temptation.

Now let us think, however, about why we decide to do the 'right' thing when we do. Although sometimes we just decide it is wrong to cheat and leave it at that – acting on our judgment that it is wrong – how do we respond when people confide in us, expressing their temptation to behave otherwise (when someone says, 'I really want to cheat. I don't think I will get caught or feel guilty'), or indeed, when they tell us they have already given into temptation ('I cheated on my test')? Aside from simply insisting it is wrong, we typically try to convince the person that the behavior is unwise – that cheating is a kind of risk they should not engage in, a form of action that 'puts their future in jeopardy.' And we are right. Indeed, as we will see in more detail in Chapter 3, the problem of possible future selves – the very problem we struggle with when we are tempted to do wrong – entails that immoral behavior is unwise. It is unwise because, when one behaves immorally, although the future could turn out the way one wants (one cheating successfully, without guilt), there are possible futures – very real possibilities – in which one's actions turn out to be against one's interests (one is unexpectedly caught and punished, one unexpectedly finds oneself worrying, or guilt-ridden, and so on). When people come to us with temptations, we say to them things like, 'Yes, you could get away with it. But cheating is a dumb risk, one you could regret. You'd be far better off studying.' On the face of it, this is merely a prudential argument for not cheating. Yet its ubiquity – that is, how often we respond in this kind of manner – suggests that there may be something to it. And indeed, as we will see in Chapter 3, there is something to it. Immoral behavior (behavior that aims to advance one's own interests to the detriment of others') requires a great deal of luck – namely, the future turning out just as one wishes it to: luck that we typically learn early in life that we should avoid, and, if the arguments Chapters 3–6 give are correct, we *should* learn to avoid. Moral behavior, on the other hand – behavior that treats the interests of all people fairly for its own sake – does not depend on dumb luck. Morality solves the problem of possible future selves as far as it can be solved by taking away uncertainty about the future, replacing risk with the certainty that, by being fair to others, we are also fair to all of our possible future selves: both to our future selves who only care about themselves, but also those who are care about others. And, or so I will argue, trading the risks of immorality for this kind of certainty is instrumentally rational: it is the only instrumentally rational way to respond to the problem of possible future selves.

4 Is the problem too contingent?

I have just said that this book's argumentative strategy will be to argue that morality, properly understood, is the most instrumentally rational way to respond to the problem of possible future selves. Yet this invites an obvious concern. The problem of possible future selves is a contingent problem, one based on three things:

1. Our at least sometimes wanting to know and order future interests with our present ones.
2. Our ignorance of them, since the future has not yet occurred.
3. Our wanting to satisfy the above interests without 'betting' on likelihoods.

However, insofar as this is the case, my account would seem to make morality's normative force dependent on these contingencies. What if we never wanted to know our future selves' interests, or what if we could know their interests? Do I really want to suggest that morality would not apply to us under those contingencies? If so, does my theory not contradict a widespread[1–2] (if not universal[67]) assumption that morality's normative force must be inescapably 'categorical'?

My answer to this concern is as follows. First, as I argued in Chapter 1, we should not consider it the job of moral philosophy to cohere with preconceptions about what morality 'should be,' any more than we should think it is the job of physics to conform to pre-theoretic prejudices about space and time. Just as observation disproved the common-sense notion that space and time 'must be absolute,' so too should we be open to the possibilities that observational facts might disprove the 'categorical force' of moral norms. Moral philosophy should be based on firm foundations – on observational facts attested to by virtually everyone – and we should follow those foundations where they lead. Moreover, as we saw in Chapter 1, many human observers do not appear to see morality as having categorical force. Many characters in Plato's dialogues – Thrasymachus, Glaucon, Adeimantus, Callicles, and Polus – do not appear to think that moral norms are 'categorically binding': they repeatedly ask for instrumental arguments for behaving morally, since in their view one should do whatever is in one's own interests. Nor, apparently, do criminals or psychopaths appreciate morality's so-called 'categorical nature.' And again, philosophers such as Nietzsche, Joyce, and others have argued that the intuitions some have that morality 'must be categorical' are erroneous results of social conditioning or evolution. The mere fact that it seems to some (though by no means all) that 'morality is categorical' is, in itself, no reason to think that it is in fact true. For again, what seems true and what is true can be, and have proven to be many times in history, very different things.

The relevant question is whether morality's normative force being contingent on the problem of possible future selves is compelling – or something we should take seriously – given the complete class of observational facts we have, particularly the fact that instrumentalism is the most widely accepted conception of normative rationality among human beings. Interestingly, there are several converging reasons to think that morality's normative force may indeed be contingent upon our encountering the problem of possible future selves.

Let us begin with the instrumental conception of normative rationality that Chapter 1 defended as a firm foundation for moral philosophy. Now consider two types of beings who are otherwise capable of behaving in instrumentally rational ways:

> **Impulsive being**: A being who never cares about the future, and is simply motivated by their present motivational interests.
>
> **Omniscient evil being**: A being who does care about the future, has complete knowledge of what their future interests will be, and whose interests now and in the future directly violate moral norms (against theft, murder, and so on).

Would either of these beings feel the normative force of moral norms? There are reasons to think not. First, there appear to actually be impulsive beings in this world: psychopaths. Psychopaths, as we saw earlier, lack normal abilities to care about their future or past. They act on their present inclinations (if they want to murder, they murder), they do not regret their behavior in the future, and they do not experience morality's normative force. Second, consider the omniscient evil being. Although there are no such beings in our world (though perhaps some very successful psychopaths come relevantly close for some amount of time, as they go on murder sprees with abandon), there are science fiction cases that approximate them – and when we reflect on those cases, both intuitively and instrumentally, it is hard to fathom morality's so-called 'categorical' force. Indeed, an omniscient evil agent would almost certainly attest to not experiencing any such normative force. Given their interests and ability to get away with immoral behavior with impunity, they would plausibly deny morality's 'categorical force.' Indeed, we see exactly this in an episode of *Star Trek: The Original Series* entitled, 'By Any Other Name.' In this episode, the crew of the Starship Enterprise encounters a class of beings, the Kelvans, who are – at least for a time – able to satisfy their interests without the possibility of failure. Because the Kelvans can exert their will over the humans with absolute impunity, they claim to see no reason not to do so. No matter how much the humans protest, saying the Kelvans are acting 'wrongly,' the Kelvans are unmoved, failing to see any normative reason to care about the humans' moral claims. More interesting still, it is only when the Kelvans become corrupted by human emotions and uncertainties – due to assuming human form, they unexpectedly come to form attachments to humans – that they begin to 'see that what they were doing was wrong.' In short, it seems to be precisely the fact that the Kelvans become suddenly unsure of what they might care about in the future – the fact that they are confronted for the first time with the possibility of regretting their behavior in the future – that they feel morality's normative force at all.

And indeed, if we just step back for a moment from science fiction cases to everyday life, the same patterns emerge. As we saw in Section 3, our ordinary-everyday moral reasoning is similar. When we are tempted to violate moral norms (such as cheating on a test), we may initially be beset by the categorical thought that 'cheating is wrong' – yet this categorical belief may have little or no normative purchase on us unless and until we consider the possible future consequences (guilt, remorse, punishment, and so on). Finally, when we try to convince people not to give into temptations to behave immorally, this too is how we do it: we do not simply assert 'it is wrong' and leave it at that; we try to convince

70 Rightness as Fairness

the person that their behavior is unwise, given their inability to predict the future. Consequently, although some (and perhaps many) readers may want to believe in morality's 'categorical nature' – and again, treat my approach as changing the subject from morality (which is supposed to be categorical) to prudence (which in their view is not) – my final reply is: wait and see. If, as I believe, a complete theory of Rightness as Fairness can be derived from the problem of possible future selves, and if that theory satisfies all seven principles of theory selection defended in Chapter 1 better than rival theories, then we have fair reasons to doubt morality's 'categorical nature.' We should set it aside and hold instead that morality is a product of our nature: of our concern for our future selves, and ignorance thereof.

Finally, it is worth noting that the ultimate nature of reality and free will have important implications here. On the one hand, if determinism is true, then we could – at least in principle – know our future interests in advance, 'programming' ourselves to be omniscient evil beings (like the Kelvans): in which case, on my account, 'morality' would come to lack any normative force (something which, again, I do not think we can cavalierly reject). On the other hand, if either quantum indeterminacy and/or some form of irreducible libertarian free will exists – entailing that knowledge of our future interests is impossible in advance – then, on my account, the instrumental rationality of morality would indeed be 'inescapable' for us (since, on my account, the rationality of conforming to moral norms emerges from our ignorance of the future). Notice, furthermore, that these implications are broadly in line with Immanuel Kant's own notion that morality's categorical normative force is tied up with 'transcendental freedom.' According to Kant, the moral law is categorical *because* we have transcendental freedom, understood as a kind of libertarian capacity to impose it upon ourselves, and conform to it, as a categorical law.[58–60] While my account is similar, it is notably more flexible. My account holds that if we are only contingently ignorant of the future, then morality contingently applies to us (in a normatively rational sense); but, if we are beings who necessarily care about our future, wanting to know our future interests, and, if we are categorically ignorant of our future, then morality would indeed be 'categorically inescapable.' I believe this flexibility of my account to be attractive and plausible: for, as we saw above in the cases of the Kelvans, human psychopaths, and the omniscient evil agent, an agent's experience of morality's normative force (or lack thereof) does seem contingent upon these facts.

5 Two nonsolutions

Before providing my own solution to the problem of possible future selves in Chapter 3 and beyond, there are a couple of possible proposals we should examine.

5.1 Nonsolution 1: probable futures

Perhaps the most obvious way to respond to the problem of possible future selves is to appeal to probability. Yes, one might say, there are cases where we want to know our future interests and not 'bet' on likely outcomes – but there is no way to satisfy these interests, and given that there isn't, the most instrumentally rational way to satisfy one's interests on the whole is to still choose probabilistically, on the basis of one's present interests and expectations of what one's future interests are likely to be. Consider, after all, a simple act of crossing the street. Suppose I want to know what my future interests will be – for instance, I want to know whether I will make it across the street safely – and that I do not want to bet on likely outcomes (I am fearful of the mere possibility that I might get hit). Even if I cannot know the future – and even if I do not want to bet on likely outcomes – it still seems as though the most instrumentally rational option available to me is to bet on likely outcomes: otherwise, I will never cross the street.

My response is that this would be exactly right, were no better option. And indeed, when it comes to some things we want to know about the future – facts about housing markets, crossing streets safely, and so on – I think the answer is clearly right. We may want to know whether we will be happy buying a certain house, or whether we will cross an unsafe street safely – and yet we may only be able to 'bet' probabilistically on what is likely to happen. But notice that there is something obviously suboptimal about this answer that we should want to avoid, if possible. For again, there is a reason why one wants to know things about the future. Consider again, for instance, a couple thinking of buying a new home. They want to know what decision *will* make their future selves happy. If the best they can do is place a probabilistic bet on outcomes, then – no matter how conscientious their 'bet' may be – they can nevertheless fail to realize the interests they cared about. For instance, suppose they buy the house, and disaster strikes (for instance, the housing market crashes). The fact that the disaster appeared unlikely at an earlier point in time might not console the couple one bit, as they may still wish their earlier selves had known of the impending disaster. If there were a better way for their earlier selves to have known the relevant facts about the

72 Rightness as Fairness

future, rather than merely betting on probabilities, than that alternative would – on instrumentally rational grounds – be preferable.

Now again, it might seem obvious when it comes to cases like this, that there are no better options: all one can do is act on the basis of probabilities. As we will see in Chapter 3, however, this is only partly true. While there are facts about the future – about housing markets and the like – that we cannot know in advance, it is possible to know other things about the future: things about our own capacity to make choices, to whatever extent our choices are under our control.

5.2 Nonsolution 2: diachronic motivational consistency

Another possible answer to the problem of possible future selves – broadly suggested by the notion of cross-time cooperation mentioned earlier – is to argue, as Michael Smith has in relation to something very much like the problem I have presented, that rationality requires one to seek to *motivational consistency* across time. According to Smith, we should take diachronic motivational consistency to be 'partially constitutive of what it is to have an ideal psychology.'[68] Why? Smith argues that coherence is obviously a requirement of rationality, and that any theory of rationality that does not require motivational consistency – such as Bernard Williams' theory that agents' reasons for actions are relative to their desires[69] – 'purports to be one that honours requirements of coherence, but fails spectacularly to do so.'[70]

Yet, is coherence really a requirement of rationality? The problem is: it depends. It depends on what conception of rationality one is working with. This book, however, has argued that the firmest foundation for moral philosophy is instrumentalism. Yet instrumentalism, in ways that Williams affirms, cannot be straightforwardly utilized to derive coherence as a non-negotiable standard of rationality. After all, instrumentalism indexes what is rational to one's particular motivational interests. Since, or so I have argued, any other conception of normativity or rationality is controversial – only instrumentalism is uncontroversial – the question of whether we ought to have 'coherence-inducing desires' (as Smith maintains) comes down to whether we have instrumentally rational grounds for such desires. However, there are compelling reasons to doubt whether this is the case.

First, we may have strong interests, now and in the future, *favoring* motivational inconsistency. How so? One interesting feature of human life is that many of our different 'life-stages' have opposing interests, due to the kinds of life-stages they are. For instance, when we are young, we do not want to be over-burdened with responsibilities or 'maturity.'

Further, to a certain extent, our youthful irresponsibility may irk our later selves. We may wish we had been a bit more responsible than we were. However, it does not follow, instrumentally, that we should have been more responsible. After all, our earlier self had interests in being a bit irresponsible. And it may well be, hedonically, that a good human life – on the whole – has all kinds of such diachronic contradictions, ones we cannot eliminate and which, considering our lives as a whole, it might be better for us not to. To say that one's younger or older selves should 'have to' render their interests more consistent with each other for its own sake – simply for the sake of consistency – is at odds with instrumental rationality, which requires us to figure out whether consistency is the best means for satisfying our motivational interests. And again, it may not be. Here is an intuitive case where it may not be. Compare two lives: one where one's younger self lives a life of drudgery to ensure that his older self is not frustrated by his earlier decisions (and so, in which one's younger self endures sacrifices for diachronic motivational consistency), and a second life where one's younger and older selves' motivations contradict each other more (one's earlier self was a less responsible than one's older self might like), but which is happier on the whole than the first life. The latter life may be instrumentally more rational than the former, even though it has greater diachronic motivational inconsistency than the former life. The point here is simple and straightforward. Given an instrumental foundation – which this book has defended – diachronic motivational consistency is not necessarily rational. It all depends on whether a life with diachronic consistency is a better life, overall, than one with less – and, as we have just seen, this is not obviously the case.

Second, Smith's case for diachronic motivational consistency neglects the issue of costs. Although Smith argues that we should have higher-order desires for diachronic motivational consistency because (in his view) our ideally rational self would have such a desire, from an instrumental perspective the 'because' here is a non-sequitur. For even if it were true that one's 'ideal self' would have fully consistent motivations across time, one's actual self would have to endure costs associated with achieving greater coherence given the actual motivations of one's nonideal self. Instrumental rationality, however, requires us to adopt optimal means for advancing our actual motivations. And here is the problem: if we have diachronically inconsistent motivations, seeking diachronic consistency may be more costly than remaining diachronically inconsistent. To see how, consider again the young person who finds themselves wanting (as young people are often wont to do) to be a little bit irresponsible. Next, suppose that the only way for them to achieve diachronic consistency with their future selves – a self who will want them to be less irresponsible – is for them to largely restrain themselves from pursuing their desires. Such restraint is not cost free. The young person might find themselves bitter and miserable, thinking to themselves, 'Why am I being so darn responsible just to render my interests coherent with those of my likely future self?' I do not mean to say here that it is irrational for a young person to make such sacrifices, given the costs involved – indeed, as many of us know, making some sacrifices while young can be rational (being too irresponsible can lead to years, or decades, of misery later on). Rather, my point is simply that we cannot derive straightforwardly – at least from instrumental foundations – that one should have the kind of dominant desires for diachronic coherence that Smith affirms. Instrumentally speaking, whether and to what extent one should have a desire for diachronic motivational consistency – and whether it should be a 'dominant' desire outweighing all others (that all, all inconsistent motivations) – is a function of one's first-order desires and the costs involved of rendering them more coherent.

As we will see in Chapter 3 and beyond, my solution to the problem of possible future selves is somewhat similar in spirit to Smith's proposal. However, there are critical differences, among them that my solution is derived from purely instrumental foundations, and just as importantly, allows motivational consistency to be *weighed* against the costs of pursuing it.

6 Conclusion: an unsolved problem

This chapter argued that the problem of possible future selves is a real problem: one we face all too often in life. We oftentimes want to know our future interests, and how to order them with our present ones, because our future selves matter to us. And yet, or so it seems, we cannot know those things. Must we simply take our chances, hoping that we have made the right 'bet,' and that our decisions satisfy our future interests? I will now begin to argue that there is another solution: that morality itself is the most instrumentally rational way to respond to the problem.

3
The Categorical-Instrumental Imperative

Chapter 1 argued that moral philosophy should be based on Firm Foundations – on truths commonly recognized by human observers – and that the following conception of normative rationality is the firmest such foundation:

> **Instrumentalism:** if one's motivational interests would be best satisfied by φ-ing, then it is instrumentally rational for one to φ – that is, one instrumentally ought to φ.

Chapter 2 then argued that when instrumentalism is combined with other commonly recognized facts – facts about how we can care, and oftentimes do care, about our past and future – the result is a deep problem that pervades everyday life: the problem of possible future selves. The problem is simple. In some cases, we worry about the impact our decisions will have on our future selves. More specifically, we worry that our decisions might result in outcomes our future selves will not want – outcomes that are contrary to our future interests. And because we do not want to make such choices – because we want to make sure that our choices will not frustrate our future selves (or worse, be positively disastrous for them) – we want to know our future selves' interests, so that we can avoid risking future disappointment. But, or so it seems, this is impossible. We cannot know our future interests for the simple reason that the future has not yet happened.

This chapter argues that although the problem of possible future selves presumably does not have a full solution – since we cannot, presumably, know all of our future interests – it nevertheless has a partial one. Our present and future selves can cooperate across time to agree upon and mutually act on a set of shared interests: a set of interests it is instrumentally rational for each self to act on for their own sake, simply because they are agreed to by both selves as a solution to the problem, thus enabling one's present self to know and advance at least some interests of their future self, no matter how the future turns out. More specifically, this chapter argues that because our present and future selves can mutually recognize the problem of possible future selves, as well as three types of interests they both can have – voluntary interests which are under our control, involuntary interests which are not, and semivoluntary interests which are partially under our control – it is instrumentally rational for both to cooperate according to the following principle:

> **The Categorical-Instrumental Imperative:** voluntarily aim for its own sake, in every relevant action, to best satisfy the motivational interests it is instrumentally rational for one's present and every possible future self to universally agree upon, given their voluntary, involuntary, and semivoluntary interests and co-recognition of the problem of possible future selves, where relevant actions are determined recursively as actions it is instrumentally rational for one's present and possible future selves to universally agree upon as such when confronted by the problem – and then, when the future comes, voluntarily choose your having acted as such.

This chapter argues, in other words, that the Categorical-Instrumental Imperative solves the problem of possible future selves, at least to the extent that the problem can be solved. Finally, although this principle and the argument for it are admittedly complex, and this chapter does not yet show in detail how it amounts to a moral principle (as that is the topic of future chapters), the concluding sections of this chapter show, in down to earth terms, how it coheres with and accounts for a variety of aspects of moral experience, including (1) the roles that conscience and fear of punishment play in moral deliberation, (2) the notion that 'morality is its own reward,' (3) the notion that morality, in some sense, is infinitely more valuable than immorality, and (4) the notion that prudent decisionmaking requires being 'fair to oneself,' advancing one's present interests while 'not putting one's future in jeopardy.'

Section 1 begins by arguing that because a solution to the problem of possible future selves would enable one's present self to satisfy their present and future interests, it is instrumentally rational for one's present and future selves to cooperate to solve it. Section 1 then argues, however, that because one's present and future selves can mutually recognize that one's present self cannot know which future self they will be, a solution to it would have to involve a mutual agreement on interests for both selves to act on for their own sake, simply as a solution to the inability of one's present self to know any of the (other) particular interests of their future self. Third, Section 1 argues that because both selves (present and future) can mutually recognize that one's present self cannot know which future self will exist – that is, which particular interests their future self will have – it is instrumentally rational for both selves to seek and uphold a mutual agreement on shared interests that are instrumentally rational for one's present and *all* possible future selves to agree to given their particular interests and co-recognition of the problem of possible future selves. Finally, Section 1 argues that insofar as some of one's possible future selves can have interests concerning the problem itself – wanting their past selves to encounter the problem in some circumstances but not others – one's present and future selves share a higher-order interest in arriving at and upholding a mutual agreement on whether, and when, one should encounter the problem of possible future selves to begin with.

Next, Section 2 argues that because one's present and possible future selves can have three different types of motivational interests – (Section 2.1) involuntary interests, which are experienced first-personally as out of one's voluntary control, (Section 2.2) semivoluntary interests, which are experienced first-personally as partially but not wholly within one's control, and (Section 2.3) voluntary interests, which are experienced first-personally as entirely within one's control – such an agreement (between one's present and future selves) must be one that is instrumentally rational for all such selves to agree to given co-recognition of the problem (the inability of one's present self to know which future self they will be) and all three types of possible interests.

Section 3 then argues that the interests one's present and future selves have in cooperating to solve the problem of possible future selves, combined with co-recognition of the three above types of interests, entail that it is rational for both selves to cooperate according to the Categorical-Instrumental Imperative. Specifically, Section 3 argues that once we fully spell out the interests and mutual assumptions of one's present and future selves in problem of possible selves cases, we can see that while behavior that does not conform to the Categorical-Instrumental Imperative may have better likely outcomes, conforming to the Categorical-Instrumental Imperative nevertheless has better overall expected outcomes, as it is only by conforming to it that one's present and future selves can advance their shared interest in enabling one's present self to know one's future interests – thus avoiding the kinds of harmful unlikely outcomes that, in problem cases, one is interested in avoiding for certain. In the process, I show how the Categorical-Instrumental Imperative explains the instrumental attractiveness of immoral behavior, while providing a compelling explanation (to be developed further in subsequent chapters) of how immoral behavior is actually irrational – illuminating (1) the roles that conscience and fear of punishment play in moral deliberation, (2) the notion that 'morality is its own reward,' and (3) the notion that morality is infinitely more valuable than immorality.

Section 4 then responds to a concern that my argument for the Categorical-Instrumental Imperative essentially appeals to our having, and developing, a 'conscience.' I show that in one sense, this is right: that my argument does depend on our at least sometimes worrying about the future – about the possible consequences of our actions. However, I show that unlike traditional appeals to conscience by moral sentimentalists – which involve controversial appeals to things like sympathy, empathy, or a 'moral sense' (which not everyone clearly has in sufficient measure to make moral behavior instrumentally rational) – my argument is based on *uncontroversial* concerns about the future that all nonpsychopaths, including people without 'much of a conscience,' have. My argument, in other words, does not appeal to 'moral sentiments': rather, it merely appeals to interests we all have concerning our future.

Finally, Section 5 illustrates how the Categorical-Instrumental Imperative speaks both to our everyday experience of the problem of possible future selves, and how many of us tacitly try to solve it: namely, by attempting to advance our present interests in ways that are fair to our future selves – ways that they can rationally endorse voluntarily – given that we do not know how the future will turn out.

I am not the first to suggest that we can in some sense cooperate diachronically across time with our past or future selves. Roman Altshuler,[1] Adina Roskies,[2] and others[3] have argued that such cooperation may be a critical part of agency or moral responsibility. Nor am I the only one to suggest that moral responsibility has something to do with our possible selves across different worlds.[4-5] What I am the first to do is to argue that a very specific kind of human motivational concern about the future – the kinds of interests that give rise to the problem of possible future selves – entail a compelling new conception of morality, Rightness as Fairness, as a diachronic agreement between our present and all possible future selves. And, or so I shall maintain, we can respect the principle of Firm Foundations in defending Rightness as Fairness on these grounds. For although the argument provided for obeying the Categorical-Instrumental Imperative is complex, it is ultimately based upon facts about our capacities to care about our future and past, engage in 'mental time travel,' engage in moral imagination (about possibilities), and make and uphold voluntary agreements, that satisfy Firm Foundations: facts that are commonly recognized both in everyday life and in modern science.

1 Interests in diachronic cooperation

The problem of possible future selves is generated, once again, by the interest we sometimes have in knowing our future interests and ordering them with our present ones – so that we can act in ways that are certain to advance our present and future interests. When we have this kind of interest, we typically have it for a reason: because we are worried about possible (even if unlikely) outcomes. For while we may know that some path of action is likely to lead to a good result for our future selves, we worry that it might not: that the action might result in a future that our future selves do not want. When we worry in this way, we sometimes want to act on something better than mere judgments of what is likely to satisfy our future interests – for, in these cases, we do not simply want to know what is likely to make our future selves well off: we want to *know* what actually will. That is, we want certainty. We want to know our future interests so that we 'do not risk making the wrong decision.'

But can we possibly achieve such certainty? Is it possible for our present selves to truly know our future interests, given that the future has not happened yet? As we will now begin to see, the answer is yes. We can know some of our interests in advance: a certain class of voluntary interests it is instrumentally rational for our present and every possible future self to voluntarily agree to – interests which, insofar as we have voluntary control over them now and in the future, we can voluntarily choose now and in the future as shared interests, no matter which future self we actually turn out to be.

As we will see in more detail in Section 2, some of our present and future interests are, either in part or in whole, not under our voluntary control. We are in many respects 'reactive beings' with emotions and drives that we simply find ourselves with. For instance, we may find ourselves, here and now, wanting to buy a beautiful home. Further, if we buy the home and the housing market crashes, we may find ourselves – quite against our will – upset or heartbroken at how things turned out. Although (as we will see in Section 2) we appear to have some 'semi-voluntary' control over our emotions – we can act in ways that alter or modify our emotional responses and the like – it is nevertheless the case that some of our interests appear entirely out of our voluntary control. When it comes to these two types of interests – which I will call 'involuntary' and 'semivoluntary' interests – we cannot solve the problem of possible future selves. We cannot know in advance what our involuntary or semivoluntary interests will be, since they both depend – in part or in whole – on visceral reactions that are out of our voluntary control. There is nothing our future selves can do to help us know them in the present, because which involuntary or semivoluntary interests our future selves have depends on things out of their – and our – control.

There is, however, a different type of interest that our present and future selves are capable of having that both selves can exploit to solve the problem of possible future selves, to the extent that it can be solved: namely, the kinds of voluntary interests that we experience ourselves having voluntary control over. As we saw in Chapter 2, although we experience ourselves with emotions, desires, and other inclinations, we also experience ourselves as making voluntary choices: as (at least ordinarily) deciding what our dominant motivational interests are, the interests that lead us to actually act. For instance, consider again the example from Chapter 2 of not wanting to get out of bed. There you are, feeling like staying in bed. You are strongly inclined not to get up. Nevertheless, you experience yourself as having a choice: you can voluntarily choose to get out of bed, 'overriding' your initial inclination not to. It is these types of interests – our voluntarily chosen interests – that we experience ourselves as having control over, and it is them, or so I will argue, that our present and future selves can voluntarily cooperate to share, given their mutual recognition that our present selves cannot know the other (involuntary and semivoluntary) interests of their future selves. In short, although there may be nothing our present or future selves can do to ensure that our present selves know some of their future interests – whether, for instance, their future self will be involuntarily or semivoluntarily disappointed (or even miserable) with the home they bought – our present and future selves can voluntarily cooperate with one another to arrange that they share voluntary interests: interests to share precisely because both selves recognize the problem of possible future selves.

Before we proceed any further, notice how commonsensical this notion is: that there is something special, and important, about our capacity to voluntarily decide, both now and in the future, how we respond to our desire to know our future, given our ignorance of it. It is often said that 'one should concentrate on those things over which one has control.' We all recognize that there is so much in this life over which we do not have complete voluntary control. We do not have full control over whether our investments turn out well, for instance: we can at best try to make a good investment, given the information we have at our disposal. And of course we do not have full voluntary control over our emotions: sometimes we get angry, or sad, or joyous, whether we like it or not. Yet although there are many aspects of life over which we lack complete voluntary control, there are also aspects of this life over which we do have voluntary control: we have control over our choices. And, or so I will argue, it is these interests – our dominant ones, the ones we choose to act on – that our present and future selves can come to a shared agreement on given their other (involuntary and semivoluntary) interests, so as to partially solve the problem of possible future selves (solving it, that is, so far as our responses to it are under our control).

Now, as we also saw in Chapter 2, the experience of voluntary choice that my account depends upon – our experience of being able to voluntarily decide what our dominant motivational interests are – may ultimately be a kind of cognitive illusion. Ultimately, it may well be that all of our choices – including the ones we experience as 'voluntarily up to us' – are causally determined by laws of physics over which we have no control.[6] What should we make of this concern? Does it threaten the argument I will provide for the Categorical-Instrumental Imperative? It does not. The ultimate nature of our capacities for voluntary choice – that is, whether our 'voluntary choices' are causally determined by forces of physics out of our control – merely concern whether we in fact make and uphold the kind of agreement with our future selves that this chapter defends as a solution to the problem of possible future selves. It is irrelevant to the normative question of whether such an agreement is the solution to the problem of possible future selves that our present and future selves *should* adopt, so far as it is within their power to do so. To see what I mean, consider the sense in which causal determinism 'threatens' any normative or moral theory. Consider, to begin with, the simple instrumental claim that if one wants to lose weight, one should eat fewer calories than one's body expends. If causal determinism is true, whether we actually eat fewer calories than we expend is in some ultimate sense out of one's control: one either will eat fewer calories than one expends (if the laws of nature cause one's brain to make that decision), or one will not (if the laws of nature cause one's brain to make the opposite decision). Although causal determinism makes it ultimately 'out of one's

82 Rightness as Fairness

control' what one does, it does not threaten the normative claim that if one wants to lose weight, one should eat fewer calories. That claim is still true, especially if understood in the reductive sense suggested in Chapter 1 (where instrumental 'oughts' are simply reduced to claims about what is optimal for achieving what one wants). All that determinism does is threaten one's ability to actually do what one (normatively) ought to do. And, of course, this is an issue that any normative or moral theory encounters. If utilitarianism were the true moral theory, determinism would simply call into question one's ability to act as utilitarianism says one ought to. Accordingly, we can set aside concerns about determinism and take our first-personal experience of voluntary choice at face value: as expressing our experience of our capacity to make voluntary choices. My argument will simply be as follows: insofar as we experience ourselves as having the capacity to make voluntary choices, it is instrumentally rational for us to try to arrive at and uphold a mutual agreement between our present and future selves on interests to share, and pursue, for their own sake given mutual recognition of the problem of possible future selves. As such, whether and to what extent we truly have causal power to follow through on what is instrumentally rational is another issue.

With these caveats in place, let us examine the problem of possible future selves from the perspectives of our present and future selves. On the one hand, it is clearly instrumentally rational for one's present self to want to voluntarily cooperate with their future self in problem-cases. The problem of possible future selves, after all, is defined by one's present self wanting to know (and advance) their future interests. Given that the future has not happened yet, there is one – and only one – way for one's present self to know their future interests: namely, their being assured in advance by their future self of what their interests will be. But there is only one way for them to have such an assurance: namely, their future self voluntarily cooperating with them to arrive at shared interests. As such, one's present self has a rational interest in their future self voluntarily cooperating with them in precisely this way. On the other hand, one's future self – whichever one actually comes into existence – has complementary grounds for wanting to voluntarily cooperate. Their past self, after all, is looking to know and advance their future interests. That is the whole point of the problem of possible future selves: one's past self is looking to know one's future interests so that they cannot disappoint one's future self. Since one's future self has the interests in question – interests that they, one's future self, do not want to see disappointed either – voluntarily cooperating with their earlier self is instrumentally rational for them: it is the only way to enable their earlier self to know (and be certain to advance) their interests in the future.

Thus, one's present and future selves share the following instrumentally rational interest: an interest in cooperating diachronically (or across time) to arrive at a set of shared voluntary interests – interests that would enable one's present self to know their future interests, and order them with their present ones, before the future comes.

Next, both selves should recognize that the problem of possible future selves itself – because both recognize that one's present self cannot know the particular interests they will have in the future (whether they will want or not want to buy a home, whether they will be happy or unhappy having bought one, and so on) – means that they cannot cooperate given knowledge of one's particular future interests. Rather, both sides must recognize that because one's present self is ignorant of the future, the only way that both can cooperate diachronically to arrive at a set of shared voluntary interests is for one's present and future selves to voluntarily commit to acting on voluntary interests that it is instrumentally rational for one's present and *every* possible future self to universally agree to, given mutual knowledge of the problem. For it is only in this way that, no matter which future self is actualized, the shared interests one's present and future selves act upon are necessarily in both selves' interests, enabling one's present self to know them, despite the countless possible ways the future might go (and despite which future self is actualized).

Third, since one's present and future selves both know that one's present self cannot know future events in advance (one's present self cannot know whether the housing market will crash, or whether one will get caught cheating on an exam, and so on), and both know that which interests one's future self has may depend greatly on those events (whether one's future self will be happy or disappointed by one's home purchase depends on things one's present self cannot know), both selves have grounds to seek a set of shared interests that one's present self can know, and satisfy, for certain: interests, that is, that both selves pursue *for their own sake* given their mutual recognition of the problem of possible future selves (as opposed to for the sake of something else, such as satisfaction of buying a home, which cannot be assured).

Finally, although one's present and future selves share such interests – interests in coming to a mutual agreement on interests to pursue for their own sake, as a solution to the problem – this shared interest entails a higher-order interest in determining together, vis-à-vis a similar agreement, whether one's present self should have encountered the problem of possible future selves to begin with, and indeed, what kinds of future cases in which one should encounter that problem. For as we will now see, one problem we face in encountering the problem of possible future selves is that some of our possible future selves may not want us to encounter the problem at all. Indeed, there are some cases in which, when the future comes, one wishes that one's past self hadn't wanted to know one's future interests. Sometimes, when the future rolls around, we wish that our past selves had just acted rather than concerned themselves worrying about the future. Allow me to explain.

Consider Michael Stocker's famous case concerning visiting a sick friend at the hospital.[7] Suppose I find out a dear friend is dying in the hospital, and I find myself encountering the problem of possible future selves: I want to know whether my future self will approve of me going to the hospital (I sit and think to myself, 'Should I go to the hospital? I wonder whether my future self will be happy with that decision. I really wish I knew!'). Here is the problem: my future self may turn out to be appalled by this very fact – by the fact that my present self is uncertain at all about his future interests, wanting to know them. Indeed, my future self may think to himself, 'What an awful person I was. I shouldn't have been uncertain about what I would want, or want to know whether I would be happy with me visiting the hospital. I should have taken it for granted that I would want me to visit, and simply visit out of love for my friend.' And indeed, this sort of reaction is not uncommon. We are in fact sometimes disappointed that our earlier selves regarded certain things as questions to begin with ('Why in the world was I thinking of whether I would be happy giving my friend a ride to the airport? My friend has helped me out so many times. I should not have been thinking of myself at all. What an awful, selfish friend I am to even think like that!').

Consequently, whenever one encounters the problem of possible future selves, one's present and future selves share two interests: an interest in forging and upholding a voluntary agreement on whether and when one should encounter the problem of possible future selves, and, if it is mutually agreed that one should encounter the problem in certain cases, an interest in forging and upholding a diachronic agreement on shared interests to pursue for their own sake a solution to it.

We may sum up our investigations thus far as follows. Whenever we encounter the problem of possible future selves – whenever we find ourselves having an interest in knowing and advancing our future selves' interests (and ordering their interests with our present ones) – our present and future selves have interests in seeking and upholding:

1. An instrumentally rational agreement with all of our possible future selves on whether and when our present selves should encounter the problem of possible future selves (wanting to know their future selves' interests, and so on), and, if such an agreement is reached,
2. An instrumentally rational agreement with all of our possible future selves on a set shared interests to pursue for their own sake as a solution to the problem of possible future selves.

The question now is what such an agreement will look like. As we now see, there are complicating factors: namely, the fact that one's present and possible future selves can come to the table (in attempting to forge and uphold such an agreement) with three possible types of interests: voluntary, involuntary, and semivoluntary interests – interests that one's various selves should want to take into account in forging and upholding such an agreement. For whatever agreement our present and future selves come to, it must be one based on the realization that reaching and upholding the agreement can impose costs on both one's present self and future self (whichever possible one is actualized). To see why, suppose my present self has an interest performing action W, one of my possible future selves has an interest in doing action X, another possible future self has an interest in doing Y, and so on. Given that all of these possible selves 'come to the table' with different interests, an agreement on which interests one's present and future selves should share (for the sake of solving the problem of possible future selves) may require one's present or future self (whichever one is actual) to modify their interests in a way that might be costly. After all, wanting one thing, X, and then forcing oneself to adopt some other motivation Y for the sake of an agreement, can be irksome or even painful. One may really want to do X, and doing Y instead might be a significant sacrifice. As such, an instrumentally rational solution to the problem should not abstract from such costs, but include them.

2 Three types of interests

In order to solve the problem of possible future selves, determining what is an instrumentally rational way to respond to situations in which (A) we want to know our future selves' interests and (B) order them with our own, but (C) we are ignorant of the future, we need to clarify precisely which kinds of motivational interests our present and future selves can have.

2.1 Involuntary interests

Some, indeed many, of our motivations afflict us involuntarily. For instance, one may simply find oneself wanting something to eat thanks to hunger. Similarly, one may find oneself wanting to watch something else on the television because one is bored by what one is watching. Moreover, all too often, one simply finds oneself reacting to things one has done in the past. Consider an example in which I accidentally drop my computer on the ground, and it shatters. I may find myself struck by anger and dismay, as well as a wish that I hadn't been so clumsy. And, of course, sometimes we just find ourselves wanting things for our future (these days, I often find myself wanting a particular future for myself: a future where I have written a good book!).

Let us call these types of motivational interests – interests that simply happen to us, impinging upon us in the present whether we like it or not – 'involuntary interests.' Clearly, our lives are full of them. Indeed, most of our interests are arguably of this sort. I find myself wanting to get up and work on this book today. I find myself wanting to check my email. I find myself upset when I have worked on this book all day but accomplish little more than confusing myself. Further, in these very respects, these interests seem to be what define us as individuals. Not everyone finds themselves waking up in the morning wanting to write a book called *Rightness as Fairness*. I do. Others find themselves inclined to do other things. Some find themselves inclined to be firefighters, others find themselves inclined to be criminals, and so on. Or consider our emotional inclinations. Some of us are more temperamental than others. I find myself upset by things that do not upset my spouse, and she finds herself upset by things that do not upset me. Our emotional inclinations – interests that also just afflict us – in large part seem to define who we are, as they too drive us to make the choices we do (more on this shortly).

I think it may be worth dwelling a bit more on just how suffused our lives are with involuntary interests. Throughout today, I have found myself beset by motivations – including emotional reactions – that I never 'asked' for, and which I find myself unable to avoid. For instance, no matter how much I reflect and tell myself that I should not get upset if I have had an unproductive day at work, I may find myself upset. Similarly, when I get on an airplane that experiences severe turbulence, I may tell myself that I should not experience fear – that airplanes are a safe way to travel, almost never crashing due to turbulence – and yet I may feel fear whether I like it or not. Indeed, even if I believe that it is irrational, I may find myself wishing I had never boarded the plane to begin with (this has happened to me many times). We are, in many respects, reactive beings, besotted by emotional reactions and inclinations despite our best efforts.

At the same time, it may be possible to influence which 'involuntary interests' we have. To illustrate, if we notice that we are beset by fears that do not serve our interests on the whole – if one fears public speaking, for instance, but wants to pursue a career that involves a great deal of it – then there may be things we can do to prevent or influence the kind of 'involuntary interests' our future selves will have (one can practice speaking in public). But even though our involuntary interests may be prospectively modifiable in such a way – we can modify which involuntary interests we will have in the future – the critical thing with involuntary interests is that their existence is involuntary. Even if I practice public speaking so that I have less fear than I might have otherwise have, the lesser fear I experience when I speak in public is still, in a very real sense, involuntary: it happens to me, whether I like it or not. As such, there is still a sense in which – even though we may influence which interests afflict us in the future – those interests still afflict us. Whatever (lesser) fear I have of public speaking right now may be a result of past training. But fear may still thrust itself upon me, unchosen, when I speak publicly.

There are several important things about these kinds of interests for the purposes of our discussion: that is, for solving the problem of possible future selves. First, and most obviously, involuntary interests are *interests*. However much we may like or dislike them – however rational or irrational they may be – they are interests that our various possible selves in fact find themselves with, and which must therefore be taken as a kind of 'given' in instrumental deliberation. We should not pretend that they do not exist or idealize away from them. And indeed, insofar as we have them, they define certain costs and benefits for us (if I find myself angry, there are certain things that may be in my motivational interest than would not be if I never found myself that way). Second, cases of compulsion and 'acting without thinking' aside – cases where we find ourselves unable to resist our involuntary interests (compulsion), or where we simply act on our involuntary interests without any reflection (acting without thinking) – we do not experience our involuntary interests as comprising or settling either (i) our dominant motivational interest (the interest we actually act upon), or (ii) the ordering of our motivational interests as a whole. For instance, I may find myself with two involuntary interests: simultaneously wanting to perform an action (give a public speech to obtain career success), and not perform it (I fear giving speeches). Yet, for all that – provided I do not experience myself as compelled to act against my will or without thinking – I experience myself as having the ability to choose which involuntary interest to act upon or prioritize: I experience myself as having the capacity to choose whether to put my interest in avoiding something I fear in front of my interest in career success (and not give the speech), or conversely, to put my interest in my career in front of my fear (giving the speech). This, again, is our first-personal experience of free choice.

2.2 Semivoluntary interests

In addition to involuntary interests, we also have 'semivoluntary' interests: interests that we can modify through voluntary choice, but only within certain bounds, and at certain costs to ourselves. For instance, consider once again the case of me dropping my computer on the ground and breaking it, and experiencing a rush of anger and dismay – motivations that cause me pain and immediate regret for my clumsiness. Although these interests, this pain and regret, may initially impose themselves on me, I do not ordinarily experience myself as completely powerless against them. Instead, I experience myself as having some power over them in two separate respects. First, as I just mentioned, I experience myself as having the choice of whether to act upon my pain and regret – as having the ability to choose whether I sit here and sulk (which I am inclined to do), or whether to go purchase a new computer (which I am not inclined to do). Additionally, insofar as I experience myself as having this capacity for free choice, I also experience myself as having a limited ability to modify the involuntary interests I find myself with into other ones. For instance, in addition to choosing to buy a new computer, I can try to control my anger. I can tell myself, 'Try to calm down,' and actively work to lessen my anger. Of course, being a human being, I am typically only able to succeed in this to a limited extent. Whereas I find myself free to choose to go purchase a new computer, I find myself struggling with my anger – not free to choose precisely how angry I am, but able to somewhat influence how angry I am – and, indeed, with great fallibility. One minute I may be able to calm myself, but the next moment my anger and dismay may bubble up again – in which case I can try to calm myself again (or alternatively, allow my anger and dismay to rage out of control). Such experiences, I argue, are universal: most, if not all, of us have experienced times in which we struggle with our emotions and inclinations in this way. This struggle is 'what makes us human.'

Indeed, just like involuntary motivational interests, our daily lives are full of these types of semivoluntary interests. Here is one case: I find myself perturbed at a driver who cuts me off in traffic. I may find myself beset by an involuntary urge to yell, curse, or honk my horn. Yet it is at this point that I experience myself as having a choice: namely, to either give into my anger, giving it full reign over my behavior, or to calm down. I can tell myself to calm down, and, while I may not have full voluntary control over how I feel – I may not be able to simply 'make my anger go away' – I can reduce it through force of will. Similarly, recent studies on empathy indicate what commonsense already suggests: that we can control, at least to some extent, how much empathy we feel and towards whom.[8] For instance, we can proactively try to imagine how someone else feels by 'putting ourselves in their shoes' – something which can lead to us feel more for them and care more about their interests than we did before. Conversely, we can also proactively try to avoid putting ourselves in others' shoes, avoiding feeling empathy for them.[9] Next, consider shame and guilt. Although whether we feel any shame or guilt at all may or may not be under our control, when we do experience these emotions, we are plainly able to take voluntary steps to make ourselves feel more or less of them, at least within some bounds. For example, after cheating on an exam, one may feel just a little bit bad about doing so, but not much – and yet one may tell oneself that one should feel worse than one does ('I should really feel bad about what I did') and, through some effort, make it so: making oneself feel worse about what one did through conscious effort. And, of course, one can often alter one's feelings in the opposite direction, initially empathizing with the interests of others ('I really feel bad about the laborers who work in the hot sun for poverty wages') but then convincing oneself not to care so much ('What can I do? Nothing. I guess I will just put it out of my mind'). Here is another case: you said something embarrassing many years ago, and something you experience now reminds you of it, involuntarily rekindling your shame and embarrassment about it. You can then tell yourself, 'There is no point in continuing to be embarrassed about that. Try to forget it!,' as it is in the past. You may even be able to push it out of your mind temporarily, only to have the embarrassment return in somewhat lesser form a few minutes later. These are the kinds of struggles we have with ourselves, day in and day out, throughout our lives. It would be nice if we had perfect voluntary control over how we respond to involuntary motivational interests – to anger, shame, or embarrassment that impress themselves on us. Often enough, however, we are only able to modify these interests throughout voluntary choice, lessening the anger, shame, or embarrassment through conscious effort.

This brings us to a critical feature of these types of interests. Our semivoluntary interests are not 'cost free.' To modify a semivoluntary interest – to change it from what it previously was – in a certain way thwarts the initial interest. For instance, when I find myself angry at someone, there are certain things I may want to do: it might feel very good, for instance, to yell at them or say something mean-spirited. If, however, I decide to control my anger (enough so I do not yell at them), then I force myself not to do that – the thing that, in the first instance at least, I was inclined to do and would have made me feel good: a cost. Such costs are something we experience often. We control our anger, or our laughter, and so on, begrudgingly. We do not really want to control them, but we choose to for the sake of something else (say, not suffering later consequences of acting angrily or laughing inappropriately). Whether it is instrumentally rational to make that choice is (at least in part) a function of the costs of altering the semivoluntary interest. It may be advantageous on the whole to control one's anger, but if it is, it is only because the advantages of doing so outweigh the costs of controlling it.

2.3 Voluntary interests

Finally, we experience ourselves, first-personally, as having fully voluntary motivational interests – interests that we do not experience as simply happening to us or merely modifiable, but which we experience ourselves as fully free to choose. I may not want to get out of bed (an involuntary interest), but I can tell myself that I ought to get out of bed, and ordinarily, if I have strength of will, I can make it so: I can will myself out of bed. Similarly, although you may be struck by anger during an argument – and in some cases experience yourself as compelled to act involuntarily by your anger (something that even the best of us are guilty of!) – you typically experience yourself as having the capacity to decide whether to act on that interest. These voluntary interests have several critical features that are relevant to our discussion.

First, to the extent that we experience ourselves as having voluntary interests, we experience them as defining our highest motivational interest: the motivational interest that we act upon, and thus take a stronger interest in than any of our other (involuntary or semivoluntary) interests. Again, I may find myself very angry, but to the extent that I experience myself as having voluntary control over my behavior,

I experience myself as having the capacity to act against my anger (I can tell myself, 'I know it would feel really good to lash out in anger right now, satisfying my thirst for anger, but do not do it' – and make it so). Now, of course, we sometimes find our voluntary interests 'overcome' by involuntary ones, as when we act compulsively or 'out of control.' In such cases, however, we do not experience ourselves as acting voluntarily; we experience ourselves as compelled to act involuntarily.

Second, insofar as we have voluntary motivational interests, we experience them as capacities to order and modify our semivoluntary interests within the bounds they can be ordered and modified. For example, when I feel a rush of fear and excitement before jumping off a high diving board, I can voluntarily tell myself, 'Focus on the excitement over the fear' – and to some extent make it so: I can choose to prioritize one of my semivoluntary interests over the others.

Finally, we experience our voluntary motivational interests as capacities to impose costs on ourselves (vis-à-vis controlling or modifying some involuntary and semivoluntary interests) for the sake of realizing other benefits. It may not feel very good right now, for instance, for me to restrain my feelings of dismay upon dropping and breaking my computer. It may feel good at present to wallow in self-pity (an emotion that I involuntarily find myself beset with). Still, I can tell myself that I shouldn't wallow in that pity because it will prevent me from achieving other things I have decided (voluntarily or semivoluntarily) that I want even more: namely, writing a good book. If I judge that wallowing in pity will accomplish very little in terms of accomplishing this other thing that I decide I want more – if I decide I want to write a good book more than I want to wallow in self-pity – then I can (at least ordinarily) decide to voluntarily impose costs on my present self (depriving him of the enjoyment of momentary pity, which may disappoint me) so that my future self can enjoy something I have decided to want more than that: writing a good book.

3 The Categorical-Instrumental Imperative

We are now in a position to establish the instrumental rationality of obeying the Categorical-Instrumental Imperative. We saw, in Chapter 2, that we encounter the problem of possible future selves when our present selves are uncertain about the future, wanting to know our future interests and order them with our present ones. We have now seen, in this chapter, that there is one – and only one – way for our present selves to do so. We can know our future interests, and order them with our present interests, if and only if our future selves cooperate with us to arrive at a set of mutually agreed upon interests for both (present and future selves) to voluntarily pursue for their own sake: for, if our present and future selves agree to some such interests and voluntarily uphold them, then there is no possible way one can fail to know, or satisfy, those agreed upon interests. For instance, if one's present and future selves agreed on one telling the truth for its own sake (and let us speak hypothetically here for the time being), and then both voluntarily adopted that as a shared end (telling the truth for its own sake), then, no matter what else the future holds – crashed housing markets, divorces, whatever – one's present self can know that they share that interest (telling the truth for its own sake) with their future self, and further, know that neither self can possibly fail to achieve it (since it is pursued by both for its own sake, nothing further).

Alas, things are not quite this simple. For as we saw in Section 2, not all of our interests – now or in the future – are under our voluntary control. One has many possible futures with many possible interests that one does not have full voluntary control over – some futures in which you find yourself involuntarily angry, others in which you do not, some in which you find yourself inclined to lie, some in which you do not. Thus, if your present and future selves are to come to a rational agreement on shared interests to pursue for their own sake, they must do on the basis of mutual recognition of the fact that your present self cannot know which future self will exist. Fortunately, as we saw in Section 1, no matter which future self comes into existence, they share an interest in enabling their previous self to know their interests. Thus, in cases where one encounters the problem of possible future selves, the only way one's present and future selves can cooperate to solve the problem is for both to voluntarily commit themselves to acting on interests one's present and every possible future self can universally agree to given (A) mutual recognition of the problem of possible future selves, and (B) mutual knowledge of the many possible voluntary, involuntary, and semivoluntary interests one's various possible selves can have.

But this is just to say that cooperating on the basis of the following principle is the only way for one's present and future selves (whichever one comes into existence) to solve the problem, insofar as it can be solved (vis-à-vis one's voluntary interests):

> **The Categorical-Instrumental Imperative:** voluntarily aim for its own sake, in every relevant action, to best satisfy the motivational interests it is instrumentally rational for one's present and every

possible future self to universally agree upon given their voluntary, involuntary, and semivoluntary interests and co-recognition of the problem of possible future selves, where relevant actions are determined recursively as actions it is instrumentally rational for one's present and possible future selves to universally agree upon as such when confronted by the problem – and then, when the future comes, voluntarily choose your having acted as such.

Although the argument just given for this principle is complex, it can be simplified as follows: in cases where one wants to know one's future interests (call them 'problem-cases'), one's present and future selves necessarily share an interest in solving the problem, and it can only be solved if both voluntarily commit themselves to acting in ways that one's present and *every* possible future self could universally agree to, given their other interests and co-recognition of the inability of one's present self to know which future self will be actual. Since this argument is still complex at present, I believe we can explicate it further and make its complexities more intuitive by carefully examining a specific instance utilizing causal decision theory.[10]

I have not yet explained how the Categorical-Instrumental Imperative is supposed to be a moral principle (this is the subject of following chapters). However, let us think about it now in the context of a putative moral decision: the case in which one is tempted to cheat on an exam.

Cheating on an exam can appear instrumentally rational, at least in certain circumstances. Consider a situation where a student can expect to fail an exam and the class they are taking if they do not cheat (they have not studied adequately, let us suppose). Furthermore, suppose that this student knows that they are unlikely to get caught: that their teacher rarely catches cheaters (the student, we may suppose, has plenty of good evidence for this – such as friends who cheated successfully). Then suppose the student knows they have little to no 'conscience' in cases like this – that they will not feel guilt or remorse later on – and that they are not very worried about getting caught or feeling guilty. Finally, suppose the student expects that the worst that will happen to them if they get caught cheating is that they will fail the exam and class (as this is the teacher's known policy). In this situation, when we look at their interests, it certainly appears that the student has everything to gain (doing well on the exam through cheating) and little to nothing to lose (since, in the worst-case scenario in which they get caught, they get exactly what they would have gotten if they had not risked cheating at all: failing the exam and the class). Cheating looks instrumentally

94 *Rightness as Fairness*

rational because, taking the situation in isolation, it is instrumentally rational. Given the interests they have in the situation at hand, the expected outcome of cheating (possibly passing the exam) is better than the expected outcome of not cheating (failing the exam with certainty, which they do not want). This example demonstrates why we human beings often tend to violate moral norms: when we are in a given situation and look at the costs and benefits from the interests we have within it, it can look altogether rational to behave immorally.

Here, however, is the problem. Generally speaking, our decisions – and the situations in which we find ourselves – do not exist in isolation. They exist in the broader context of our lives: a life, that is, that extends into the past and future. And as we all well know, an action that looks instrumentally rational in a narrow context – when one focuses only on one's present interests – can be instrumentally irrational all things considered, taking into account the person's full set of interests. For instance, suppose the student in our example wants to be a doctor. Indeed, let us suppose that this is among their strongest interests, one that, if you asked them, they would say they want to satisfy above almost all else. Now suppose our student is in the situation they are in now – the situation in which they are tempted to cheat on their exam – precisely because they have made a string of bad decisions vis-à-vis becoming a doctor (they habitually fail to study, and so on). In other words, they are in the situation they are now because they are a person who has not worried appropriately about their future. Should they cheat? Is it instrumentally rational for them to cheat? Perhaps, but only in the sense that they do not have the habits they instrumentally should have: habits that would have placed them in a better position to achieve their interests (of becoming a doctor). We want to say (and they might even say, if we got them to think about their long-term career plans), that they shouldn't cheat in the sense that, instrumentally speaking, they should not have gotten themselves into that position in the first place if their most prized goal is to become a doctor. We want to say that they should be the kind of person who is not tempted to cheat in the first place.

Notice that I have not made any reference to the problem of possible future selves or the Categorical-Instrumental Imperative here. This is by design, because before we see how these things might apply to this case, it is first important to see how, instrumentally speaking, we evaluate our actions and those of others in a broader context: the context of a *life*. When we think about people like our proverbial student we want to say two things: (1) it is instrumentally rational for them to cheat, looking at their present interests alone, but (2) it is not instrumentally rational (or 'wise' for them to do so) in the broader context of their life.

Now let us turn back to the problem of possible future selves. Why do we run into the problem? We run into it because we are certain types of beings. Unlike nonhuman animals, young children, psychopaths, and (to a lesser, but significant extent) teenagers, we all worry about the future, at least sometimes. We worry about it for all kinds of reasons – not the least among them that we learn from experience how unwise it can be not to worry. Indeed, the idea that we should worry about the future consequences of our actions is one of the most common lessons we teach our children in order to live 'like mature adults.' It is a most common lesson of 'after-school special' television programs, which typically present the viewer with a teenager who is tempted to violate a moral norm (a norm against, say, lying to their parents), because it looks likely they will benefit. But then the unlikely happens: the teenager is unexpectedly caught and punished, or otherwise ends up feeling guilty or remorseful about their behavior. The general lesson we teach our children, to make them live wisely (in terms of living a successful life, one in which they are not imprisoned for crimes, and so on), is to care about their future. But, now it is precisely this disposition – a disposition that all of us have to some extent, provided we are not complete psychopaths – that generates the problem of possible future selves. Our disposition to care about our future – to live 'wisely' – manifests itself from time to time as a desire to know our future interests. We want to know whether we will get away with cheating on an exam, or feel guilty, and so on, because we have learned to worry or be concerned about these things.

The fact that we only sometimes have these concerns – and encounter the problem of possible future selves – might once again give rise to the worry that the argument and theory I am providing is too contingent: that it makes the rationality of moral behavior dependent on our having 'good habits,' the kinds of habits that give rise to the problem of possible future selves. However, this fact actually coheres well with a broad range of phenomena: among them the fact that nonhuman animals, children, psychopaths, and to some degree teenagers do not experience morality's normative force. It may well be, then, that morality does depend on our having certain types of inclinations: namely, the kinds of concerns about the future that give rise to the problem of possible future selves. It also coheres very well with recent studies showing that the more one gets a person to focus on their future (presumably increasing their worries about it), the more likely they are to behave morally.[11] Finally, as we will see in future chapters, I want to argue that insofar as we all encounter the problem of possible future selves from time to time – not necessarily in exam-cheating cases, but in cases as simple as wanting to know whether one will be happy with buying a home – the rationality of obeying the Categorical-Instrumental Imperative in those cases makes it instrumentally rational, in a recursive fashion, to become the kind of person who encounters and solves the problem of possible selves with the Categorical-Instrumental Imperative in other cases as well (namely, the kinds of cases we ordinarily recognize as 'moral decisions'). In short, even though we may 'come to the table,' as it were, only worrying about the future in some cases – the child lying to their parents might worry about whether they will get away with it (wishing they could know it!) – I will argue that the rational solution to those cases, the Categorical-Instrumental Imperative, makes it instrumentally rational to have the very worries that give rise to the problem in other cases, making it rational to encounter and solve the problem in those cases as well. We can, as it were, normatively 'bootstrap' morality as a whole out of isolated, even 'nonmoral' cases in which we encounter the problem of possible future selves. For indeed, as we will see in Chapter 6, the Categorical-Instrumental Imperative requires us to develop dispositions of various sorts: dispositions to encounter the problem when, and only when, *fairness* requires it.

With these caveats in mind (which we will return to in later chapters), let us finally turn to the rationality of obeying the Categorical-Instrumental Imperative in cases where one has the worries – that is, the interests in knowing one's future – that give rise to the problem of possible future selves. In particular, let us revisit our case of the student tempted to cheat on an exam. In the case as we first described it, the student had few worries about their future. Their thoughts were occupied with likely outcomes: with the facts that they would likely get away with cheating, and the direct consequences of their getting caught (failing the class) are no worse than the consequences if they did not choose to cheat (since they would fail anyway). Now, however, consider a student who is concerned about their future: they want to know what their future interests will be, not merely in the next day or so, but in general. They might worry, for instance, that even if they cheat on the test successfully, they are pursuing a very dangerous path in life: a life of poor study habits, habitual cheating, and so on, which might at some point in the future 'blow up in their face' in a way that their future self might profoundly regret. Indeed, they might worry that although cheating on their exam might benefit them in the short term, if they do not cease their cheating ways at some point (such as, perhaps, now), they will never learn the abilities or knowledge they need to succeed later in life. They might think to themselves, 'I want to be a doctor someday. But how can I be successful if all I do is cheat?' Or they might worry about the kind of person they are becoming ('What if I regret becoming such a cheater someday?'). And so on. It is this student – the one plagued by doubts – who encounters the problem of possible future selves. They are tempted to cheat, but worry about the possible consequences of doing so, even the unlikely ones ('I probably won't feel guilty if I get away with it. But what if I am caught? I may feel terrible. I might regret it.'). It is this student who wants to know their future: they want to *know* whether cheating will advance their future interests, or whether their future self, at some point or other (perhaps only in the distant future, if their career or life does not go as they wish), will regret their having done so.

If this is how one encounters the present case in which one is tempted to cheat, is it still instrumentally rational to cheat? The answer is no. In cases where one encounters the problem of possible future selves, one is not most interested in likely outcomes: one is more interested in all possible outcomes. One wants to *know* which – of the many possible outcomes that could occur – will occur. But once this is established as one's dominant interest, then it is – by definition – not instrumentally rational to bet on likely outcomes. For as we will see momentarily, any such 'bet' leaves open an infinite number of ways in which one could fail to know one's future interests – an infinite number of ways in which one could fail to satisfy one's interest in knowing one's future interests. Consequently, it is instrumentally rational, in true problem-cases – cases where one wants to know one's future interests – to act in ways that will advance one's interests no matter how the future goes, likely outcomes and unlikely outcomes alike. This is exactly what the Categorical-Instrumental Imperative requires one to do: to arrive at a set of shared voluntary interests with *all* of one's possible future selves, to pursue for their own sake in response to the problem.

We can see this more clearly – that is, how immoral behavior is instrumentally irrational even though it can initially appear rational in problem-cases – by applying decision theory to such cases. In decision theory, rational behavior is understood in terms of the sum total of relevant outcomes multiplied by their respective probabilities of occurrence (where relevant outcomes are demarcated in terms of the agent's interests). In *non*-problem-of-possible-selves cases, where one is not worried about remote, unlikely possibilities, it can be instrumentally rational to cheat on an exam. For, let us suppose in a given case that a student has a high (.6) probability of benefiting greatly from cheating (gaining, let us say, 100,000 'satisfaction units' if they do so successfully, indicative of a very strong interest in cheating). Then let us say that the only other possibilities the student is concerned with are the case where they cheat and get caught (a .3 probability of being punished with a failing grade, losing them 100,000 satisfaction units), the case where they cheat and feel a bit guilty (.1 probability of losing 10 satisfaction units), and finally, two cases where they do not cheat: the extremely unlikely case that they do not cheat but do well on the exam (.001 probability of +500,000 satisfaction units), and the far more likely case (.999 probability) that they will fail if they do not cheat (once again losing 100,000 units). If this is the student's situation, then decision theory entails that it is instrumentally rational to cheat. For whereas the expected utility of cheating is $(+100,000).6 + (-100,000).3 + (-10).1 = +29,999$ satisfaction units, the expected utility of not cheating is far worse: namely $(+500,000).001 + (-100,000).999 = -998,500$.

Now, however, consider the student who is tempted to cheat on an exam but who encounters it as a problem-case: a case in which, because they are concerned about possible outcomes (including unlikely ones), they want to *know* their interests in advance, not merely bet on likely outcomes. In this case, although the probability of them cheating successfully (gaining 100,000 satisfaction units) may still be .6, there is an infinite number of relevant alternative futures that the individual cares about, including the possible but unlikely future that their cheating behavior will negatively affect them later in life – as might be the case if they become a 'cheater' who is ultimately convicted of fraud later in their career (−5,000,000 satisfaction units multiplied by a .000000001 probability, let's say). There are also possible, if unlikely futures, in which their cheating results in entirely unexpected positive benefits, as could possibly happen if, after cheating, they discover they never want to cheat again, start to work hard, and this transformative experience leads them to become enormously successful (+1,000,000 satisfaction units multiplied by an infinitesimal .000000001 probability). And of course there are many other possibilities as well (one even more remote possibility is that they could live an entire life cheating successfully, which we might represent as having a $.1^{10}$ probability of giving them +1 billion satisfaction units).

The point here is simple. In problem of possible future selves cases, while the likely expected utility of cheating might be positive (see Table 3.1), there is nevertheless an infinite number of ways in which one's

Table 3.1 Expected utility of immoral action in a problem-case

---

Cheating successfully: (100,000 satisfaction units [SU]) × .6 [high probability]
Cheating unsuccessfully, failing course: (–100,000 SU) × .2 [medium probability]
Cheating successfully but feeling guilty afterward: (–5 SU) × .1 [low probability]
Cheating successfully but suffering a criminal conviction later in life because of developing cheating habits: (–5 million SU) × .000000001 [very low probability]
Cheating successfully, cheating successfully for life, enjoying fame and fortune: (+1 billion SU) × .1^{10} [infinitesimal probability]
.
.
. (infinite series of possible positive and negative outcomes)
'Likely utility' (focusing on top three most likely outcomes) = +39,999.5 satisfaction units
Total Expected Utility (sum of infinite number of possible positive and negative outcomes times their probabilities of occurrence) = zero

---

dominant interest – in knowing one's future interests in advance – can go unsatisfied. There are an infinite number of possible (if only unlikely) positive outcomes, and an infinite number of possible (if unlikely) negative outcomes. Since in a problem-case one cares about all of these possibilities, this means that the *total expected utility* of any action in which one 'bets' on outcomes is exactly zero: an infinite number of possible positive outcomes (+infinity) added to an infinite number of possible negative outcomes (–infinity).

These results might sound strange at first glance, and some readers may be concerned that I am exploiting the nature of infinity as a kind of mathematical trick (since the sum of any infinite series of positive numbers, no matter how small their probabilities are, is +infinity, and the sum of any infinite series of negative numbers, no matter how small their probabilities, is –infinity). Yet the results of this case are not a mathematical trick. They simply illustrate the nature of the problem of possible future selves: the fact that a person who encounters a decision in such a situation – a person who wants above all to know their future interests – cannot expect to benefit from 'betting on probabilities.' Yes, they may in fact benefit if they do make such a bet (as, in this case, they are likely to gain 39,999.5 positive satisfaction units). But again, the problem is that they are not interested in what they are likely to gain. They want to know what they will *actually* gain – and, since there is an infinite number of possible ways their future could go, it follows that no bet is instrumentally rational. Indeed, while I have used the resources of decision theory to illustrate this, it is simply an expression of the problem of possible future selves: namely that, in 'problem-cases,' the person involved does not *want* to bet (because they are worried about all possible, including unlikely, futures).

Further, as we will see in future chapters, the Categorical-Instrumental Imperative can be used to derive the conclusion that insofar as we sometimes face the problem of possible future selves in our lives, we should face it in other specific cases (namely, in decisions where concerns of fairness to oneself or others arise). As such, our present results sit well with how we often speak about morally good people. For instance, one thing we note about people who make morally good decisions is that they do not consider the likely benefits of a behavior such as cheating as outweighing the possible risks (to themselves and others) of them doing so. Indeed, as we will now see, the decision-theoretic argument given above can be extended to account for and explain another related thing that we often say about moral people (and indeed, something they often say themselves): namely, that to them the value of behaving morally is infinitely greater than the value of behaving immorally. Allow me to explain.

Given the argument above, some readers might wonder how moral behavior solves the problem of possible future selves. After all, isn't it true that we can draw up the same result for moral behavior in problem-cases: that since there is an infinite number of possible ways that moral behavior can benefit a person, and an infinite number of ways in can backfire, the total expected utility of moral behavior in problem-cases is zero as well (as illustrated in Table 3.2)?

In other words, it now looks like even if moral and immoral behavior have the same total expected utility – zero, due to there being an infinite number of improbable ways both actions could go well or

Table 3.2 Expected utility of moral action?

Not cheating, and failing the exam: (–100,000 SU) × .9 [high probability]
Not cheating, but barely passing the exam: (+10,000 SU) × .5 [low probability]
Not cheating, but doing surprisingly well on the exam: (+100,000) × .01 [very low probability]
Not cheating, but developing better personal habits for success in life: (+1,000,000SU) × .000001 [very low probability]
.
.
.(infinite series of possible positive and negative outcomes)
'Likely utility' (three most likely outcomes) = –84,000 SU (less than in Table 3.1)
Total expected utility = zero (same as Table 3.1)

poorly – immoral behavior is still more likely to result in good outcomes (in which case, shouldn't one choose immorality, since its likely outcomes are better?). Further, some readers might protest that neither table can be correct – for, given the way I have formulated our decisions and possible outcomes, all of our actions have an expected value of zero, as there are in principle, always an infinite number of ways things can go well or poorly, not just in problem-cases but in *every* case.

These concerns are mistaken, however. Let me begin by addressing the latter concern first: the concern that neither table can be right, as (if my analysis is correct) all actions have an expected utility of zero. My analysis does not entail this. As we saw earlier, in some cases one is not concerned with all possible outcomes. The student who is tempted to cheat in a non-problem case – a case where they do not want to know their future interests in advance – is concerned merely with likely outcomes. Indeed, this is presumably the case with many and probably most of our decisions. One does not stop to concern oneself with every possible future outcome when simply drinking a glass of water, for instance, nor – at least ordinarily – when crossing the street. Typically, one is simply concerned with likely outcomes, in which case the infinite number of possibilities that give rise to the expected outcome of zero in problem-cases is not generated. The expected outcome of zero is only generated in problem-cases, because it is only in those cases that one is concerned with all possible outcomes.

Now let us turn to the other concern, which is that in problem-cases, moral behavior has an expected utility of zero as well, since – just as with immoral behavior – there is always an infinite variety of possible ways that moral behavior can turn out well or poorly for the person performing the action. While this concern is understandable, it actually enables us to see more clearly why, although immoral behavior can be tempting even in problem-cases, properly understood moral behavior has greater expected utility in such cases: indeed, infinitely greater expected utility. Notice that Tables 3.1 and 3.2 both analyze expected outcomes in terms of things *external* to the action itself. In Table 3.1, one's interest is in cheating successfully: that is, in achieving something beyond cheating itself, namely, doing well on an exam (or enjoying some other less likely gain from cheating). Similarly in Table 3.2, one's aim is to achieve something above and beyond not cheating: one's aim is to do well on the exam by not cheating. Now, when framed this way, moral behavior can indeed look less likely to be beneficial than immoral behavior. If my dominant aim is to do well on an exam, then cheating may be more likely to benefit me than not. But according

102 Rightness as Fairness

to the Categorical-Instrumental Imperative, this is fundamentally the wrong way to respond to problem-cases, and by extension, the wrong way to understand the expected benefits of moral behavior.

The Categorical-Instrumental Imperative states that the only rational way to solve the problem of possible future selves is come to an agreement with all of our possible future selves on interests to pursue *for their own sake*. As we will see in future chapters, these turn out to be interests in fairness (norms of fairness turn out to be the only interests that satisfy the Categorical-Instrumental Imperative's satisfaction conditions). Let us assume, then, for the moment, that this is correct: that, following the Categorical-Instrumental Imperative, the only ends we can agree to with all of our possible future selves are ends of pursuing fairness *for its own sake* (again, the argument for this comes later). If this is correct, then the right way to frame moral behavior in a decision-theoretic framework is not as illustrated in Table 3.2. One must instead represent outcomes in terms of the dominant, voluntary interests of each possible future self: who, by obeying the Categorical-Instrumental Imperative, make their dominant interest pursuing fairness for its own sake, as its own reward. If this is correct – if what it is to obey the Categorical-Instrumental Imperative is for each possible self to make their dominant interest fairness for its own sake, as its own reward – then the correct representation of the expected benefits of moral behavior is Table 3.3.

Since each possible future self in this case has the same intrinsic, voluntarily chosen end – not cheating for its own sake – then there is no possible way for any of the selves to fail to satisfy their dominant end. Instead, there is an infinite number of possible future selves, all of whom are assured to satisfy their dominant end: fairness for its own sake. And in that case the total expected outcome of the action of not cheating is +infinity, infinitely greater than immoral behavior in problem-cases and

Table 3.3 Expected outcomes of obeying the Categorical-Instrumental Imperative

---

Possible future self #1 (not cheating for its own sake): (>0 SU) × .7 [high probability]
Possible future self #2 (not cheating for its own sake): (>0 SU) × .1 [low probability]
Possible future self #3 (not cheating for its own sake): (>0 SU) × .01 [very low probability]
.
.
.(infinite series of possible selves all adopting the same end as above)
Total Expected utility = +infinite SU

infinitely greater than 'moral' behavior that aims at particular outcomes (as in Table 3.2).

I imagine two concerns arising here. First, couldn't one apply the same reasoning to the conclusion that immoral behavior voluntarily pursued for its own sake has infinite expected utility? Second, even if we suppose that truly moral behavior aims at fairness for its own sake (which future chapters will argue), one might worry that Table 3.3 only lists the expected outcome of certain voluntarily chosen interests (choosing not to cheat for its own sake). However, can't moral behavior – even when it is chosen for its own sake – result in disappointment when it comes to one's other interests (such as disappointment one might involuntarily or semivoluntarily feel from doing poorly on an exam)?

My reply to both concerns comes mostly in the form of a promissory note: namely, that I will show in Chapter 6 that one cannot expect infinite utility by committing oneself to voluntarily pursuing immoral behavior 'for its own sake.' For, as we will see, moral behavior (actions that conform to the Categorical-Instrumental Imperative) renders the interests of different possible future selves more consistent (taking into account costs), thus enabling an infinitely larger number of possible future selves to more effectively satisfy their voluntary, involuntary, and semivoluntary interests. Thus, although immoral behavior can still (as I have allowed above) result in better likely outcomes (not getting caught or feeling bad for cheating) than moral behavior chosen for its own sake, moral behavior chosen for its own sake promises something that neither immoral behavior in general, immoral behavior 'chosen for its own sake,' or moral behavior for a specific purpose can promise: an infinitely greater number of possible futures in which one can successfully satisfy one's interests.

Furthermore, even if immoral behavior might result in 'better likely outcomes' in isolated cases (as in Tables 3.1–3.2), there are grounds for believing that this is not generally the case. Indeed, there are ample reasons to believe we are better off in the long term if we become the kinds of people who encounter the problem of possible future selves and solve it by way of the Categorical-Instrumental Imperative – rationally discounting larger 'likely outcomes' in favor of wanting smaller but certain outcomes of moral behavior pursued for its own sake. First, prioritizing 'likely short-term gain' has been shown to be a strong predictor of criminally delinquent behavior – behavior that lands people in prison (or worse).[11] Second, much empirical research has demonstrated that human beings tend to be far more sensitive to negative outcomes than positive ones, experiencing negative outcomes as more harmful than positive outcomes beneficial.[12-13] Our proclivity to this 'negativity bias' is widely recognized among psychologists. Indeed, in a highly influential article, Roy Baumeister and colleagues review a wealth of empirical evidence and conclude that a general principle of the 'bad being stronger than the good' exists 'across a broad range of psychological phenomena,' including 'in everyday events, major life events (e.g., trauma), close relationship outcomes, social network patterns, interpersonal outcomes, and learning processes.'[14] Broadly speaking, these are the very the notions we appeal to when we teach our children (and ourselves) the benefits of morality. We commonly recognize that although the 'likely benefits' of immorality may appear greater than those of moral behavior in isolated cases, becoming the kind of person who sees things this way is unwise in the long-run, increasing both the likelihood of reckless behavior as well as (because of the law of large numbers) the probability that immoral behavior will end up resulting in detrimental negative outcomes that could have been avoided through moral behavior. For instance, even if the probability of getting caught and punished severely is only one in 100, if one cheats one hundred times, the probability that one will suffer those severe consequences is *1*.

Finally, as we will also see in Chapter 6, the Categorical-Instrumental Imperative is sensitive to the costs that morality imposes upon us. Unlike many moral theories, which hold us to very strict standards (and, some argue, impossibly strict standards of 'moral sainthood'[15]), the Categorical-Instrumental Imperative entails it is rational – and morally permissible – to weigh moral ideals of fairness against the costs of pursuing them. Indeed, we will see that morality turns out to be a kind of equilibrium point: one that requires one's present and possible future selves to jointly arrive at norms of fairness that, taking all possible costs involved into account, maximize the probability that all of one's possible future selves will be able to successfully satisfy their interests given mutual recognition of the problem of possible future selves.

With these concerns addressed (or, in part, forestalled to Chapter 6), let us return to the notion that truly moral behavior has infinite expected value. One further, natural question to ask here is: how could morality have this amazing property without it having been noticed (or explicated) before? The surprising answer is that many of us have realized it before, if only dimly. Allow me to explain.

Consider first the reaction that it is 'surprising' or 'counterintuitive' that the expected utility of moral behavior is infinite. Is it really? First, it is often said that 'morality is its own reward.' We often teach our children that if one does what is right because it is right, then, no matter what happens, 'one can look oneself in the mirror at night.' And indeed, contrast the possible futures of people who do moral things for their own sake against those who do immoral things. Consider people like Nelson Mandela and Martin Luther King – people who stood up for what was right and just, come what may. Although Mandela was imprisoned for decades, we recognize that there is something about his moral behavior that cannot be possibly taken from him: his 'dignity' in doing the right thing. In contrast, consider the immoralist. Some immoralists get away with immoral behavior, winning fame and riches. Yet, some of them face the worst futures imaginable. Consider Bernie Madoff, the infamous Ponzi-schemer who defrauded investors of billions of dollars. Madoff ended up in prison, one of his sons committed suicide, his second son suffered a fatal relapse of cancer that he attributed to stress arising from the scandal, and his wife was publicly disgraced – and there is nothing he can do to undo the past. Similarly, consider the student who, because she was caught cheating on one test, has too low of a grade-point-average to attend law school. Like Madoff, this student has to pay for her immoral actions, in ways she can never fully undo. Or consider the husband who neglects his spouse. He may get away with it for decades, only to suffer a miserable divorce. All of these individuals can rationally regret their behavior. But the person who does not cheat investors or on tests, or neglect their spouse, out of fairness, for its own sake? Things can of course go wrong in this person's life (the person can face bad luck, do poorly on exams, and so on) – but they are still assured something the immoralist is not: internal satisfaction that they did what is fair and right for its own sake, out of 'fairness to themselves' (and, by extension, out of fairness to others, as we will see in Chapters 4–6).

Indeed, many of us already recognize that there is great depth to the notion that morality has infinite expected utility. For while we recognize that many things in life are beyond our control – one's marriage could fail despite one's best efforts, one's spouse could die, one could come down with a deadly disease, and so on – the thing about morality, about being fair for its own sake, is that one's present and future selves can control it. If I neglect my spouse and she divorces me, or if I neglect her and I come down with a deadly disease, and so on, I could regret to my dying day that I did not treat her better: my future self could wish more than anything that they could go back in time and behave differently. On the other hand, however, if I treat her well – if I am fair to her and to myself for its own sake – then no matter what happens, I can know, in every part of my soul, that I treated both of us the way I should have.

106 *Rightness as Fairness*

I cannot look back and wish, in an instrumentally rational fashion, that I had been horrible to her – for my past and future selves have made it their dominant interest to be fair to her for its own sake. This, I believe, is the infinite value of morality: the expected utility of morality is infinite because it advances interests that one's present and every possible future self (literally an infinite number of possible future selves) rationally agree to pursue for their own sake. As such, the notion that morality has infinite expected utility is not strange or counterintuitive. It in fact embodies the oft-asserted notion – long defended by moral sages (from Jesus Christ onward) – that morality, properly understood, can 'never fail.' The Categorical-Instrumental Imperative finally explicates this notion in full. It is only when one acts on interests that one's present and every possible future self rationally agree upon that, no matter what the future holds, one cannot fail to achieve what one wants. Although I am far from alone in defending such a notion (Elizondo argues that Kant's practical philosophy has similar implications, assuring one of inner-contentedness[16], Socrates argued that morality comprises psychological health in *The Republic*[17], and so on), my particular argument for it – as we will now see in more detail – is unique and, I believe, more nuanced and compelling than existing ones.

Indeed, the Categorical-Instrumental Imperative does more than validate Immanuel Kant's famous assertion that the only thing that could be good without limitation is a 'good will' – a will that conforms to the moral law for its own sake.[18] It also synthesizes two claims about infinity that Kant set against one another in the following famous passages concluding the *Critique of Practical Reason*:

> Two things fill the mind with ever new and increasing admiration and reverence, the oftener and the more steadily one reflects on them: the starry heavens above me and the moral law within me… The first begins from the place I occupy in the external world of sense and extends the connection in which I stand into an unbounded magnitude with worlds upon worlds and systems of systems, and moreover into the unbounded times of their periodic motion, their beginning and their duration. The second begins from my invisible self, my personality, and presents me in a world which has true infinity but which can be discovered only by the understanding, and I cognize that my connection with that world (and thereby with all those visible worlds as well) is not merely contingent, as in the first case, but universal and necessary. The first view of a countless multitude of worlds annihilates, as it were, my importance as an animal creature,

which after it has been for a short time provided with vital force (one knows not how) must give back to the planet (a mere speck in the universe) the matter from which it came. The second, on the contrary, infinitely raises my worth as an intelligence by my personality, in which the moral law reveals to me a life independent of animality and even of the whole sensible world, at least so far as this may be inferred from the purposive determination of my existence by this law, a determination not restricted to conditions and boundaries of this life but reaching into the infinite.[19]

Kant's thoughts in this passage cohere with my argument for the Categorical-Instrumental Imperative. First, Kant writes that he stands in awe of the heavens – the unbounded 'worlds upon worlds' and 'systems of systems' that he can comprehend. Second, he notes that it is his intelligence that enables him to see that he is not merely 'connected' with this world (the world he actually finds himself in), but with 'all those visible worlds as well.' As such, he affirms that even though he is infinitely small in relation to all of those possible worlds, it is his ability to act on the moral law – his ability to not be 'restricted to conditions and boundaries of this life' but rather reach 'into the infinite' – that gives the moral law infinite value. This has been exactly my argument. It is our infinite 'smallness' in the present, the fact that our future could go an infinite number of ways, that makes morality infinitely valuable: it is only by reaching out to all of our possible future selves, and coming to a universal agreement on interests to pursue for their own sake, that we bridge the infinite gulf between us and them. However, there are a number of critical differences between my argument and Kant's, which – I believe – firmly favor mine over his. Among other things, whereas Kant argues for the infinite value of his categorical imperative on the basis of a very controversial conception of practical reason – one that does not reduce reasons to obey the moral law to instrumental normativity[16–21] – my argument is based on an uncontroversial conception of instrumental normativity combined with other clear facts: facts regarding our capacity to care about our past, present, and future; our sometimes wanting to know our future interests; and experiencing ourselves as capable of having three distinct types of interests (voluntary, involuntary, and semivoluntary ones). Thus, I hold that my argument is on firmer foundations than Kantian ethics – and, as we will see in future chapters, has many other advantages as well.

Finally, the Categorical-Instrumental Imperative provides, as we have seen, a unique explanation of why the infinite value of morality can be so hard to see. First, because we are human, we tend to focus on likely outcomes – outcomes in 'close-by' futures (where we might get away with cheating, neglecting our spouse, and so on) – rather than all possible futures. Secondly, because we are human, we have the tendency to focus on 'extrinsic' interests: on achieving things like doing well on tests, making money, and so on. Both tendencies explain why the infinite value of conforming to the Categorical-Instrumental Imperative is hard to see. It is only when we encounter the problem of possible future selves – being concerned about possible futures, and wanting to know our future interests – that that infinite value of acting on the Categorical-Instrumental Imperative becomes evident, at least insofar as we truly act on it for its own sake, both now and in the future. For it is precisely in these cases – cases where one worries about not knowing what one's future interests will be – that acting in ways that every possible future self can voluntarily accept has clear value: in these cases, the only way to ensure that you can 'look in the mirror' later on and not regret your decisions, to the extent that this is within your voluntary control, is to ensure that you act in ways that every possible future self can voluntarily accept. This, I believe, is the 'secret' about morality that many of us already recognize: that it is only when one does what is truly right for its own sake, acting in ways that (as the Categorical-Instrumental Imperative states) we could voluntarily agree to no matter how the future turns out, that we assure ourselves, to the extent that it is in our voluntary power to do so, that our choices have a kind of 'dignity' – a *categorical rightness* that we can recognize as the right way to act, vis-à-vis all possible futures, in light of one's ignorance of how the future will go.

In short, the Categorical-Instrumental Imperative itself – and by extension, the principles of fairness we will see it generates – explains both why immoral actions are tempting but also irrational. Immoral actions (such as lies, cheating, and so on) typically stem from our natural tendency to focus on likely, desirable outcomes (such as, perhaps, being tempted to cheat and enjoy doing it successfully). Morality, on the other hand, requires us to do something that is much more difficult, but infinitely more valuable: focusing on all possible outcomes, and acting in ways that all our future selves can voluntarily accept. Furthermore, as we will see in later chapters, morality is 'difficult' – and the infinite expected value of morality hard to see – because, in cases where we encounter the problem of possible selves, the Categorical-Instrumental Imperative requires us to develop dispositions (or interests) to encounter the problem, and obey the Categorical-Instrumental Imperative, in other cases: including cases where we might not initially encounter the problem. This is also very intuitive. After all, a big part of the reason that cheating might appear so tempting to the would-be cheater is that they lack the 'conscience' – or concerns about the future that make morality rational – that, recursively, on the basis of their earlier actions, they *should* have according to the Categorical-Instrumental Imperative. Indeed, as we will see in future chapters, the recursive structure of the Categorical-Instrumental Imperative entails that one should be disposed to be concerned about cheating, and not cheat, due to internalizing certain virtues of fairness that we should have acted on in earlier instances in our lives. This is an intuitive idea: the reason why we ordinarily want to say the cheater shouldn't cheat is that they should have developed a better conscience than we actually have. That is, we believe that we should approach the question of whether they should cheat from different motives: namely, with concerns about the consequences of their actions – concerns they should have, and would have, if they had made more sound moral choices previously in their lives. We will return to this in Chapter 6.

I believe the above case for the Categorical-Instrumental Imperative to be sound. The only instrumentally rational way to solve the problem of possible future selves (to the extent that it can be solved) is to conform our actions now, and in the future, to the Categorical-Instrumental Imperative, acting on interests it is instrumentally rational for our present and future selves universally agree upon, given their particular contingent (voluntary, involuntary, and semivoluntary) interests and co-recognition of the problem. Acting on such interests has infinite expected value because, given our ignorance of the future and infinite number of possible selves, there is an infinite number of ways for our actions to succeed: no matter which future happens, our actions will satisfy the interests our future selves choose to share with us (provided they too uphold the agreement).

Thus far, I have been speaking of the Categorical-Instrumental Imperative as a moral principle – assuming that it justifies the kinds of actions I have been discussing (not cheating on exams, being fair to one's spouse, and so on). However, I have not yet shown this. The Categorical-Instrumental Imperative, at least as this chapter has defined it, simply states that we are to seek and uphold a universal agreement with all of our possible future selves. We will see in subsequent chapters exactly how this is a distinctly moral notion. Before we do, however, I would like to address a concern and then examine the more general plausibility of the Categorical-Instrumental Imperative as a prudential principle.

4 Just conscience?

One worry readers might have is that the problem of possible future selves, and argument for the Categorical-Instrumental Imperative, both appear to come down to a matter of conscience. Consider first the problem: one's interest in knowing one's future interests, and ordering them with one's present ones. This problem was introduced as stemming from concerns we sometimes have about the future: concerns about getting caught or punished for cheating for instance, or feeling guilt, and so on. More generally, the problem appears to stem from a general concern to avoid regretting one's choices in the future, by ensuring that one makes the right choices (choices that one's later self will be able to accept, regardless of how else the future turns out). This certainly sounds like 'conscience' – and indeed, so does the positive argument for the Categorical-Instrumental Imperative: the argument that obeying this principle has infinite expected positive value for the person who encounters the problem of possible future selves. For again, as we saw above, it is precisely the individual's interest in knowing the 'right decision' before the future comes that functions in my argument to entail the infinite expected value of obeying the Categorical-Instrumental Imperative.

If, in these respects, the problem the Categorical-Instrumental Imperative is intended to solve, and the argument for obeying it as a solution to that problem, are ultimately simply a matter of conscience – of one wanting to know what 'the right decision' is, rather than risking behavior contrary to the Categorical-Instrumental Imperative – one might wonder: why didn't I just say so? Why go through all of the argumentative contortions involved in getting there? Why not just straightforwardly appeal to conscience as morality's foundation?

The answer to this concern is as follows. Although in one respect my argument is an appeal to our capacity for having 'a conscience' – our worrying, at least in some cases, about our future – the argument was necessary for several reasons. First, unlike bare appeals to conscience (or a 'moral sense') – unlike the kinds of appeals to sympathy, empathy, or a 'moral sense' often appealed to by moral sentimentalists[20] (moral emotions which not everyone clearly has in sufficient measure to make morality instrumentally rational) – the argument I have provided is not predicated on our having a controversial kind of conscience, such as our feeling guilty for wrongdoing (for, as we all well know, not everyone does feel guilty for wrongdoing). Instead, my argument has been based on a simple form of conscience that we all experience from time to time: being concerned about the future and wanting to know our future interests. This is critical, because rather than positing some kind of 'moral sense,' my argument for the Categorical-Instrumental Imperative is constructed out of a problem we *all* encounter. We encounter it not because we have 'moral emotions,' but simply because, in some cases, we simply worry about possible outcomes (including 'getting caught' by our teachers for cheating, or punished by others for lying, and so on). In other words, my argument shows how – psychopaths aside – we all have a 'conscience' in a sense that is sufficient to generate morality: conscience not as a moral emotion per se, but simply as a capacity to be concerned about and want to know the future. Second, the particular argument I have given for the Categorical-Instrumental Imperative – locating its basis in our sometimes encountering, and having an interest in solving, the problem of possible future selves – enabled us to arrive at it as a solution to the problem. As we will see in the chapters that follow, the Categorical-Instrumental Imperative is an important and unique principle indeed: one that ultimately reconciles a number of traditional approaches to moral philosophy (deontology, consequentialism, virtue ethics, and contractualism), but which also reconciles a number of leading approaches to political philosophy (libertarianism, egalitarianism, and communitarianism), in addition to having many other theoretical and practical virtues. Thus, the 'argumentative contortions' we have gone through to derive the Categorical-Instrumental Imperative have been for good reason.

5 An intuitive solution to the problem of possible future selves?

The Categorical-Instrumental Imperative is a complicated principle. Its central notions of coming to an instrumentally rational agreement with 'all of our possible future selves,' given our and their 'voluntary, involuntary, and semivoluntary interests,' are abstract and tough to parse. Still, however, we have already seen how the principle is an intuitive one. It is intuitive to think that morality is somehow a matter of 'not putting one's future in jeopardy,' and of acting in ways that one's future selves can rationally accept rather than regret. Further, as we will see in future chapters, the conception of morality that emerges from it – Rightness as Fairness – is intuitive as well. Since the Categorical-Instrumental Imperative is complex, however, I think it may be helpful to conclude this chapter by bringing it still further down to earth, considering its central notions not in relation to paradigmatically moral decisions, but rather in simple decisions about what is prudent for a person to do in the present, given uncertainty about the future.

We do not always encounter the problem of possible future selves. Indeed, many of our daily actions and decisions are so banal that we do not worry in the slightest what our future selves will want or think about them. For instance, there are many things I did earlier today that I simply cannot remember. I took a number of different sips of coffee, but I do not remember each and every one of them. They were not exactly life-changing decisions. And so I did not think about them at the time, and I cannot recall them now. Decisions like those are not ones in which we face the kind of uncertainty – and concerns about the future – that define the problem of possible future selves.

Now, however, consider a case where you do run into the problem. Allow me to share one of my own. While writing this book, I have repeatedly found myself wanting to write a good book and wanting to put all of my energy into it, for the sake of my future self. I want my future self to be happy with the book I write. At the very same time, I recognize that there are other things my future self might care about as well: among other things, my spouse, family, friends, and health. And it might just be that if I put all of my energy into this book – thereby ignoring my spouse, family, friends, and health – my future self could regret it. Perhaps, despite investing all of my time into it, I won't write a good book. Or perhaps I will, but only by alienating my spouse, friends, and family by ignoring them. Or perhaps I will write a good book but, because I ignored my health, failing to get a skin cancer check, end up coming down with undiagnosed cancer. And so on.

In short, as I sit here wanting to write a great book for the sake of my future self, I recognize that if I put all my energy into realizing that goal alone – to the exclusion of others – I put my possible future selves in jeopardy. For instance, if I neglect my spouse, I may find that I wrote a great book but damaged our relationship severely, and regret having done so. Indeed, even if I write a great book, my future self might wish above all else that he could go back in time and not neglect his spouse. Similarly, suppose I neglect my health. Things could turn okay: I could write a great book and suffer no misfortune. But this is only one possible future, and if another, less likely one occurs – one in which I am diagnosed with untreatable cancer because I did not go for a routine skin check – then my future self might wish, more than anything in the world, that he could go back in time and not neglect his health.

Because of all of these uncertainties – all of these possible futures – I face a problem: the problem of possible future selves. I care about my future. I want to realize a future that my future self will want. But I do not know which future self will be actualized. Anything could occur, including unlikely possibilities. Moreover, as we saw in Chapter 2, simply betting on likely outcomes – on not getting cancer, for instance (which I hope is unlikely) – is not instrumentally rational, because I do not know whether my future self will want me to take such risks. If an unlikely event happens – such as my getting cancer – my future self may wish for all the world that I had not taken even that tiny risk. And so, it seems, there is only one rational way to respond: the way that I have responded – trying, for its own sake, to be fair to each of my possible future selves. I have put hard work into this book for the sake of my future selves who care about that, I have given attention to my spouse, friends, and family for the sake of my future selves who care about them, I have looked after my health for the sake of future selves who care about my health; and so on. I have not 'bet' on one future self over the others. I have instead tried to behave in ways that put *all* of my possible future selves in a position to advance their own interests, whatever their interests would be. Although this juggling act has not been without costs for my present self, it is broadly the kind of juggling act we generally consider to be prudent, in light of worries about possible ways the future could go. We often tell ourselves and others 'not to put all of your eggs in one basket,' but rather to try to act in ways that put 'yourself in a good position to succeed' in the future despite the fact that things could go many different ways. There is intuitively something prudent, indeed commonsensical, about this approach to living. We often tell people to 'be fair to themselves' by balancing their present concerns against their future concerns, where this balancing act involves not recklessly betting on a particular future (one in which everything turns out as one expects), but instead 'putting oneself in a good position' to be satisfied in life despite life's unexpected vicissitudes. Although sometimes things still do not turn out the way we may like, we can nevertheless recognize when the future comes whether we were reckless, or whether we were 'fair' to our future selves. If one cheats one's way through school and later finds oneself languishing in a dead-end job, one is apt to regret one's earlier behavior. But, if one works one's way through school 'the right way,' working hard to develop skills that will be beneficial no matter how the future goes, then, even if things do not turn out well in the future, one can voluntarily appreciate and endorse that: the fact that one's past self did what they could to ensure that they were well prepared for the future, come what may. Finally, of course, to the extent that we do so, we also prepare our future selves to deal with whatever outcomes – good or bad – occur. If one develops mental strength, intelligence, and fortitude, then even if bad things happen, one is better prepared to deal with them than if one had been unfair to one's future selves (by simply cheating one's way through school, never developing adaptive habits to enable their future self to respond to life's unexpected turns).

And so it is. It is true that no matter what I do, external things may or may not turn out the way I like. I may write a great book, I may not. I may have a happy family, I may not. I may have good health, I may not. Still, whatever happens, I can choose to treat all of my possible future selves fairly for their own sake, and they can all endorse me having done so, together, as a mutual agreement between me and all of them, as a rational response to the problem I face. As such, when the future comes – whatever it may hold – my future self can say, and know, that his past self did what was fair and right, given his ignorance of the future. I believe that there is infinite value in this, for reasons I have already defended. There is an infinite dignity in being fair to your present and possible future selves.

This, again, is not to say that fair actions – those that conform to the Categorical-Instrumental Imperative – can 'erase all disappointment.' I am certain, for instance, that Nelson Mandela faced great pain in prison as a result of his decision to stand up for justice. And, in a much more banal case, I could be disappointed if I do not write a good book. The point is not that our present and future possible selves can bring all of our interests into line with how things turn out, such that our future selves will not be disappointed with some of the results of our actions. The claim, rather, is that when one does what is fair for its own sake – conforming one's actions to the Categorical-Instrumental Imperative for its own sake – there is always an element of one's action that one cannot rationally regret when the future comes: namely, the fact that one acted fairly for its own sake. Again, this is perfectly intuitive and in line with the common saying that 'doing the right thing is its own reward.' I may be unhappy with the results I achieve on a test by not cheating, but if I decide not to cheat for its own sake, then no matter what happens, in that respect I can 'hold my head high' and know that I did what was fair with respect to my future – and I can choose to endorse my action in the future for that reason alone. No matter what happens, one's future selves can choose – with dignity – for one's earlier self to have behaved fairly for its own sake. Although things may not turn out as we like – thanks to our inability to control the future – we can still say, 'Things may not have turned out exactly as I want. But I was fair to myself, and all of the selves I could have been. I was fair to the self who wanted to write a good book. I was fair to the self who wants to maintain good relations with family and friends. I was fair to the self who has interests in maintaining good health. Given my ignorance at the time, I put every self I could be in a position to achieve their own ends later on.' And there is great power to this. When one does wrong, one can rationally regret it (one can say to oneself, 'I should not have cheated'). When one treats all of one's possible selves fairly, however, there is a sense in which, no matter which future self is actual, that future self can say: 'I did exactly what I should have done. I was fair to every self I could have been, given my ignorance of which future would occur.' And this just is, I believe, our moral experience. We do not always like doing the moral thing, and the moral thing does not always lead to consequences that satisfy us – but there is something intrinsically rational about doing the right thing: it is the only rational way to solve the problem of possible future selves, to the extent that it has any solution at all.

6 Conclusion

This chapter argued that the Categorical-Instrumental Imperative is the only instrumentally rational solution to the problem of possible future selves. It also argued that this principle explains, and justifies, the dim sense that many of us have that morality is infinitely valuable – as well as why the infinite value of morality is so hard to see. Finally, this chapter argued that the Categorical-Instrumental Imperative embodies an intuitively compelling sense of fairness to one's future self: a sense of 'not putting one's future in jeopardy' that many of us identify, in real-life, with reasons to behave morally. We will now begin to see just how far this idea leads. We will see that being fair to one's possible future selves is identical to being fair to others, and therefore, that – to the extent that we sometimes encounter the problem of possible future selves in our lives (as we all in fact do) – fairness itself is instrumentally rational. It is instrumentally rational for us to become certain types of people: people who disposed to encounter, and solve, the problem of possible future selves when, and only when, it is *fair* to do so, through Four Principles of Fairness.

4
Three Unified Formulations

Chapter 3 argued that instrumental rationality requires responding to the problem of possible future selves by way of the following principle:

The Categorical-Instrumental Imperative: voluntarily aim for its own sake, in every relevant action, to best satisfy the motivational interests it is instrumentally rational for one's present and every possible future self to universally agree upon given their voluntary, involuntary, and semivoluntary interests and co-recognition of the problem of possible future selves, where relevant actions are determined recursively as actions it is instrumentally rational for one's present and possible future selves to universally agree upon as such when confronted by the problem – and then, when the future comes, voluntarily choose your having acted as such.

Although this principle is admittedly complex – containing many complications, which the following chapters will clarify – we also saw that it is surprisingly intuitive, amounting to a strategy that many of us already exploit for dealing with uncertainty about the future: the strategy of being fair to one's present and future selves, advancing one's present interests while not 'gambling away one's future.' Finally, I suggested (but did not argue) that the Categorical-Instrumental Imperative is also a moral principle that identifies fairness to oneself with fairness to others.

The present chapter begins to develop these implications explicitly. Section 1 argues that insofar as we have capacities to identify our future interests with the interests of other human and nonhuman sentient beings, it is instrumentally rational to interpret the Categorical-Instrumental Imperative as follows:

> **The Humanity and Sentience Formulation:** voluntarily aim for its own sake, in every relevant action, to best satisfy the motivational interests it is instrumentally rational for one's present and every possible future self to universally agree upon, given co-recognition that one's voluntary, involuntary, and semivoluntary interests could be identical to those of any possible human or sentient being(s), where relevant actions are determined recursively as actions it is instrumentally rational for one's present and possible future selves to universally agree upon as such in cases where one's present self wants to know and advance their future interests – and then, when the future comes, voluntarily choose your having acted as such.

Section 2 then argues that the Categorical-Instrumental Imperative and its Humanity and Sentience Formulation are in turn identical to a third formulation:

> **The Kingdom of Human and Sentient Ends Formulation:** voluntarily aim for its own sake, in every relevant action, to abstract away from the interests (or ends) of particular human or nonhuman sentient being(s), acting instead on interests (or ends) it is instrumentally rational for all human and nonhuman sentient beings to universally agree to share given their different voluntary, involuntary, and semivoluntary interests, where relevant actions are determined recursively as actions it is instrumentally rational for one's present and possible future selves to universally agree upon as such in cases where one's present self wants to know and advance their future interests – and then, when the future comes, voluntarily choose your having acted as such.

Finally, Section 3 argues that these formulations of the Categorical-Instrumental Imperative and the arguments for them have advantages over traditional Kantian ethics, a conception of morality which, as we will see, bears some broad similarities to the one this book has so far defended. Specifically, I show that my formulations of the Categorical-Instrumental Imperative have advantages on the principles of (Section 3.1) Firm Foundations, (Section 3.2) Internal and External Coherence, (Section 3.3) Explanatory Power, Unity, and Parsimony, and (Section 3.4) Fruitfulness over Kant's formulations of his categorical imperative.

118 Rightness as Fairness

1 The Humanity and Sentience Formulation

Let us assume that Chapter 3's argument for the Categorical-Instrumental Imperative is sound. Our task is now to determine which types of actions satisfy it: that is, which types of voluntary aims (in problem of possible future selves cases) would best satisfy motivational interests it is instrumentally rational for one's present and all possible future selves to universally agree to given their other motivations and co-recognition of the problem (co-recognition, that is, that one's present self cannot know which future self will be actual). Consequently, we need to clarify two things: (1) who one's 'possible future selves' are in problem-cases, and (2) what their voluntary, involuntary, and semivoluntary interests may be.

Let us begin with the notion of possible future selves. Who are one's possible future selves in problem of possible future selves cases? The answer is that they are the same as 'one's possible future selves' in general. At any point in time, whether we are considering a problem-case or not, there is a vast and possibly infinite number of ways one's future could possibly go. For example, as I sit here, I have an immense number of possible futures. Some, of course, are far more likely than others. Tonight, I will very likely be in Tampa, Florida. It would be a big surprise if I ended up anywhere else, as I have no plans to walk, drive, or fly anywhere tonight. However, sometimes the unlikely happens. It is possible, albeit extremely unlikely (we hope), that there will be a terrorist attack in Tampa today, forcing its residents (including me) to flee from the city. Or, alternatively (Heaven forbid), one of my family members in California could have a health emergency today, leading me to get on the soonest flight out of Tampa. And so on.

We can perhaps better understand the notion of our 'possible future selves' by further considering some of the putative moral cases discussed earlier. Suppose, again, a student knows it is very unlikely they will be caught cheating, as they have reliable evidence that their teacher lacks vigilance in spotting cheaters. Suppose, furthermore, that the student knows they are unlikely to feel guilty, either if they do get caught or if they do not (they are not 'the remorseful type'). Be that as it may, such a student nevertheless has many possible futures, including the unlikely futures just alluded to: futures in which they are unexpectedly caught, and perhaps punished far more than they expect (not only failing the class, but being expelled from school, for instance); futures in which they are not caught but unexpectedly feel some pangs of guilt; futures in which they are not caught but their cheating behaviors catch up to them later in life, in ways they do not want (for instance, by their becoming a habitual cheater who eventually commits, and is convicted for, financial fraud, or is perhaps divorced by their spouse for habitual infidelity – all of which might trace back to cheating habits that started far earlier in their life, including on the current exam); and so on.

Now consider some other cases. As I sit here, it is intuitively far more likely that I will be concerned today with the well-being of myself and my family than with the interests of some animal on the other side of the world. Yet, is it possible that I will be concerned with the interests of some such animal? Indeed it is. The other night, my spouse happened to turn on the BBC documentary series, *Planet Earth* (a series that just happened to be on television and we do not normally watch) – and it led to a variety of experiences I did not expect. We saw particular animals in the most remote parts of Earth struggling for survival, and in many cases failing: suffering and dying from starvation, exposure to the elements, and predation. And although my 'prior probability' for caring about the interests of any of those animals prior to watching the program was surely miniscule (I have never seen those particular animals before, and may never see them again), on this occasion I cared for them (indeed, we both did). We found ourselves hoping that a particular mountain goat would escape the clutches of a snow leopard, and feeling horrified when it was eventually caught, imagining what it would be like to *be* that goat, dying on a snowy mountainside in the jaws of a powerful predator. At the same time, though, we both remarked that we empathized with the leopard as well: we understood and to a certain extent identified with its interests in living (imagining, as it were, just how much we would want to live if we were in its position, starving for a meal and needing to provide for a hungry cub). Similarly, although I had never personally met a migrant farmworker – and never would have expected to identify my interests with theirs – last Spring I watched a public screening documentary film on the plight of migrant workers, which was then discussed by one of the filmmakers, a migrant worker. Here again I found myself moved. I found myself caring not only about migrant farm workers in general – identifying my interests with theirs, resolving to do something to help their cause – I also found myself identifying my interests with those of particular workers, experiencing some of their hopes and suffering by proxy, almost as though they were my own (though of course I cannot come close to truly experiencing the full extent of their experiences.). Finally, consider perhaps an even more surprising example. A television series, *Catfish*, follows real-life stories of people who have been deceived or otherwise harmed by individuals assuming false identities on the Internet. A recent episode told the story of 'Falesha,' a young woman who had her online identity stolen at the age of 15. Over a period of several years, a woman calling herself 'Jacqueline Linkwood' used publicly available photos of Falesha to create a false Facebook profile in which she routinely made vulgar comments and conducted personal attacks on complete strangers. 'Jacqueline' eventually progressed to full-on online identity theft, creating a false Facebook profile in Falesha's name (still using her pictures), 'friend-requesting' individuals from Falesha's school and community, and proceeding to harass them. As a result, Falesha was ostracized and mistreated by many of her classmates who believed that she was bullying them online. On one episode of *Catfish*, however, series producers were able to track down 'Jacqueline,' and brought Falesha to her house to confront her. Although Falesha was expecting to experience anger prior to the meeting (and even worried about having a physical confrontation), after the meeting she admitted that she 'wanted to cry' out of pity for the young woman, who clearly displayed troubling signs of mental illness – identifying with her perpetrator's suffering in an entirely unexpected way. Indeed, Falesha was so moved that she even returned with the series producers the next day to stage an intervention to help 'Jacqueline' and her mother.

We can now begin to see how the Categorical-Instrumental Imperative has the flavor of a moral principle. We are concerned about possible futures, wanting to know our future selves' interests, not only for self-interested reasons (for instance, because we want to make a good housing investment). We also worry about the future because we learn, over time, that as human beings we can end up caring about others' interests: sometimes only as a result of punishment (our instructors failing us for cheating, our friends shunning us for lying), other times as a result of rewards (such as social recognition for helping someone), but also for other reasons still – because of unexpected emotions, such as empathy, guilt, or remorse. As we will now see in more detail, there are all kinds of possible ways – both 'selfish' and 'unselfish' – that we can come to unexpectedly identify our interests with those of others: with those of not only other human beings, but also nonhuman animals, and even other possible sentient beings we have not yet encountered (such as artificial intelligences or alien creatures). The Categorical-Instrumental Imperative, in other words, will be revealed to be a moral principle because of who our possible future selves are: selves who may (but also may not) care for others.

1.1 Possible other-human-regarding interests

It is presently an open question when we encounter problem of possible future selves cases, and (more importantly) when we *should* encounter them (for, as we will see in Chapter 6, the Categorical-Instrumental Imperative recursively requires us to encounter the problem in certain types of cases: namely, cases where fairness requires it). For now, however, I want to set aside this issue and simply focus on the ways in which our future selves can end up identifying our interests with the interests of others.

We have already seen some cases where it is possible (even if unlikely) for one's future self to care about the interests of other human beings. Sometimes we unexpectedly end up caring about others' interests for purely selfish reasons: because of reward or punishment. Consider again the cheating student. Although it may be unlikely that they may get caught, and that they will feel guilty even if they do, it is always possible for them to end up caring about what their instructor or other students care about (namely, them having not cheated) – if only for selfish reasons. This could happen in various ways. For example, their instructor could punish them far more than they expect, not only failing them from the class but also seeking their expulsion from school – something which could, in principle, lead the student to wish they had not cheated: wish, that is, that they had identified their interests (in not cheating) with their instructor's. Alternatively, the student might simply have to go through hassles they end up wishing they would have avoided (having to meet with the dean, perhaps). Or alternatively still, their cheating ways to could catch up to them far later in life, leading them to develop cheating habits that lead to career ruin (getting caught and imprisoned for financial fraud) or even personal ruin (getting caught and divorced for infidelity). All of these possible outcomes could lead the student to wish that they had identified their interests with those of their instructor: that is, their instructor's policy against cheating, and interests in his or her students not cheating. Indeed, if the student were to suffer greatly later down the road (as in the case of being criminally prosecuted for financial fraud), the student might even wish they had never become a cheater, tracing back their habits to the exam in question ('I started to become a cheater in college, and never stopped,' they might say to themselves. 'I wish I had never started').

Notice that I am not arguing that many – if any – of these outcomes are likely. Again, they may be profoundly unlikely. The student in question may very likely get away with cheating in the given case scot-free, without any short- or long-term consequences. The point is simply that, from one's standpoint in the present, they are undoubtedly *possible*. The student cannot know for certain that they will not occur – as again, part of what it is to be human is for the 'unexpected to happen' sometimes. Some people cheat repeatedly, never getting caught or feeling guilty. But unless they are a complete psychopath (a kind of being who, for reasons discussed in Chapter 2, appears unable to care about their future, and unable to appreciate the normative force of moral demands), they are capable – as are we all – of recognizing that their actions *can* 'blow up in their face,' leading to possible outcomes their future selves might wish they had avoided. We recognize these as possibilities for the simple reason that we are not omniscient, and because, in this world, we know through experience that things of small probability sometimes do occur (sometimes people do get caught, even when it is unlikely; sometimes people do feel guilty, even though they never felt guilty in similar cases previously; and so on).

The point in these cases is this: because of our ignorance of the future, in problem-cases we must recognize that there are many possible ways in which – literally or by proxy – we can come to identify our interests with those of other human beings. However, the qualification here, 'by proxy,' is important. Although some of one's possible future selves might literally identify their interests with the interests of others (as when we feel others' pain as though they are our own, wanting to not hurt them because we experience their pain 'as our own'), in many cases the relevant identification is by proxy: by the person coming to align their interests the interests of others. Indeed, these cases may be far more common or likely: ones where one wishes one hadn't cheated on an exam, as one's teacher wished, simply because one (now, in the future) wishes one had not been caught and punished. Although one's future self does not literally identify their teacher's interests as their own in this case, the student nevertheless does so by proxy, wishing that they hadn't cheated (which is 'in line' with what their teacher wants).

Nevertheless, although some of our possible future selves only 'identify' their interests with those of other human beings by proxy, some of our other possible selves do so literally, adopting others' interests as one's own. The most obvious example of this involves experiences of conscience. Sometimes, when we treat others badly, we find ourselves with a 'sinking feeling' that we should have done otherwise: feeling their pain as if it were our own, experiencing their interests as our own. For instance, it may only be after decades of a person coldly ignoring their spouse – never feeling any guilt – that, in the midst of horrific argument, seeing their spouse break down and sobbing, that empathy can unexpectedly 'hit' a person, overwhelming them with guilt they never expected to have: seeing themselves, and how selfish they have been, through their spouse's eyes for the very first time, and wishing, above all else, that they could go back in time and make their spouse's wants and needs *their* wants and needs. Indeed, such transformative experiences appear to be a very important part of moral experience. For instance, one may see a person in need – a person in an automobile accident on the street – and unexpectedly feel for them, experiencing their terror as if it were one's own: terror that drives you to rush to their aid.

Second, these same types of shifts that cause us to literally identify our interests with others' interests – the remorse we experience as a result of getting caught for bad behavior, or alternatively, unexpected feeling of empathy – are sometimes experienced by our future selves as semivoluntary (that is, as partially under our voluntary control). Indeed, recent research on empathy shows that empathy is not fixed but malleable: we can change how much empathy we feel in a given situation through concerted effort.[1] For example, after cheating on an exam, one may feel just a little bit bad about doing so, but not much – and yet one may tell oneself that one should feel worse than one does ('I should really feel bad about what I did'), and through some effort, make it so: making oneself feel worse about what one did through conscious effort. And of course, one can often alter one's feelings in the opposite direction, initially empathizing with the interests of others ('I really feel bad about the laborers who work in the hot sun for poverty wages') but then convincing oneself not to care so much ('What can I do? Nothing. I guess I will just put it out of my mind').[2] Our ability to alter our reactions to others' interests – making ourselves feel for them more or less than we do – is, indeed, a pervasive part of moral experience. Within at least some bounds, we can make ourselves feel things, in part by engaging in imaginative simulation (choosing whether or not to imagine someone else's plight from their perspective).

Finally, setting feelings aside – which we appear to only have semivoluntary control over (my anger or empathy are, intuitively, partly in my control and partly out of it) – insofar as we experience ourselves as having voluntary interests and the capacity to make choices, we experience ourselves as free to *choose* whether we identify our dominant motivational interests (the ones we act on) with the interests of others. I can tell myself, 'I will not shop at Supermarket X any more to support the striking migrant workers,' and experience myself as choosing to follow through on this judgment, identifying my dominant motivational interests with theirs. Similarly, if one finds wanting to say something mean-spirited to a spouse during a disagreement (out of anger), one can tell oneself, 'I will respect their feelings,' and choose to do so, saying something constructive instead. In other words, some of our possible future selves can voluntarily choose to make other human beings' interests our own.

Although I have thus far been focusing on ways in which our present and future selves can expectedly or unexpectedly identify their voluntary, involuntary, and semivoluntary interests with the interests of particular other human beings (one's teacher, spouse, or friend) and groups thereof (fellow students, migrant laborers), we can also expectedly or unexpectedly identify our interests with those of others in general. In some instances, we simply find ourselves involuntarily empathizing with our fellow human beings ('I really wish everyone could be happy and that there wasn't so much suffering in the world'). Other times, we actively choose to care about human beings in general ('I will do unto others as I would have them do unto me, as the Golden Rule requires'). This may not be the usual case, of course, as we all may not be so inclined – due to our involuntary and semivoluntary inclinations – to care about the interests of humankind at large (we are often naturally much more inclined to identify our interests with those of particular others: our family, friends, fellow citizens, and so on). The point, however, is that it is always *possible* for our future selves to care about the interests of wider classes of human beings, including (as the limiting case) the interests of all human beings.

In sum, although many of our future selves may not identify their interests with the interests of other human beings – some of our possible future selves may be profoundly selfish – our possible selves include selves who voluntarily, involuntarily, or semivoluntarily identify their interests with the interests of other human beings, both particular human beings and groups thereof (in the limit, all human beings). Accordingly, if we are to apply the Categorical-Instrumental Imperative properly – that is, if we are to determine which motivational interests it is rational for our present and *all* possible future selves to universally agree upon in problem-cases – we must do so on the assumption that our possible future selves may, for a variety of different reasons, identify their interests with the interests of any or every possible human being.

1.2 Possible nonhuman-animal-regarding interests

Our future selves can, in similar ways, end up aligning or identifying their interests with those of nonhuman animals.

First, in a variety of ways, we can – and sometimes do – find ourselves involuntarily identifying our interests with the interests of nonhuman animals. When we see an animal suffering, for instance, we may involuntarily have feelings of empathy: we find ourselves not wanting to see that animal suffer anymore. Further, although some (and perhaps many) of us may have muted feelings of empathy for animals in general – caring about our own interests and the interests of other human beings far more than those of animals – there are other ways in which our future possible selves can find themselves involuntarily identifying their interests those of animals. For instance, sometimes other human beings who care about nonhuman animals impress upon us the importance of doing so, even going so far as to be angry at us for not doing so (one may find oneself continually getting into heated arguments with 'moral vegetarians,' for instance). Similarly, one can unexpectedly find oneself sickened by a documentary on factory farming: a documentary showing one just how badly animals used for human consumption are treated (for the record, this happened to me). Indeed, this kind of experience can in some cases be transformative, getting one to empathize with a single animal or multiple animals in a totally unexpected way. Consider again my previous example of going on a fishing trip. Although I had never felt much empathy for fishes, and had been fishing a few times before, when I saw the fish I caught on this particular trip staring back at me, I found myself feeling unexpected empathy and regret for what I did. I (involuntarily) found myself imagining myself in the fish's position on the hook, staring back at me, about to die – and at that moment, I found myself wanting to throw it back into the water, identifying my interests with its own. This was not something I expected (again, I had gone fishing before in the past, and never had such an experience before). It simply happened to me. With respect to my earlier selves, my feeling this way was a very improbable outcome – and yet it happened: it was a possible future that, in this case, was actualized. I unexpectedly identified my interests with those of the fish.

Second, and in much the same way, our present and possible future selves can always end up having semivoluntary interests in the interests of nonhuman animals. I may find myself feeling only a bit guilty about the fish I just caught – wanting to throw it back – but choose to actively suppress my guilt, keeping the fish, and seeing my guilt dissipate over time. Conversely, I may experience the horror of watching a documentary on factory farming, resolve never to consume animal products again, and voluntarily choose to focus on that earlier experience, 'reliving' the experience of watching the documentary, increasing the amount of empathy I feel so that I do not eat meat even when I am tempted to. Although I may never fully rid myself of my desire to eat meat, one may experience one's empathy for nonhuman animals as partly under one's voluntary control.

Finally, however much we may or may not empathize with the interests of nonhuman animals, we nevertheless experience ourselves – in many if not all of our actions – as having the capacity to voluntarily decide what our dominant motivational interests are with respect to them. Indeed, even if one does not feel much empathy for animals, one may choose not to consume animal products on principle, on the judgment that it would be wrong to. Similarly, to take a less extreme case, I may not want to take my dog out for a walk – I may not empathize much with his desire to go out for one, given that he has already been out several times today – and yet judge that I should, choosing to take him out merely out of a sense that I owe it to him.

Thus, just as many of our possible future selves may not identify their interests with the interests of other human beings, but other possible future selves do, so too is it the case that many of our possible selves do not identify their interests with the interests of nonhuman animals, but other of our possible future selves do. Some of our possible future selves voluntarily, involuntarily, or semivoluntarily identify their interests with particular animals (our pets, for instance), whereas other possible selves (perhaps less likely ones, but still possible ones) identify their interests with the interests of nonhuman animals generally. As such, if we are to apply the Categorical-Instrumental Imperative properly – if we are to determine which motivational interests our present and all possible future selves might agree upon our acting on – we must do so on the assumption that our possible future selves may, for a variety of different reasons, identify their interests not just with the interests of other human beings, but also nonhuman animals.

1.3 Possible sentient-being-regarding interests

Finally, in the same ways, our possible future selves can unexpectedly – voluntarily, involuntarily, or semivoluntarily – find themselves identifying their interests with the interests of other possible sentient beings we have not yet encountered, including sentient aliens from other worlds and artificial intelligences. Indeed, the fact that we could unexpectedly end up identifying our interests with the interests of such beings is one of the most common tropes in science fiction. For example, in the film *AI: Artificial Intelligence*, human beings systematically treat the artificially intelligent androids (called 'Mecha') they have created horrifically, setting up 'flesh fairs' in which they torture, maim, and kill them. Unexpectedly, however, one of the newest and most human-like androids – a young 'boy' named 'David,' the film's protagonist – suddenly gives rise to feelings of empathy and guilt in the audience. His shrieks, 'Don't burn me, don't burn me...don't make me die, I'm David, I'm *David*!' lead members of the audience to turn on the fair's organizers. One audience member shouts, 'Mecha don't plead for their lives. Who is that? He looks like a boy!' and the audience riots, suddenly treating David's interests as – literally or by proxy – their own.

Although in this case the audience's coming to align their interests with David's appear to result from sudden, unexpected experiences of empathy for him (since he appears like a human boy), another common, compelling trope of science fiction is that, as with other human beings and animals, we have a choice. We can choose to make the interests of nonhuman aliens or sentient artificial intelligences our own. While of course we may be strongly disposed by evolution to care far more about human beings than such creatures, insofar as we experience ourselves as having the capacity to make voluntary decisions, we experience it as within our power to decide whether, and to what extent, we make nonhuman sentient creatures' interests our own.

1.4 Derivation of the Humanity and Sentience Formulation

We are now in a position to derive the Humanity and Sentience Formulation of the Categorical-Instrumental Imperative. We have just seen that it is possible – even if unlikely – for one's future selves to care about and identify their interests with the interests of any other human or nonhuman sentient being(s). Accordingly, since the Categorical-Instrumental Imperative requires us, in problem of possible future selves cases, to come to a universal agreement on shared interests with *all* of our possible future selves, we can simply restate the principle by explicitly stating that one's possible future selves *may* identify their interests with any or all such beings – as follows:

> **The Humanity and Sentience Formulation:** voluntarily aim for its own sake, in every relevant action, to best satisfy the motivational interests it is instrumentally rational for one's present and every possible future self to universally agree upon, given co-recognition that one's voluntary, involuntary, and semivoluntary interests could be identical to those of any possible human or sentient being(s), where relevant actions are determined recursively as actions it is instrumentally rational for one's present and possible future selves

to universally agree upon as such in cases where one's present self wants to know and advance their future interests – and then, when the future comes, voluntarily choose your having acted as such.

Notice that this does not say that all, or even most, of one's possible future selves identify their interests as such. It merely states that the universal agreement required by the Categorical-Instrumental Imperative must be based upon mutual recognition – between one's present and possible future selves – that their interests *may* be identical to those of any possible human or nonhuman sentient being.

Now, we still do not know exactly what this formulation – and by extension, the Categorical-Instrumental Imperative – requires: that is, what kind of agreement between our present and possible future selves might actually satisfy it. We will turn to this question in Chapters 5 and 6. The point for now is simply that the Humanity and Sentience Formulation is just another way of stating the categorical-instrumental imperative: a way of disambiguating its central notion of 'possible future selves.'

2 The Kingdom of Human and Sentient Ends Formulation

Once we have arrived at the Humanity and Sentience Formulation, we can directly derive a third formulation of the Categorical-Instrumental Imperative:

> **The Kingdom of Human and Sentient Ends Formulation:** voluntarily aim for its own sake, in every relevant action, to abstract away from the interests (or ends) of particular human or nonhuman sentient being(s), acting instead on interests (or ends) it is instrumentally rational for all human and nonhuman sentient beings to universally agree to share given their different voluntary, involuntary, and semivoluntary interests, where relevant actions are determined recursively as actions it is instrumentally rational for one's present and possible future selves to universally agree upon as such in cases where one's present self wants to know and advance their future interests – and then, when the future comes, voluntarily choose your having acted as such.

The principle follows straightforwardly from the first two formulas. Given that (A) the Categorical-Instrumental Imperative requires one to seek an instrumentally rational, universal agreement with all of one's possible future selves given mutual co-recognition of the problem of possible future selves (that is, the inability of one's present self to know which possible future self they will be), and (B) the Humanity and Sentience Formula identifies one's possible future selves in terms of their possible interests – interests which may be identical to those of any possible human or nonhuman sentient being(s), it follows that (C) an instrumentally rational agreement between one's present and every possible future self cannot be one that favors any particular beings' interests – say, your interests, or mine, or Fido's – but instead abstracts away from their particular interests, discovering instead *shared interests that are instrumentally rational for all to agree to together*, given whatever voluntary, involuntary, or semivoluntary interests they each might have. Accordingly, the Categorical-Instrumental Imperative, Humanity and Sentience Formulation, and Kingdom of Human and Sentient Ends Formulation are all identical: they are three different ways of stating the same solution to the problem of possible future selves.

At this point, we still do not know what kind of shared interests might satisfy the Categorical-Instrumental Imperative's formulas, if any exist at all. Chapters 5 and 6 will argue that there are in fact interests that it is instrumentally rational for all to share, despite the differences between their possible ends. Specifically, Chapter 5 argues that we can model the Kingdom of Human and Sentient Ends Formulation's (and so, the Categorical-Instrumental Imperative's) satisfaction conditions by way of a 'Moral Original Position'; and Chapter 6 then argues that we can derive Four Principles of Fairness from it. Before we turn to those tasks, however, I believe it is worthwhile to briefly compare the results we have arrived at so far to an influential moral framework to which it has some obvious affinities: Kantian ethics.

The Categorical-Instrumental Imperative's name – and the names of its two other formulations – bear clear similarities to Kant's famous moral principle, the categorical imperative, and the three formulations he gave of it: the universal law, humanity, and kingdom of ends formulas. These nominal similarities are by design, for there are obvious content similarities between the principles I have defended and Kant's formulations of his principle. First, whereas Kant's universal law formula states that we are always to act on maxims (or subjective principles of action) that we could will to be universal laws of nature[3], my Categorical-Instrumental Imperative states that we are to seek and uphold, in all of our 'relevant' actions, a universal agreement between our present and all possible future selves. Second, whereas Kant's humanity formula states that we are to always treat the 'humanity' in ourselves and others always as an 'end in itself' and never merely as a means[4], my Humanity and Sentience Formulation states that, in all of our 'relevant' actions, we are to act in ways that is instrumentally rational on the supposition that our interests might be identical to those of any possible human or sentient being (thus modeling a kind of 'respect' for them). Third, whereas Kant's kingdom of ends formula states that we are always to act 'as lawgiving in a kingdom of ends,'[5] where a kingdom of ends is 'a whole of all ends in systematic connection' arrived at 'if we abstract away from the personal differences of rational beings as well as from all the content of their private ends'[6], my Kingdom of Human and Sentient Ends Formulation says something similar: namely, that, in all of our 'relevant' actions, we are to act on shared interests that are instrumentally rational when abstracting away from different human and nonhuman beings' ends: interests that are instrumentally rational whatever one's ends could possibly be.

Because of these similarities, and the fact that Kantian ethics is widely recognized as a predominant moral framework in Western moral philosophy, I would like to pause to compare the three formulations of the Categorical-Instrumental Imperative, as I have so far defended them, to Kant's theory. I will do so using the seven principles of theory selection defended in Chapter 1.

3 Advantages over Kantian ethics

Kant's moral theory is arguably the most influential moral theory in the history of Western philosophy. It is widely recognized as such in introductory texts in ethics, and a wide variety of moral and political philosophers self-identify as Kantians. Moreover, Kant's theory has a number of deeply attractive elements, including perhaps most notably its unique (albeit opaque) account of 'human dignity': the notion that morality requires us to respect the human capacity for free, autonomous choice.[4]

Despite its attractions, however, Kant's theory is also recognized as facing a number of interpretive and philosophical challenges. First, it has never been clearly established that we ought to actually obey his supreme moral principle, the categorical imperative. Although Kant appears to have given several different arguments for obeying it[7–9] – arguments which many neo-Kantians have attempted to clarify, defend, and improve[10–14] – these arguments have never enjoyed widespread acceptance. As I will argue shortly, this is at least partly because Kant's and neo-Kantians' arguments for obeying his categorical imperative are based on controversial claims (about practical reason, humanity, and so on) that do not satisfy Firm Foundations, the principle of theory selection which Chapter 1 argued is the most critical requirement of sound theorizing. Second, there are a number of longstanding controversies over how to interpret (and apply) Kant's theory. For instance, Kant defends several different formulations of the categorical imperative, claiming they are all identical (the 'very same law'[15]), and uses its first two formulations (the universal law and humanity formulas) as moral tests of right and wrong.[16] There is great disagreement in the literature, however, over whether Kant's formulas are in fact identical (although the general consensus is that they are not[17], there are still those who argue that they are[18-19]). Furthermore, there is great disagreement on how to interpret Kant's formulas and use them as moral tests, and what their implications are.[18-34] For instance, while some (including, arguably, Kant himself) have interpreted his theory as entailing absolute prohibitions (specifically, that it is always wrong to lie)[35-37], many others interpret his theory the opposite way: as permitting context sensitive accounts of when specific behaviors (such as lying) are wrong.[38-41] Finally, while many 'neo-Kantians' have attempted to refine and revise Kant's theory in a variety of ways[42-44], these theories are alleged by their critics to run into similar problems of their own.[45-49]

In short, while Kantian ethics – both in its original form and its 'neo-Kantian' variants – has many attractions, it also encounters significant interpretive and philosophical challenges that, in the eyes of many, have never been adequately surmounted. I will now argue, in part because of those challenges, that the moral theory defended in this book thus far – the Categorical-Instrumental Imperative, in its three formulations – has advantages over Kant's theory on the seven principles of theory selection defended in Chapter 1.

3.1 Firmer foundations

Chapter 1 argued that we should prefer theories that are based on Firm Foundations – on premises that are generally recognized as being clearly true by human observers – over theories based on controversial premises.

Kant's theory and its neo-Kantian counterparts fare weakly on this principle. First, Kant bases his theory on controversial claims about the nature of practical reason, motivation, and deliberation that many critics have called into question.[50-55] The same is true of neo-Kantian theories. Consider, for instance, Christine Korsgaard's attempt to found morality on the notion that 'unified practical agency' is the constitutive

132 Rightness as Fairness

end of practical deliberation.[44] As intriguing as her account is, many critics question its basic presuppositions (why, they ask, must deliberation normatively commit one to having a 'unified practical identity'? Why couldn't a person – a practical agent – simply have a disconnected array of interests?).[45–46] Similarly, Barbara Herman has argued that we should obey Kant's categorical imperative because the constitutive aim of practical deliberation is to determine what is 'unconditionally good.'[42] Yet this claim is controversial as well.[48–49]

Indeed, we have seen in this book additional reasons to question such accounts. In Chapter 2, I argued that our first-personal experience of deliberation is ambiguous between two models: a Kantian Model in which we always base our intentional actions on 'categorical' judgments of what we ought to do, and a Hybrid Model where this is only the case some of the time – a model where, other times, we simply act on whatever 'disconnected' interests or drives we might have any particular time (such as when we simply walk to get a glass of water or beer 'without thinking'). Furthermore, we discussed how contemporary neuroscience appears to better support the Hybrid Model, as human action is known to be generated by two distinct brain circuits: a 'habit'-circuit in the limbic system that is more or less automatic, and a 'regulatory' system in the frontal cortex that, sometimes but not always, intervenes in a way that gives rise to 'deliberation.' In short, while Kant and neo-Kantians base normative arguments for obeying Kant's categorical imperative on claims about 'the constitutive features of action,' there are grounds for doubting those accounts – grounds for thinking that there is no one constitutive feature of action – because, or so it appears, human beings have two different systems that generate intentional action, one of which appears Humean (or 'automatic') and another that appears broadly Kantian. Importantly, my arguments for the Categorical-Instrumental Imperative considered these apparent differences in the nature of human action. Rather than assuming (as Kant and neo-Kantians do) that all of our actions stem from a single conception of practical deliberation, I argued that when we look at human interests – that is, at actual human motives – there appear to be two fundamentally different types of actions: those in which we simply act on our present motives, and those in which we want to know our future interests, regulating our present actions in light of concerns about what our future motivations might be.

I therefore submit that my theory has an advantage over Kantian ethics on the principle of Firm Foundations. Whereas Kantian ethics employs highly debated claims about the nature of practical reason, the value of humanity, and the like, the argument I have given for the

Categorical-Instrumental Imperative in its three formulations has been based on (A) an instrumental conception of normative rationality that (as we saw in Chapter 1) virtually all human observers accept, (B) observations about the kinds of things that human beings plainly do seem to care about, at least in some cases (observations which empirical neuro-behavioral research on mental time travel and future-directed behavioral regulation supports[56–59]), and finally (C) observations about the kinds of involuntary, voluntary, and semivoluntary interests we experience ourselves as having – observations which I submit respect Firm Foundations.

3.2 Greater internal coherence

My theory also fares better than Kantian ethics on the principle of Internal Coherence. First, there are questions about whether the transcendental philosophy that Kant bases his theory on – his conception of 'pure practical reason' and its relationship to the sensible world – is internally consistent (although it certainly may be consistent, many have worried that it is not).[60–61] Second, as we saw earlier, there are longstanding questions over whether Kant's different formulations of the categorical imperative are consistent, either in meaning or in application (in terms of their moral implications). For again, although Kant claims that the various formulations of his categorical imperative express the same law, the general consensus is that they are identical neither in meaning nor extension.[17] And if this general consensus is correct, then Kant's theory is in fact internally inconsistent, presenting several different principles as the 'fundamental principle of morality.'

In contrast, I believe that my arguments for the Categorical-Instrumental Imperative – and its three formulations – are internally consistent. I have argued that all three formulas are clearly identical to one another. Furthermore, in Chapter 5, I will show that the formulas entail a single, unified moral test of right and wrong.

3.3 Greater external coherence

My theory also has advantages on the principle of External Coherence. First, whereas Kantian ethics is based on a controversial conception of practical deliberation which arguably conflicts with empirical science[52] – or, in Kant's specific case, may be neither verifiable nor falsifiable in principle by empirical science, since his entire account of 'pure practical reason' holds that it is a nonempirical phenomenon not reducible to empirically observable human motivations[8–9] – my account coheres well with observed, known facts: facts attested to by common human observation and empirical science. On my account, the normative force of morality emerges from a specific sort of concern we have for our future: our wanting, at least in some cases, to avoid possible futures that we will regret. In addition to cohering with commonsense, we have already seen (in Chapter 3) that it also coheres very well with recent empirical results linking morality and prudence to concern for one's future,[56–59] as well as with observed facts regarding the relationship of moral responsibility to having capacities of 'mental time travel.' Thus, given that my theory bases morality's normative force on concern for the future and the ability to imagine one's possible future selves, my theory predicts what we do in fact empirically observe: namely, that the less a given being cares about the future or engages in mental time travel, the less they should experience morality as having normative force. Indeed, normal adults, who care about the future and possess mental time travel capacities, tend to feel morality's normative force strongly; teenagers, who have difficulty caring about their future and engaging in mental time travel, feel morality's normative force far less,[62–65] and beings who appear to lack any apparent mental time travel capacities (nonhuman animals and psychopaths) appear not to feel the normative force of morality at all.[66–71]

Conversely, Kant's moral theory and its neo-Kantian counterparts do not appear to cohere with these facts, with how we actually experience morality's force, or how we deliberate morally. According to Kantian moral theorists, when we deliberate morally we are to think about which sorts of principles we could 'universalize' or 'respect humanity.' However, as the above empirical research demonstrates – and everyday experience verifies – it is concern for our future, as opposed abstract rumination, which comprises moral deliberation. This is evident in recent empirical research as well as in simple examples. Consider first a simple example. Just the other day, I was about to pass by my spouse's computer, which I saw to be plugged into an electrical outlet during a lightning storm. I briefly thought about unplugging it to protect its contents from being destroyed in the event of a power-surge caused by a lightning strike – but then I immediately dismissed the concern and walked by. A moment later, however, it occurred to me that I could regret it in the future if I did not walk back and unplug it (and indeed, that it would be wrong not to, given how little effort it would take to do so). Why? Because I began to worry about what *might* happen: a lightning strike could cause a power-surge, erasing my spouse's hard earned work, leading to great possible regret on my part (as I imagined how bad I might feel for her if it happened). This is, I believe, a more natural way to construe moral deliberation – not in terms of abstract Kantian reasoning, but in terms of possible futures, and the ways in which our actions might affect us in the future. Finally, this is not only a clearly natural and intuitive way to construe moral reason: science has shown that failures to reason in this way appear to be among the strongest predictors of immoral behavior.[56, 71-74] Science shows, in other words, that to the extent that people tend to behave morally, they tend to deliberate in the kind of future-directed manner my theory predicts – and, to the extent that people fail to behave morally, they fail to do so (at least in part) because they fail to deliberate in the manner delineated by my theory.

Furthermore, as we saw in Chapter 2, my theory coheres with intuitive connections between morality's normative force and our ignorance of the future. Whereas Kant and neo-Kantians hold that morality applies to us categorically – completely irrespective of our motivations or ignorance – my theory predicts that beings who know their future interests with complete omniscience should experience morality as having no normative force. Yet, although we have never encountered such beings, science fiction cases reveal that the implications of such omniscience are powerful. As we saw concerning the *Star Trek* episode entitled, 'By Any Other Name,' when the human crewmembers of the Enterprise encounter the Kelvans – a race so powerful and self-controlled that they can seemingly know their interests in advance – they find that the Kelvans experience moral claims as having no normative force. Although this is merely a science fiction example, it is telling. It indicates, among other things, that the show's writers – ordinary people, nonphilosophers – see natural and important connections between our ignorance of the future and conformity with moral norms.

As we will see in more detail in future chapters (Chapters 6 and 7), my theory also coheres with and explains the attractiveness of several predominant moral frameworks (consequentialism, deontology, contractualism, and virtue ethics) and several predominant political philosophical frameworks (libertarianism, egalitarianism, and communitarianism). Finally, we will now see that it coheres with some other common moral beliefs and practices that have traditionally been thought to raise problems for rival theories.

First, many critics of Kantianism have complained that it 'over moralizes' human life. One common critique is that the theory requires 'one thought too many,' always requiring us to in some sense act on moral motives rather than motives we intuitively consider more appropriate, such as love.[75-77] Another trenchant critique by Susan Wolf is that Kantianism, like many other predominant moral theories, counterintuitively requires us to be 'moral saints,' turning all of our choices in moral ones, and requiring us to always 'do the right thing.'[78] Despite Kantians' repeated responses to these concerns,[42–43,79] these concerns have not gone away. Further, the idea that morality requires us to 'always do right' (in Kant's case, to always act on maxims one could will to be universal laws of nature) seems to fit poorly with our ordinary self-conception, which is that morality should only require a fair amount of effort from us – that is, 'B+' effort, rather than 'A+,' saintly effort (though 'moral saints' may well be people to admire).[80] Indeed, empirical research shows that people tend to index their beliefs and attitudes about norms, and their level of compliance to them, to the willingness of *others* around them to comply with the same norms.[81] Finally, as Dorsey argues, some of our actions (such as simply intentionally blinking one's eye) are arguably 'amoral,' having nothing to do with morality at all.[82] As we will see in Chapter 6, the Categorical-Instrumental Imperative coheres better with these facts, as it entails that morality itself is partly a matter of negotiating with others which of our actions it is fair to subject to moral evaluation.

Second, I hold that my arguments fare better than Kantian ethics regarding the moral status of nonhuman animals. Kant's theory, as he formulated it, ascribes no intrinsic moral status to animals: we are to treat animals well only as a means to treating other human beings properly.[83] And although some Kantians have attempted to account for the intrinsic moral value of animals, they tend to understand the moral value of nonhuman animals in abstract terms: that is, in terms of universalizable maxims or the 'unconditional value' of sentience.[84–85] However, our everyday experience of the moral status of nonhuman animals coheres better with my theory: namely, that it is often when we see animals suffer, such as when we watch slaughterhouse documentaries, that we begin to see their interests as *possible* interests of our own.

Finally, while Kantians may argue that by reducing morality to a kind of prudence, my theory fails to cohere with or explain morality's 'categorical,' absolutely binding nature, I have already argued (in Chapter 1) that moral philosophers are not epistemically entitled to hold this as a requirement a moral theory must satisfy. Moral theorists are no more epistemically entitled to maintain that morality 'has' to be categorical any more than physicists are epistemically entitled to maintain that space and time 'must' be absolute. Both claims may be nothing more than prejudices – and it is the job of a good theory to determine whether the prejudice is true. And, or so I will argue in Chapter 8, Rightness as Fairness – a theory that affords morality quasi-categorical status (applying close-to-categorically to all of us who have the capacities that give rise to the problem of possible future selves) – fares better on the seven principles of theory selection than rival theories. I thus submit that we should reject the notion that morality must be categorical.

3.4 Greater explanatory power, unity, and parsimony

I also believe that my theory fares better than traditional Kantian ethics with respect to the principles of Explanatory Power, Unity, and Parsimony.

First, whereas Kant's theory and its neo-Kantian counterparts bifurcate the normative domain world into two independent domains – the moral (categorical imperatives) and the prudential (hypothetical imperatives)[86] – my analysis provides a unified explanation of both, reducing morality to a kind of prudence (prudence in handling the problem of possible future selves). My theory is also simpler (that is, more parsimonious) than Kant's theory and its neo-Kantian counterparts. Whereas traditional Kantian ethics requires positing a number of controversial metaphysical entities and properties – such as 'pure practical reason,' 'transcendental freedom,' and an entire class of categorical imperatives which are held to be true but irreducible to imperatives of prudence – my theory accounts for morality in terms of commonly observable facts and properties: our interests in the present and future, our ignorance of the future, our concept of instrumental normative rationality, and our experience of ourselves as having voluntary, semivoluntary, and involuntary interests.

Second, rather than appealing to special metaphysical entities – such as pure practical reason that distinguishes us in kind from nonhuman animals – my theory (as we have already seen) provides a simpler, more unified account of the moral value of human and nonhuman sentient creatures, showing how they both emerge from the same problem: the problem of possible future selves.

Finally, as we will see in subsequent chapters, my theory reconciles unifies a variety of traditionally opposed moral insights (those of consequentialism, deontology, contractualism, and virtue ethics); provides a unified test of right and wrong (the Moral Original Position); and finally, unifies three traditionally opposed political frameworks: libertarianism, egalitarianism, and communitarianism.

3.5 Greater fruitfulness

Although we have yet to determine precisely what the Categorical-Instrumental Imperative requires, we can already begin to see that it has advantages on the Fruitfulness principle over traditional Kantian ethics.

As noted earlier, whereas Kant defended multiple formulations of his categorical imperative and tried to use them as moral tests of right and wrong, Kant scholars have been unable to come to a consensus on how to interpret his formulas, how his formulas relate to one another, and whether they can be used to provide compelling tests of right and wrong. For instance, Kant scholars have spent a great deal of time attempting to interpret Kant's universal law formulation[18-24] and apply it to issues ranging from abortion[87] to suicide.[88] Yet no clear consensus has been reached on any of these issues. Similarly, theorists continue to debate the interpretation and application of Kant's humanity[25-32] and kingdom of ends formulas,[19,33-34] without any clear consensus.

The Categorical-Instrumental Imperative promises greater fruitfulness in several ways. First, as we will see in Chapter 5, all of its formulations entail a single moral test: a Moral Original Position. Second, as we will see in Chapter 6, that moral test generates Four Principles of Fairness that unify deontological concerns with autonomy and consequentialist concerns with achieving good results, while providing a contractualist method for applying these principles through fair negotiation. Finally, my theory unifies three attractive but traditionally opposed orientations in political philosophy – libertarianism, egalitarianism, and communitarianism – providing a method for negotiating and reconciling conflicts between these theories.

Finally, as I have already suggested and will argue in more detail throughout the rest of this book, my theory provides a fruitful answer to the question that many philosophers and ordinary people have about morality: namely, why we should care about it. For whereas traditional Kantian ethics answers this question in abstract, rationalistic terms – either in terms of transcendental freedom,[8-9] unified practical agency,[44] unconditional goodness,[42] the unconditional value of humanity,[11-13] and so on – my theory explains why we should be moral in terms of our *interests*, specifically our interests concerning our future selves. And indeed, such concerns are something that emerging empirical results strongly suggest is tied to improving moral behavior.[56-59] Rightness as Fairness, via the Categorical-Instrumental Imperative, explains why focusing on our future selves appears to improve human moral behavior, and suggests fruitful ways for going about improving it.

4 Conclusion

This chapter showed how that the Categorical-Instrumental Imperative – a principle which requires us to seek and uphold a universal agreement with all of our possible future selves – is identical to two other formulations comparable to, but having advantages over, Immanuel Kant's various formulations of his categorical imperative. We will now see that the formulations of the Categorical-Instrumental Imperative have a variety of other advantageous implications: they entail a clear test of right and wrong (Chapter 5) and Four Principles of Fairness (Chapter 6) that reconcile traditionally opposed normative frameworks in political philosophy (Chapter 7), and satisfy Chapter 1's seven principles of theory selection better than alternative moral theories (Chapter 8).

5

The Moral Original Position

Chapter 4 showed that the Categorical-Instrumental Imperative – a principle that I have argued solves the problem of possible future selves – can be restated as follows:

The Kingdom of Human and Sentient Ends Formulation: voluntarily aim for its own sake, in every relevant action, to abstract away from the interests (or ends) of particular human or nonhuman sentient being(s), acting instead on interests (or ends) it is instrumentally rational for all human and nonhuman sentient beings to universally agree to share given their different voluntary, involuntary, and semivoluntary interests, where relevant actions are determined recursively as actions it is instrumentally rational for one's present and possible future selves to universally agree upon as such in cases where one's present self wants to know and advance their future interests – and then, when the future comes, voluntarily choose your having acted as such.

This chapter shows that we can model this principle's satisfaction conditions, determining what it requires of us, by way of a hypothetical thought experiment: a Moral Original Position similar to the 'original position' that John Rawls famously defended as a method for arriving at principles of justice.[1] Furthermore, we will see that the Moral Original Position addresses and resolves several concerns about Rawls' model.

Section 1 of this chapter briefly reviews Rawls' original position and several rationales he gave for deriving principles of justice from it. Section 2 then discusses several critiques of Rawls' original position.

The Moral Original Position 141

Section 3 argues that a revised version of Rawls' original position – a Moral Original Position dropping Rawls' focus on (A) human beings alone[2] and (B) the 'basic structure' of a domestic society,[3] assuming (C) closed borders,[4] (D) 'strict-compliance,'[5] and (E) differences between justice in domestic and international affairs[6–7] – successfully models the Categorical-Instrumental Imperative's satisfaction conditions, thus specifying what the Categorical-Instrumental Imperative requires of us. Finally, Section 4 uses the Moral Original Position to contend that many of Rawls' critics have been broadly correct, and argues that the Moral Original Position must be used to properly resolve those critiques.

1 Rawls' Original Position

In *A Theory of Justice*, arguably the most influential work of political philosophy in the twentieth century, John Rawls argues that 'justice is fairness.' First, Rawls argued that the primary subject of justice is the 'basic structure' of a domestic society: a society's 'political constitution,' or 'the way in which the major social institutions distribute fundamental rights and duties,' and its 'principal economic and social arrangements.'[3] Second, Rawls argued that we should understand the principles of justice that should govern this structure as the result of a fair agreement between all of society's citizens: an agreement from a hypothetical 'original position' of fairness.[7] Third, Rawls argued that this original position should be defined partly in virtue of a 'veil of ignorance,' a device that withholds from every citizen any and all information relating to their own identity – information regarding their race, gender, social class, talents, and so on – to ensure that no one can arbitrarily privilege themselves in the agreement.[8] Fourth, Rawls specifies that every citizen in the original position is to deliberate to principles of justice for a closed, well-ordered society without immigration or emigration,[4] whose citizens and institutions 'strictly comply' with whichever principles are selected.[5] As Rawls explained, the purpose of these seemingly strange idealizations is to derive an ideal theory of a fully just domestic society: that is, a theory of ideal domestic social and political fairness that sets aside complications such as immigration, emigration, international affairs, and failure to comply with its principles, leaving these matters for later theorizing.[5–6] On the basis of these assumptions, Rawls used the original position to argue for the following two 'liberal-egalitarian' principles of domestic justice (below, I list Rawls' final statement of these principles in *Justice as Fairness: A Restatement*[9] – for earlier formulations, see *A Theory of Justice*[11] and *Political Liberalism*[12]):

> (a) Each person has the same indefeasible claim to a fully adequate scheme of equal basic liberties, which scheme is compatible with the same scheme of liberties for all; and
>
> (b) Social and economic inequalities are to satisfy two conditions: first, they are to be attached to positions and offices open to all under conditions of fair equality of opportunity [Rawls' 'fair equality of opportunity principle']; and second, they are to be to the greatest benefit of the least advantaged members of society [Rawls' 'difference principle'].[9]

Finally, Rawls extended the original position to international law and practice, arguing that parties to an international original position would agree to several principles comprising a 'Law of Peoples.'[13]

Over the years, Rawls gave three broad justifications for his conception of justice as fairness and the original position: a Kantian justification, a 'reflective equilibrium justification,' and a public reason justification. Allow me to briefly explain each.

1.1 Rawls' Kantian rationale

Rawls makes it clear throughout *A Theory of Justice* that his conception of justice is intended to make sense of the moral 'inviolability' of each individual person.[13] Given that Kant's moral theory – the theory that says that our humanity has unconditional value[14] – is largely considered the most influential theory of such inviolability, it is unsurprising that Rawls invoked it. Specifically, Rawls held that his original position models Kant's notions of universal lawgiving, autonomy, and a kingdom of ends,[15] and that the original position's output principles of justice are 'analogous to categorical imperatives.'[16] We can see Rawls' rationale here by briefly summarizing the similarities between his and Kant's theories that Rawls draws attention to. First, insofar as the parties to Rawls' original position are seeking a universal agreement on principles to govern their society, their task – and output principles – seem broadly analogous to Kant's idea that morality is a matter of acting on universalizable maxims.[17] Second, insofar as the original position's veil of ignorance requires citizens to deliberate in a manner that abstracts away from their own contingent ends, the original position and its output principles seem broadly analogous to Kant's notion of a 'kingdom of ends,' which holds that we must always regard ourselves as legislators and subjects of 'a whole of all ends in systematic connection' arrived at 'if we abstract away from the personal differences of rational beings as well as from all the content of their private ends.'[18] Finally, since Kant argued that our 'humanity' consists of our capacity to set and pursue ends on principle[19] – in a manner that some Kant scholars (including myself) have argued is identical with the notion of a kingdom of ends[20–21] – the original position and its output principles seem broadly analogous to respecting each individual's humanity.

1.2 Rawls' reflective equilibrium rationale

In addition to arguing that the original position and its output principles have a Kantian interpretation, Rawls defended them using 'reflective equilibrium': a method of systematizing and revising our moral and political beliefs until we reach a stable theory that best satisfies our considered moral judgments.[22–23] Rawls' case for reflective equilibrium is relatively straightforward. He argues (as many other theorists have[24–26]) that we should judge moral and political theories not simply in terms of their moral foundations (as in the Kantian interpretation), but also in terms of how well they cohere with our moral beliefs or considered convictions, more generally. Although Rawls notes[27] that we should obviously not expect a good moral or political theory to cohere with all of our moral or political beliefs – as some of our beliefs might be mistaken – he holds that a good moral theory should aim to systematize our beliefs, draw tensions between different beliefs into the open, and perhaps lead us to revise our beliefs in order to bring them into a more stable equilibrium with each other.

Rawls then argued that the original position and its output principles fare well in reflective equilibrium. Specifically, he argued that the original position and its output principles (both domestically and internationally) cohere with a wide variety of beliefs that citizens of liberal-democratic regimes tend to share: domestically, with beliefs that justice is a matter of freedom and equality, that society is (or should be) a cooperative endeavor for mutual gain, and so on;[28] and internationally, that peace and toleration of moral and religious differences are valuable, provided they occur within a scheme that respects and protects a few very basic human rights.[29] Although, as we will see in Section 2, many of Rawls' critics have denied that his theories (particularly his international theory) fare well in reflective equilibrium, the point for now is simply that this is a second way in which he defended his theories.

1.3 Rawls' public reason rationale

Finally, Rawls argued that his domestic and international original positions coheres with a very specific and important idea that he thought citizens in modern liberal-democratic regimes generally share: a notion of public reason that requires political principles to be publicly justified to all those that fall under them on terms they can all accept, as a kind of 'overlapping consensus.'[30–31] Indeed, in his later work, Rawls repudiated his earlier attempt to base the original position on Kantian foundations, arguing that because citizens in liberal-democratic regimes do not share the same 'comprehensive moral doctrines' – some citizens may believe morality comes from God, others may believe morality is relative, and so on – a stable liberal political philosophy must be based on a shared public conception of what is reasonable, both domestically[30] and internationally.[31] Rawls then argued that the domestic original position and principles of domestic justice embody public reason domestically, and that his international original position and principle of a 'Law of Peoples' embody it internationally.

2 Some common critiques

As influential as Rawls' theories have been, they have long been the subject of critiques. Although we have neither the time nor need to summarize all such critiques here – nor, importantly, will I take any stance in this section on whether the critiques I discuss are correct (as this book is concerned with developing a systematic new critique) – it well be helpful for our present purposes to briefly summarize several of them. For as we will see in Section 3, the Categorical-Instrumental Imperative broadly corroborates these critiques, while at the same time providing a new method – the Moral Original Position – for resolving the concerns they raise.

2.1 Kantian critiques

One longstanding critique is that Rawls' 'Kantian interpretation' of the original position is mistaken – that is, that Rawls misinterprets Kant's moral theory. Broadly speaking, this complaint has come from two directions.

On the one hand, libertarian philosophers such as Robert Nozick have argued that Rawls' theory violates Kant's categorical imperative because it treats people as mere means, contrary to Kant's humanity formulation of the Categorical Imperative.[32] According to Nozick, Rawls' original position models a conception of justice that forces people to interact 'fairly.' Yet Nozick suggests that this is anathema to the spirit of Kant's notion of respect for humanity, which requires respecting people's autonomous choices. According to Nozick, in order to truly respect humanity in a Kantian sense – respecting, that is, each person's ability to set and pursue their own ends – we must understand each person as having absolute rights to life, liberty, and property that serve as side-constraints on the behavior of others. Therefore, on Nozick's account, individuals should be viewed as having rights *not* to enter into Rawls' original position or a society governed by its output principles.

On the other hand, so-called cosmopolitan critics of Rawls have alleged that the opposite is true: that both Rawls and Nozick misinterpret Kantian ethics, and that true respect for humanity – and a true Kantian 'kingdom of ends' – would involve a cosmopolitan original position in which all human beings deliberate behind a veil of ignorance to principles of global justice, not just human beings within a given domestic society.[33–35]

2.2 Reflective equilibrium critiques

Second, there have been many 'reflective equilibrium' critiques of Rawls' theory. Among other things, scholars have raised concerns that the theory provides inadequate analyses of what justice requires with respect to persons with disabilities,[36] gender and families,[37] animals,[36] the actions of individuals,[38] and so on. According to these philosophers, Rawls' original position arbitrarily restricts considerations of justice to healthy human beings who can accept and reciprocally uphold a social contract, wrongly ignoring animals and persons with severe disability. Similarly, they argue that the original position arbitrarily restricts justice to the basic structure of society, ignoring justice within families and the actions of individuals more generally outside of the basic structure.

Other theorists have challenged Rawls' strict-compliance assumption, arguing that it restricts his theory of justice to 'ideal theory' without any clear bridge-principles to determine what justice requires in a nonideal world,[39–40] others still have argued that his way of distinguishing domestic from international justice conflicts with our considered convictions regarding freedom and equality of human beings,[33–35] and so on.

2.3 Public reason critiques

Finally, there have been a number of critiques of Rawls' public reason-based defense of his theory. On the one hand, critics from two directions – libertarian and cosmopolitan critics – have objected to Rawls' attempt to base political philosophy on public reason, holding that instead political philosophy should be based on a comprehensive moral conception of the freedom and equality of persons (though, of course, libertarians and cosmopolitan-egalitarians have differing conceptions of what the right comprehensive moral theory is).[32–35] Conversely, there are those who argue that Rawls was right to try to base political philosophy in public reason, but that he defended an incorrect conception of it, and that insofar as his theory of justice is based on an incorrect conception, he derives incorrect principles of justice.[41–42]

3 The case for a Moral Original Position

I have deliberately avoided evaluating the above critiques. For although I believe some of the critiques are technically flawed, at least as traditionally formulated (I have argued that Rawls' theory can be extended to nonideal theory in ways that may deal more adequately with gender, families, and other forms of oppression, such as racial oppression[40]), we will now begin to see how many of the critiques are accurate in spirit. We can see this by explicating in more detail what the Categorical-Instrumental Imperative requires.

Let us reflect on the final formulation of the Categorical-Instrumental Imperative that we arrived at in Chapter 4:

> The Kingdom of Human and Sentient Ends Formulation: voluntarily aim for its own sake, in every relevant action, to abstract away from the interests (or ends) of particular human or nonhuman sentient being(s), acting instead on interests (or ends) it is instrumentally rational for all human and nonhuman sentient beings to universally agree to share given their different voluntary, involuntary, and semivoluntary interests, where relevant actions are determined recursively as actions it is instrumentally rational for one's present and possible future selves to universally agree upon as such in cases where one's present self wants to know and advance their future interests – and then, when the future comes, voluntarily choose your having acted as such.

If this principle is correct, instrumental rationality in problem of possible future selves cases requires us to (A) abstract away from the particular ends of human and nonhuman sentient beings, and (B) seek and uphold a universal agreement on interests to pursue for their own sake given

The Moral Original Position 147

the different voluntary, involuntary, and semivoluntary interests that different human and nonhuman sentient beings can have.

We can model these two notions – the notion of abstracting away from specific beings' ends and of seeking and upholding a truly universal agreement on interests to pursue for their own sake given the differences between different beings' possible voluntary, involuntary, and semivoluntary ends – by way of a *Moral Original Position*. The Moral Original Position is a hypothetical situation in which we (moral agents) deliberate behind (1) an *Absolute Veil of Ignorance*, requiring us to treat the ends of any and every possible human or nonhuman sentient being as though they could be our own, without (2) any of Rawls' idealizing assumptions, except for the requirement that we are to seek a set of interests that are instrumentally rational to pursue for their own sake given the Absolute Veil of Ignorance (as this situation models one deliberating as though *all* possible ends could turn out to be one's own). If there are any such interests – interests that are instrumentally rational to act on for their own sake from behind such a veil of ignorance – they will, by definition, satisfy the Categorical-Instrumental Imperative, as they will be interests that are instrumentally rational for one's present and all possible future selves to universally agree upon. Allow me to explain.

First, given the Categorical-Instrumental Imperative's various formulations – each of which has us aim to seek and uphold a universal agreement with all of our possible future selves – the Moral Original Position's Absolute Veil of Ignorance should be applied to us, moral agents, so that we must treat the interests of other human and nonhuman creatures as though they could be our own. As such, the Moral Original Position models a universal agreement on how 'moral agents' should treat human beings and other nonhuman sentient creatures as 'moral patients' (that is, as beings whose interests may be affected by our actions). Although the Moral Original Position only treats other human beings and nonhuman sentient creatures as 'moral patients' insofar as we can identify our interests with theirs – something that readers who want to defend the 'intrinsic moral value' of human beings or animals may find unattractive – the task of this book (as explained in Chapter 1) is not to defend preconceptions about morality, but rather show what conception of morality can be defended on Firm Foundations.

Second, in order for the Moral Original Position to embody the Categorical-Instrumental Imperative's satisfaction conditions – satisfaction conditions that require us to seek an instrumentally rational agreement on interests to pursue for their own sake given the assumption that our interests could be identical to those of any possible human or nonhuman sentient creature(s) – we must not impose any ends upon those in the Moral Original Position above and beyond the end of seeking a universal agreement on (1) whether they should seek a universal agreement on first-order interests, and if so, on (2) which first-order interests we should have. Allow me to explain both elements: that is, why the parties to the Moral Original Position should have a universal agreement as a shared end, but why no other ends should be assumed beyond this (particularly none of the ends embodied in Rawls' assumptions, such as a closed society, strict-compliance, and so on).

First, there is a simple explanation as to why every party to the Moral Original Position (one's present self and every possible future self) should share the end(s) of (1) seeking and upholding a recursive, higher-order agreement with all of one's possible future selves on whether one's present self should seek an analogous agreement on first-order interests, and if so, (2) seeking and upholding a first-order agreement with all of one's possible future selves on a set of shared interests to pursue for their own sake. The reason is that these are simply the ends explicitly required by the Categorical-Instrumental Imperative.

Second, because this is all the Categorical-Instrumental Imperative states – that we are to seek and uphold these agreements with all of our possible future selves – the Moral Original Position should not assume any further ends. Specifically, it should not assume ends such as (i) the Rawlsian end of reciprocal social cooperation (since not all of one's possible future selves may wish to engage in such social cooperation), (ii) Rawls' assumption of closed borders (since not all of one's possible future selves may wish to have closed borders), (iii) the assumption that only people (rather than animals) fall under the domain of justice (since some of one's possible future selves may have an interest in animals being treated as falling under the scope of justice), (iv) the assumption that we must justify political principles to others through public reason (since not all of our possible future selves may have that as an end), (v) the assumption that moral or political theories should be judged according to a process of reflective equilibrium (since not all of our possible future selves may have that as an end), (vi) the assumption that justice primarily concerns the 'basic structure' of society (since not all of one's possible future selves may have that as an end), and so on. In short, only a Moral Original Position similar to Rawls' original position, but one which (1) eliminates all of Rawls' specific assumptions about justice and (2) requires us to treat ourselves as though our interests could turn out to be identical to any human or nonhuman sentient creature, correctly models the Categorical-Instrumental Imperative's satisfaction conditions. Thus, we can derive another, fourth formulation of the Categorical-Instrumental Imperative:

> The Moral Original Position Formulation: voluntarily aim for its own sake, in every relevant action, to act on interests it is instrumentally rational to act upon from the standpoint of a 'Moral Original Position' in which you assume that your voluntary, involuntary, and semivoluntary interests could turn out to be identical to those of any human or nonhuman sentient being(s), where relevant actions are defined recursively as those it is instrumentally rational to treat as such from the standpoint of the Moral Original Position.

We will now see that this formulation broadly corroborates many of the aforementioned critiques of Rawls.

4 Corroborating the critiques

Let us recall the three types of critiques that have been leveled at Rawls' theory: that he incorrectly interprets Kant's moral theory, that his theory does not fare well in reflective equilibrium, and that his theory is based on an unjustified conception of public reason. We shall examine each of these critiques through the perspective of the Categorical-Instrumental Imperative.

4.1 Corroborating Kantian critiques

In one obvious sense, the present book does not 'verify' the aforementioned Kantian critiques of Rawls (critiques that Rawls mistakenly interprets Kant's theory). This book, after all, is arguing that Kantian ethics is incorrect. However, in a broader sense, the theory being developed verifies the spirit of those critiques. For let us recall the moral concerns Rawls' critics raise. Kantian ethics enjoins us to respect the 'humanity' of all human beings, where this involves respecting human autonomy, and (on Kant's kingdom of ends formula) acting on a union of human ends abstracting away from all particular ends. Yet, as we have seen, there has been continual disagreement on precisely what these things involve. Kantian libertarians such as Nozick argue that respecting humanity is a matter of respecting a small class of rights to freedom from interference, and that Rawls' theory evinces *disrespect for humanity* by assuming (in its strict-compliance assumption) that everyone must be

150 Rightness as Fairness

interested in cooperating with others on 'fair' grounds. Similarly, Rawls' cosmopolitan critics allege that Rawls wrongly (indeed, arbitrarily) takes domestic justice to be more basic than global justice, when (in their view) proper respect for the humanity of all requires justice to be fundamentally global (or 'cosmopolitan'). Although the moral theory this book has been defending is not Kantian, as we saw in Chapter 4, it bears many similarities to Kant's theory – and, as we have seen in this chapter, the Moral Original Position entails that many of Rawls' assumptions about the scope and nature of justice, the very assumptions that Rawls' critics object to, cannot properly be assumed, but rather must be settled, through the Moral Original Position. It must be settled through the Moral Original Position whether 'respect for humanity and sentience' (*qua* the Humanity and Sentience Formulation) involves fair social cooperation as Rawls understood it, or libertarian rights as Nozick claims, whether justice is fundamentally cosmopolitan, and so on. The Moral Original Position reveals, in other words, that the very points of (broadly Kantian) contention that have existed between Rawls and his critics cannot be assumed in one direction or the other (either in favor of Rawls or against). Rather, morality is a matter of determining, *through the Moral Original Position*, whether Rawls or his critics have a correct moral understanding of 'respect for persons' (and sentient beings more broadly).

4.2 Corroborating reflective equilibrium critiques

The Categorical-Instrumental Imperative also undermines Rawls' use of reflective equilibrium, as well as many of his specific claims about the extent to which his theories fare well in it.

First, the Categorical-Instrumental Imperative – insofar as its satisfaction conditions are given by the Moral Original Position – entails that whether a moral or political theory should be evaluated by a process of reflective equilibrium is itself a moral question that should be settled between our present and future possible selves. Since the Categorical-Instrumental Imperative satisfies Firm Foundations, it follows that whether reflective equilibrium should be used at all is a moral question to be settled *through* the Moral Original Position, not prior to it. In other words, it entails that Rawls' use of reflective equilibrium neglected a critical question: the moral question of whether reflective equilibrium itself is fair and right to use in moral or political theorizing. And indeed, notice how this implication converges with the spirit of libertarian critiques (by individuals such as Nozick) of Rawls' use of the method. Nozick, in particular, argues that political philosophy should not be based on 'our considered convictions' about social justice, but rather on (what he believes to be) firm foundations. Nozick's objection to Rawls, in other words, is roughly as follows: Rawls' appeal to reflective equilibrium begs important moral and methodological questions against his libertarian (and other) opponents. Our inquiry verifies this. It shows that theorists who appeal to reflective equilibrium have neglected an important moral issue: namely, whether basing moral or political philosophy on the method of reflective equilibrium is itself fair.

Second, setting aside the question of whether the use of reflective equilibrium is fair, the Categorical-Instrumental Imperative undermines many of Rawls' specific claims about how well his theories fare in reflective equilibrium. As previously discussed, Rawls argues that his theories of domestic and international justice fare well in this method, but many of his critics disagree, holding that Rawls wrongly ignores the disabled, gender and families, nonhuman animals, and so on, and that his account begs important questions about the role of toleration in international affairs. Our inquiry reinforces these critiques as well, since according to the Categorical-Instrumental Imperative, all of these issues are moral questions to be settled through the Moral Original Position, not prior to its use.

4.3 Corroborating public reason critiques

Finally, the Moral Original Position also corroborates critiques that Rawls' appeal to public reason and conception of it beg important moral questions. For, if my arguments so far are correct, whether moral or political philosophy should utilize public reason – and, if so, what conception of it they should use – is yet another moral question that must be settled through the Moral Original Position, not prior to it.

5 Conclusion

This chapter showed that the Categorical-Instrumental Imperative's satisfaction conditions – and thus, what morality allows, requires, or prohibits – can be modeled in the form of a Moral Original Position: a hypothetical thought experiment broadly similar to John Rawls' famous 'original position,' but without many of Rawls' assumptions regarding the scope and ends of justice (who justice applies to, as well as what justice consists of). This chapter then showed how the Moral Original Position corroborates the spirit of many traditional critiques of Rawls' theories. Although these critiques may or may not be correct on technical details (something I have not examined), the Moral Original Position reinforces what critics of Rawls' theories have long alleged: namely, that he begs many important moral and methodological questions against those who do not share his particular conceptions of Kantian ethics, reflective equilibrium, and public reason.

6
Rightness as Fairness

We are now in a position to derive moral principles from the Categorical-Instrumental Imperative. Chapter 5 showed that the Categorical-Instrumental Imperative entails the following method for determining which actions satisfy it:

The Moral Original Position Formulation: voluntarily aim for its own sake, in every relevant action, to act on interests it is instrumentally rational to act upon from the standpoint of a 'Moral Original Position' in which you assume that your voluntary, involuntary, and semivoluntary interests could turn out to be identical to those of any human or nonhuman sentient being(s), where relevant actions are defined recursively as those it is instrumentally rational to treat as such from the standpoint of the Moral Original Position.

Section 1 of this chapter shows that we can derive the following Four Principles of Fairness from the Moral Original Position:

Four Principles of Fairness

The Principle of Negative Fairness: all of our morally relevant actions should have as a guiding ideal, setting all costs aside, avoiding and minimizing coercion in all its forms (coercion resulting from intentional acts, natural forces, false beliefs, and so on), for all human and nonhuman sentient beings, for its own sake.

The Principle of Positive Fairness: all of our morally relevant actions should have as a guiding ideal, setting all costs aside, assisting all human and non-sentient beings in achieving interests they cannot best achieve on their own and want assistance in achieving, for its own sake.

The Principle of Fair Negotiation: whether an action is morally relevant, and how the Principles of Negative and Positive Fairness and Virtues of Fairness (see below) should be applied factoring in costs, should be settled through an actual process of fair negotiation guided by the Principles of Negative Fairness, Positive Fairness, and Virtues of Fairness, where all human and nonhuman sentient beings affected by the action are afforded equal bargaining power to the extent that such a process can be approximated, and to the extent that cannot be, through a hypothetical process approximating the same, for its own sake.

The Principle of Virtues of Fairness: all of our morally relevant actions should aim to develop and express stable character traits to act in accordance with the first three principles of fairness, for its own sake.

Section 2 then combines these four principles into the following analysis of moral rightness:

Rightness as Fairness: an action is morally right if and only if it satisfies the Four Principles of Fairness, that is, if and only if it is (A) is morally relevant, (B) has coercion-avoidance and minimization, assisting human and nonhuman sentient beings to achieve interests they cannot best achieve on their own and want assistance in achieving, and the development and expression of settled dispositions to have these ends, as at least tacit ideals, and (C) is in conformity with the outcome of an actual process of fair negotiation approximating all human and sentient beings affected by the action being motivated by the above ideals and having equal bargaining power over how those ideals should be applied factoring in costs, or, if such a process is impossible, the outcome of a hypothetical process approximating the same, where moral relevance is determined recursively, by applying (B) and (C) to the question of whether the action is morally relevant.

Next, Section 2 argues that Rightness as Fairness reconciles several traditionally opposed conceptions of morality: deontology, consequentialism, virtue ethics, and contractualism. Additionally, Section 2 contends that Rightness as Fairness requires abandoning a common but problematic conception of moral problem-solving – a conception according to which we can arrive at sound answers to moral problems through principled thought or debate alone – in favor of an alternative method of 'principled fair negotiation' that requires merging principled thought and debate with actual, real-world negotiation.

Finally, Section 3 applies Rightness as Fairness to a small but representative variety of applied moral issues: (Section 3.1) Kant's famous four cases from *The Groundwork of the Metaphysics of Morals* (making a false promise, suicide, helping those in need, and developing one's natural talents), (Section 3.2) the question of whether, and if so when, morality permits or requires sacrificing the few for the many, (Section 3.3) world poverty, (Section 3.4) the distribution of scarce medical resources (e.g., transplantable organs), and (Section 3.5) the ethical treatment of nonhuman animals.

1 Derivation of Four Principles of Fairness

Our first task is to determine which interests it is instrumentally rational to act on from the standpoint of the Moral Original Position: a standpoint behind an Absolute Veil of Ignorance where one assumes one's interests could turn out to be identical to those of *any* possible human being or nonhuman sentient being(s). Any action that is instrumentally rational from this standpoint is one that is instrumentally rational for one's present and all possible selves to universally agree to act on for their own sake, thus satisfying the Categorical-Instrumental Imperative. We will now see that the Moral Original Position generates Four Principles of Fairness.

1.1 The Principle of Negative Fairness

In order to determine which interests it is instrumentally rational to act upon from the standpoint of the Moral Original Position, we must reflect carefully upon one's deliberative situation within it.

First, one knows one is a *moral agent*: someone who experiences themselves first-personally as having capacity to voluntarily motivate themselves to act on principles of one's own choice (qua the Kantian and Hybrid models of first-personal deliberation examined in Chapter 2).

Second, one is behind an *Absolute Veil of Ignorance*: one is to assume that one's interests could turn out to be identical with the interests of any possible human or nonhuman sentient being(s) – one's mother's interests, a stranger's interests, some animal's interests, the interests of many different people or animals, and so on.

Third, for reasons defended in Chapter 3, one ought not to deliberate on the basis of probabilities. For although it may be more likely that you will have some interests as opposed to others – say, your interests in your own well-being over the well-being of others – the Categorical-Instrumental Imperative requires one not to bet on 'likely future selves,' but instead forge and uphold a universal agreement with all of one's possible future selves: an agreement that satisfies the interests of every possible future person you could turn out to be, no matter how unlikely. Since you are to deliberate behind the veil as though you could have any possible set of interests – including different interests in risk-taking – you cannot deliberate on the basis of expectations about which risks are rational.

Fourth, because the Categorical-Instrumental Imperative requires one to seek and uphold such a universal agreement, one should assume that every possible future self one could turn out to be is voluntarily committed to acting on whatever interests turn out to be rational from one's standpoint behind the veil. This point is critical, because although one is to assume behind the Absolute Veil of Ignorance that one could turn out to have any possible set of interests – including the interests of people who violate moral norms, such as criminals, liars, and cheats – the Categorical-Instrumental Imperative requires one not to 'bet' on having those interests, but rather to forge and uphold an instrumentally rational agreement with all of one's possible selves. For, following Chapters 2 and 3, we are approaching these issues in problem of possible future selves cases: cases that we all experience at least sometimes in our lives, and in which we do not want to 'bet' on likely outcomes.

It is also critical to clarify that the above assumption – that one will voluntarily act on or 'uphold' whatever interests are instrumentally rational from the standpoint of the Moral Original Position, no matter which 'self' you turn out to be – is not an assumption that other people will also act on those same interests (namely, the Four Principles of Fairness that emerge from the Moral Original Position). The assumption here is not a Rawlsian assumption of 'strict compliance,' one which assumes that everyone else will comply with whichever principles one selects.[1] Instead, it merely assumes that *you* will be voluntarily committed to acting on those interests, no matter which possible future 'self' you turn out to be. It is an assumption that oneself is committed to doing what is rational in problem-cases (vis-à-vis one's possible future selves), whatever other people might do. And this, I believe is exactly what we intuitively want a moral theory to do: we want it to tell us what we should do, regardless of what others do.

Fifth, although some of the beings one could turn out to identify one's interests with – nonhuman animals in particular – may not have capacities to voluntarily tailor their own interests to the outcome of one's deliberations (the Four Principles of Fairness), one should understand one's deliberations as including their interests by proxy. In other words, one should voluntarily uphold the Four Principles of Fairness on nonhuman animals' behalf because their interests are possibly yours. The Moral Original Position thus models two notions regarding nonhuman animals: first, how we should treat them (treating their interests as possibly our own), and second, how they should hypothetically treat each other if (contrary to actual fact) they were capable of behaving morally.

Finally, one should know in the Moral Original Position that the different human and nonhuman sentient beings one could turn out to identify one's interests with can have several different types of interests: voluntary, involuntary, and semivoluntary interests. This is critical for the following reason. We saw in Chapter 2 that Michael Smith responds to something like the problem of possible future selves by affirming a rational requirement to render one's motivations consistent across time. This is not unlike Kant's notion of a 'kingdom of ends': a systematic union of the ends of all rational agents, without any conflicts between them. However, I argued in Chapter 2 that seeking such consistency is not straightforwardly rational because it fails to account for the fact that we have involuntary interests which we cannot avoid or change (for instance, we may find ourselves angry at someone whether we like it or not), as well as semivoluntary interests that we can voluntarily alter, but only within certain bounds and at some cost to oneself (as there are many possible costs to treating others fairly).

The six assumptions just discussed enable us to fully specify one's deliberative situation in the Moral Original Position. One knows, behind its Absolute Veil of Ignorance, that (i) one might turn out to have any possible set of interests, but (ii) one does not know which, and one cannot 'bet' probabilistically on any set of them over any others. For all one knows, once the Absolute Veil of Ignorance is 'raised,' one may simply be self-interested, caring about no one's interests but one's own. At the same time, however, for all one knows the opposite will be true once the veil is 'raised': one may end up caring about the interests of some, or all, other human and nonhuman sentient beings. Consequently, there is only one instrumentally rational way to proceed. Instrumental rationality requires one to adopt the best means (or instrument) for satisfying one's interests. As we have just seen, however, one cannot rationally 'bet' on any particular set of interests in the Moral Original Position (since one is 'in' the Moral Original Position precisely as a consequence of encountering the problem of possible future selves, an instance where one does not want to bet on likelihoods). What one does know is this: no matter which interests one turns out to have, one wants to advance those interests (since they are, from your perspective, possible interests of your own). Consequently, given one's ignorance from the standpoint of the Moral Original Position, one has a higher-order interest: an interest in advancing the interests of *all* the possible 'selves' one could turn out to be, without betting on any particular selves' interests (including a mere majority of selves one could be). If there are any principles of action (or interests one can voluntarily choose) that would be optimal means for advancing this higher-order interest – optimal means, that is, for enabling every possible self you could turn out to be to advance their ends from the standpoint of the Moral Original Position – then those are the principles that instrumental rationality requires from this standpoint, given the problem of possible future selves. Those are the principles that satisfy the Categorical-Instrumental Imperative.

The question then is whether there are any such principles. I submit there are. To see how, let us focus again on the three types of interests one can have: voluntary, involuntary, and semivoluntary. Insofar as we experience our voluntary interests as under our control (as interests we can choose), and our semivoluntary interests as partly under our control, one should not assume (behind the absolute veil of ignorance) that these interests are 'fixed.' One should assume instead that one can choose which voluntary interests one's possible selves (on the other side of the veil) will have, and, within certain bounds, which semivoluntary interests they will have (though, again, altering one's semivoluntary interests can be a costly affair). Consequently, we can determine that one particular strategy for advancing our higher-order interest is instrumentally rational from the Moral Original Position: namely, that all things being equal, and setting all costs and conflicts between one's possible involuntary and semivoluntary interests aside, it is rational to bring all of one's possible voluntary and semivoluntary interests into the greatest coherence possible (we will turn to costs later). For, setting costs aside, greater coherence among one's possible interests improves the capacity of every possible self to satisfy their interests. Allow me to explain.

Consider two worlds: one in which two persons (*A* and *B*) voluntarily choose interests that are incompatible with each other's, and another in which they voluntarily render their interests consistent with each other. Let us say that in the first world, *A* and *B* voluntarily choose to make it their interest in owning a particular home, but only one of them can own it; and that in the second world, *A* voluntarily chooses to let

B have the home and seek a different home for herself. All things being equal, the first world is suboptimal from the standpoint of the Moral Original Position: since *A* and *B* voluntarily set their interests against each other's, someone's voluntary interests will necessarily be thwarted (only one of them can satisfy their interest). From the standpoint of the Moral Original Position, costs aside, one should prefer the second world instead. For although *A* might have to settle for her second or third-choice home (or, worse yet, there may not be another home for *A* to own, all costs we will take into account later), *A* and *B* have nevertheless removed an obstacle to them both satisfying their interests: namely, the obstacle of their interests directly contradicting each other's.

Thus, setting aside all costs and conflicts between different possible selves' involuntary and semivoluntary interests, one should aim in the Moral Original Position to bring one's possible voluntary interests into unity, or the greatest coherence possible. Doing so minimizes the number of possible future selves whose interests one's present actions might contradict, thus maximizing the probability that every possible future self will be able to successfully satisfy their interests. Notice that this is consistent with the argument in Chapter 3 explaining why moral behavior pursued for its own sake, in problem cases, has infinite expected value, whereas immoral behavior pursued for its own sake does not. We can now begin to see why this is. All things being equal, motivational consistency across all of one's possible future selves permits all of one's possible selves – who are, in principle, infinite in number – to satisfy their interests. In contrast, motivational inconsistency entails that only some of one's possible future selves can satisfy their interests. There are *infinitely* more possible future selves who can successfully satisfy their interests in the former case than the latter. However, as we will see shortly, because there are potential costs associated with motivational consistency, this cannot be the end of the story.

For now, let us return to the question of what motivational consistency across one's possible future selves – which we have just seen is rational to want in the Moral Original Position, all things being equal – involves. If we focus on what it is to have a motivational interest, we can see that any interest possessed by a human or nonhuman sentient being entails (setting all costs aside) a higher-order rational interest in not being coercively prevented from obtaining the interest's object. Indeed, it is clearly true that if one wants *X*, then – to be instrumentally rational vis-à-vis obtaining that end – one must also want not to be coercively prevented from obtaining *X* (again, setting all costs aside). Given that one cannot possibly achieve *X* if one is coercively prevented from achieving it, if one wants *X*, instrumental rationality – in requiring one to adopt the best means for achieving *X* – requires one to want to not be coercively prevented from achieving *X*.

We can see this clearly though an example. Suppose I have eating a scoop of ice cream as my dominant, voluntary interest: I want a scoop of ice cream more than anything else. What is it for me to have this as an end? The following is obviously true: if I want a scoop of ice cream more than anything I else, I instrumentally ought to want no person or thing to coercively prevent me from getting one. If you coerce me out of getting a scoop – either by stealing my ice cream or by telling me the lie that there is no ice cream in the fridge when there actually is – then you have directly contravened my end, coercively preventing me from obtaining the object of my end. Further, coercion by other agents – force, theft, deception, etc. – is not the only way one can be 'coerced,' at least, as we will now see, relative to how it is instrumentally rational to understand coercion in the Moral Original Position. Indeed, from one's standpoint behind the Absolute Veil of Ignorance, any 'preventer' of one's satisfying one's interests – not just other human beings, but also forces of nature – is equally problematic. For instance, if I have eating a scoop of ice cream as an end but I am paralyzed – if, that is, impersonal forces of nature prevent me from obtaining it – then that too (i.e. the coercive force of nature) contravenes my end. To have something, *X*, as an end, then, is to also have not being coercively prevented – either by other agents, or by forces of nature – from achieving *X*.

There are several critical points here to clarify. First, coercion in the relevant sense (being prevented from obtaining your goals) need not merely be 'active' coercion by other intentional agents (other human or nonhuman beings). To the extent that one has an interest in something, *X*, one has an interest in avoiding both 'natural' and *self*-coercion just as much as coercion by other human beings. Allow me to explain each. Forces of nature can clearly be coercive in a sense relevant to the argument above. Suppose I want a scoop of ice cream, but the hot sun melts it before I can eat it. This contravenes my interest no less than a person stealing my ice cream. Similarly, suppose I want to live but am swept into the ocean by a rip-current and am in danger of drowning. Here, too, a force of nature contravenes my interest, forcibly preventing me from obtaining what I want. Further, a person can – through irrational impulse or mistakes of reasoning – contravene their own ends. If one has an interest in living but (falsely) believes that jumping off a cliff without a parachute will enable one to survive, and one jumps off a cliff on that basis (falling to one's death), one's own mistake leads to the forcible contravention of one's ends (the hard concrete ending one's life). Similarly, if one has an interest in living but finds oneself impelled by addiction to take an overdose of heroin, one's irrational impulse may contravene one's own end. In such cases, a person can have an interest in *being* coerced, but only to avoid greater coercion.

Consider the case where I am about to cross a bridge that, unbeknownst to me, is broken and will collapse if I try to cross it, hurtling me towards a gruesome death on the rocks below. If you coercively prevent me from crossing – by, say, physically tackling me – this would be a case of coercion. I might cry out and protest, 'What are you doing?' Still, despite the fact that you are coercing me, if I wish to live more than I want to cross the bridge, and your coercing me is the only way to stop me from trying to cross the bridge, then your coercing me does not contravene my dominant end (of staying alive): it is instrumentally *rational* for me to want to be coercively prevented from achieving my one end (attempting to cross the bridge) because I have an even stronger motivational interest in another end (staying alive). Similarly, if the dog wishes to eat poisonous meat, but I know that the dog has its continued living as a stronger interest – the dog, presumably, wishes to live more than it wishes to eat poisonous meat – then it is rational for the dog to be coercively prevented from eating the meat. Of course, the dog might not be capable of recognizing the rationality of this – but the important thing is that *we* can recognize the dog's interest in avoiding poisoning, and see its interest as possibly our own. As such, the Moral Original Position equally requires us to care about possible ways in which animals can be coerced – which is highly intuitive, as most of us think morality requires taking steps to protect our pets against things they have interests in avoiding (we will return to the topic of the ethical treatment of animals in general in Section 3.5).

Accordingly, whenever any human or nonhuman sentient being has an interest in something, *X*, they thereby have an instrumentally rational interest in avoiding all types of coercion preventing them from achieving *X*: coercion resulting from the intentional actions of other human or nonhuman beings, natural coercion (resulting from nonintentional forces of nature) and self-coercion (through mistakes of reasoning, irresistible impulses, and so on). However, because human and nonhuman sentient beings can have stronger and weaker interests, a stronger motivational interest in one thing (e.g. one's interest in staying alive) can outweigh one's interest in being free from coercion with respect to another, weaker interest (one's desire to cross a bridge one does not know will collapse). In short, humans and nonhuman beings *can* have instrumentally rational grounds to desire being coerced, but only to prevent themselves from suffering greater coercion.

Obviously, I have been using 'coercion' as a term of art here. But what exactly is coercion? Here I must simply defer to coercion theorists – philosophers who theorize about the nature of coercion.[2] Although the precise nature of coercion is an unsettled issue, we need not investigate it here for two reasons. First, we still have a relatively good working conception of coercion, including knowledge of paradigm cases (lying and fraud are coercive, murder is coercive, and so on). Second, this book's arguments enable us to demarcate a certain sense of 'coercion' as morally relevant: namely, unwanted direct contravention of one's interests (other agents, forces of nature, and one's own mistakes can all directly contradict one's ends, making those things *obstacles* to overcome in pursuit of one's ends), as this is what one has a higher-order interest in avoiding from the Moral Original Position.

Now, it might be suggested that there are clear counterexamples to the argument given above: the argument that whenever one has an end, one thereby has instrumentally rational grounds to want not to be coercively prevented from realizing that end. For instance, suppose I want a cigarette. Does it follow that it is instrumentally rational for me not to want anyone to coercively prevent me from smoking? One might think not: that however much one might want a cigarette, cigarettes are harmful; thus, perhaps one ought to want to be prevented from smoking. This, however, is not a genuine counterexample. For notice: when we say that one ought to want to be prevented from smoking, we are assuming that they have a stronger interest in avoiding the negative health effects of smoking. This brings us back to the issue of costs. Clearly, setting aside all costs (to their health), a person who wants to smoke clearly does have an instrumentally rational interest in no one coercively preventing them from smoking. It is only once costs are factored into the equation – and we consider other interests the person might have that might make smoking costly for them – that it may be instrumentally rational to desire coercion against one's ends (for the sake of, say, higher ends in longevity, health, and freedom from lung cancer).

Here, then, is what every moral agent in the Moral Original Position knows: (A) they have an interest in rendering their possible voluntary and semivoluntary interests into greater coherence, all things being equal, all costs aside, and (B) no matter which such interests they have, they necessarily have a higher-order interest in being as free from coercion as possible in pursuing their ends, setting all costs aside. These two interests entail that it is instrumentally rational in the Moral Original

Position to voluntarily choose a principle of coercion-avoidance and minimization, namely:

> **The Principle of Negative Fairness:** all of our morally relevant actions should have as a guiding ideal, setting all costs aside, avoiding and minimizing coercion in the world in all its forms (coercion resulting from natural forces, intentional acts, and false beliefs), for all human and nonhuman sentient beings, for its own sake.

Allow me to explain why.

Consider a situation in which the interests of two human beings conflict. I am drowning in a shallow pond, and you do not wish to help me. Coercing you to help me – for instance, by imprisoning you for not helping – would hamper your ability to achieve your interests (strolling by on your merry way). But not coercing you would leave me prey to coercion by natural forces (I am drowning, after all). Although one might suggest that it is rational to favor the worst off person in this position, including from the standpoint of the Moral Original Position (as drowning is surely worse than being forced to help someone), this is still suboptimal: it coerces one person for the sake of the other. If there is no better option – and there might be no better option, if the person observing refuses to help (as the person drowning may not be capable of voluntarily 'choosing to want to drown') – then, indeed, siding with the person in the worse off position is rational. For of the two worlds available, one in which one person drowns and another in which one person is forced to help the other, the latter world is less coercive. However, this is not necessarily the only option. A better option still – one we tend to favor in the real-world, on grounds of moral reciprocity – is one in which both parties negotiate with one another to render their interests consistent, so that no one has to be coerced at all. For instance, if the person walking by voluntarily chooses to save the drowning person, and then is rewarded either by the person saved or in some other way (for example, by social recognition as a 'hero') in a manner that satisfies other, stronger interests of the rescuer's, then both parties can achieve things they want – continued living (for the drowning individual) and personal satisfaction (for the person who was initially inclined to simply walk by without helping).

Indeed, there is an interesting feature of negotiating during interactions that social scientists have found in recent years: namely, that intentional agents (i.e. you, me, or even a nonhuman animal) may not even have a stable set of interests prior to acting (that they want to be free from coercion to pursue), but rather construct their interests in arriving at a decision. In traditional decision theory, an agent's preferences or ends are understood in terms of the person's revealed behavior.[3] For instance, if I choose to eat a piece of pizza over ice cream, decision-theorists have traditionally taken this to indicate that I preferred to eat the pizza over the ice cream. This is known as 'revealed preference theory.' According to revealed preference theory, intentional agents (1) have pre-existing preferences, and (2) those preferences are displayed by the agent's intentional behavior. In recent years, however, social scientists have argued that there is evidence that agents instead construct their preferences in the very process of arriving at decisions.[4–5] Call this 'constructed preference theory.' According to constructed preference theory, an agent may have no stable preference function – or ends – prior to deciding how to act. Rather, the very act of choice is a matter of arriving at a set of preferences or ends. If this is true, then although every sentient being has their own freedom from coercion as a higher-order end, some of the possible human and nonhuman beings whose interests one might identify as one's own may have negotiating their preferences – and, by extension negotiating what comprises coercing them (since what coercion involves depends on one's preferences) – as their ends, as well.

Indeed, negotiating our interests in order to accommodate the interests of others pervades human life, and for obvious reasons: one may not be able to obtain the things one desires (or not be able to obtain them very effectively) without negotiating. For instance, in the workplace, one's supervisor may have a certain amount of power of you. In order to get things you want – say, a day off work to care for your sick child – you may have to negotiate to do things you previously did not want to do (for instance, work an extra day on the weekend). Similar forms of interest negotiation are ubiquitous in human interaction: in marriages, friendships, politics, and so on. In a marriage or friendship, one often recognizes that in order for the relationship to be happy or productive – for the relationship to be satisfying for oneself – one has to negotiate one's interests with the other partner so that both parties can also obtain things they want out of the relationship. If, for instance, one does not want to invest all their discretionary income for retirement, but one's spouse feels very strongly that one should, 'sticking to one's guns' rather than negotiating a mutually acceptable set of interests (say, investing some money, but leaving enough aside for enjoyment today) can result in conflict: an unhappy situation which advances neither person's interests in the relationship. Generally speaking, in human relationships, unless one is willing to negotiate one's interests with others – unless one is willing to engage in 'give and take,' seeking mutually acceptable interests – the other party is unlikely to continue the relationship, at least not in the friendly, constructive manner one may wish. As such, we often (if not always) have interests in negotiating our interests with others, and by extension, interests in what coercing us involves (I may not initially want to do the dishes, but if my spouse convinces me it is fair for me to do so, I do not regard myself as coerced but rather as persuaded to change my interests).

A further important point here is that we cannot simply assume that a person has a pre-existing 'optimal negotiation point' prior to negotiating – one that we could simply settle through reflection or debate. For indeed, the point to which we are willing to negotiate can depend on contextual details, including the particular situation in which we find ourselves, the particular individuals we are negotiating with, and so on. To see how, consider a simple case in which one is negotiating with another person on how many cookies to share from a box of cookies. I may initially have eating all ten cookies as my interest (suppose I am very hungry). However, if we bought the cookies together, I may be willing to negotiate to an even distribution, giving you half and taking the other half for me. At the same time, if you do not feel very strongly about it, you may be willing to allow me to have more than that, saying to me, 'I know we bought the cookies together, but you are hungry: go ahead and have more.' And things could become even more complicated than this. For instance, if you were to add, 'But I want more next time,' I may or may not decide to take a larger share, no matter how much I want more. Similarly, things might be very different with other individuals. If instead the situation involves my child and I, I might be willing to give the child many cookies simply out of love for them (even though, all things being equal, I would like to eat them all myself). Alternatively, if I think it is bad for my child to eat too many sweets, I may choose to provide them with just a couple and eat just a couple myself in order to 'be a good role-model.' As all of these complexities illustrate, we cannot typically settle, ex ante – before an organic process of 'negotiation' occurs – where any given party to a negotiation may be willing to negotiate to, in terms of altering their interests. The negotiation itself creates its 'negotiation-end-point' in an organic fashion.

Finally, although children, the mentally disabled, and nonhuman animals may not possess the same robust negotiation capacities, they often do have them in some lesser degree. Our pets, for instance, often appear to learn our preferences, adapting their behavior to ours. My dog Tex, for instance, only tends to bring me toys to play with in the evening, as he appears to recognize that this is a particular time of the day I am happy to play with him. Although he only accomplished this by initially 'bugging me' to play in the evenings – he initially brought me toys when I did not want to play – the simple fact is that he ultimately got me to go along with it, and we now have a kind of implicit 'arrangement' to play in the evenings when he brings a toy. Indeed, perhaps more interesting still, he even seems to tailor his interests in how long we play to my decisions, as he does not continue to bring me toys after I have played with him for a bit and I choose to put his toy away in an open box. Similarly, our children often 'test' us, seeing which kinds of behaviors they can 'get away with without upsetting mom or dad.' Although these are admittedly crude and highly implicit forms of 'interest negotiation,' they still seem to be just that. The dog is looking to determine when it is in their interest to bring a toy to their owner to play with, by (if only tacitly) reading when their owner is interested in playing. Similarly, the child is looking to discover which of their interests they can advance without upsetting their parents too much (and, of course, when they do so poorly, or attempt to pursue interests regardless of what mom or dad think – engaging in actions their parents take to be misbehaving – they often face consequences, such as a 'time out' in the corner, thereby incentivizing them to 'better negotiate' with mom and dad in the future).

Here is why this is important. Consider again what the parties to the Moral Original Position know. First, they know that every sentient being has their own freedom from coercion as a higher-order end (an end applying to all of their first-order ends). Second, they know that they have an all-things-equal higher-order interest in rendering their ends more consistent with those of others, to the extent that doing so is in their voluntary control – avoiding coercion. Third, they know in some cases, coercion is unavoidable (if, for instance, a murderer wants to take my life, I cannot simply 'voluntarily' decide I want to die: I will find myself impelled to want to live). These three claims directly entail that, from the standpoint of the Moral Original Position, all costs aside, one should voluntarily choose the Principle of Negative Fairness: one should have the avoidance and minimization of coercion, in all of its forms, as an ideal.

1.2 The Principle of Positive Fairness

Now let us consider the flip side of coercion: assistance in pursuing one's ends. I just argued that whenever a being has an interest in something,

X, they thereby have an instrumentally rational interest in not being coercively prevented from achieving its object. Does the flip side follow: namely, that anytime someone has an interest in something, they thereby have an instrumentally rational interest in other people or beings helping them achieve it? The answer is no. If I want X and can best achieve X without any assistance, then it is instrumentally rational for me to want not to be assisted by anyone in achieving X. The only time a being has an instrumentally rational interest in being assisted in their ends is when assistance would better enable them to pursue their ends than they can without assistance.

As such, every being in the Moral Original Position shares this higher-order rational interest: an interest in being assisted in achieving their ends when, and only when, assistance would better enable them to do so than they can do on their own. Taken all by itself, one might think that this shared interest makes it instrumentally rational for the parties to the Moral Original Position to agree to an assistance-maximizing principle: namely, a principle of maximize the total amount of assistance in the world afforded to human and nonhuman beings in the achievement of ends they cannot best achieve on their own. However, there are several complications that undermine the rationality of such a principle.

First, agreeing to assist others in achieving their ends may impose costs on us. For instance, suppose you want affordable health care, and a publicly funded system of health care would better enable you to achieve that end than you would on your own (say, in a free-market system). Although my helping you (for instance, by paying additional taxes to contribute to the funding of such a system) might indeed better enable you to achieve your end, it might cost me in terms of my involuntary and semivoluntary interests. I may find myself not wanting to fund a public health care system, wanting instead to keep my money to myself. Although I could choose to voluntarily change my interests, doing so might be far from cost free for me. The parties to the Moral Original Position – if they are to choose rationally – need to be sensitive to these costs. Their task is to arrive at a universal agreement on principles of action given the assumption that their interests could be anything, including my interest in not helping you achieve what you want.

Second, agreeing to an assistance-maximizing principle is inherently incompatible with another kind of interest many of us have: an interest in *negotiating* our terms of interactions with others, or the extent to which we have an interest in helping others. For instance, although some of us may come to the table with interests in not helping others (one person may not want to fund the public health care system you want), others of us encounter this very issue with initial ambivalence: we do not have any clear ends prior to negotiation or dialogue over the extent to which we want to assist others in their ends. Indeed, this may be the case on 'both ends' of the issue. For instance, if you tell me you want publicly funded health care, I may not initially have any interests one way or the other. I may instead listen to what you have to say before I form an opinion or interest one way or the other (if you convince me that I should help you, I may form an interest in helping you; but if you fail to convince me, I may form an interest in not doing so). Similarly, the person putatively in need of assistance may form higher-interests regarding their own assistance as a result of human interaction. For instance, suppose you initially want health care, and it turns out that a publicly funded system – one assisting you – would be the best instrument for you to get it. However, in conversation with me, I convince you that this would impose undue costs on me: that I would have to pay 'too much' for your health care, which would cause me unhappiness. This might lead you to revise your interests: you may still want health care, but now want *not* to be assisted in obtaining it due to the costs that assistance would impose upon others. Since this higher-order interest you develop in interacting with me modifies your first-order interest – whereas before you just wanted health care however you could best get it (with or without assistance) – now, following our conversation, you may only want health care subject to a further motivational interest: the interest of others not assisting you to get it.

For these reasons, the parties to the Moral Original Position should agree to a principle of assistance, but one qualified by the nuances just discussed, namely:

> **The Principle of Positive Fairness:** all of our morally relevant actions should have as a guiding ideal, setting all costs aside, assisting all human and non-sentient beings in achieving interests they cannot best achieve on their own and want assistance in achieving, for its own sake.

1.3 The Principle of Fair Negotiation

The first two principles we have arrived at from the Moral Original Position – the Principles of Negative and Positive Fairness – have been based on the assumption that non-coercion and assistance of a certain sort are things that every human and nonhuman sentient being has interests in, setting all costs aside. Accordingly, these two principles should have the status of what we might call 'regulative ideals': they are principles that every one of us should have, setting all costs aside, in any morally relevant action. However, by restricting the argument in this way – by setting all costs aside – we have set aside two questions: (1) which types of actions these ideals should factor into as 'relevant' actions, once costs are brought into the picture, and (2) how the two principles are to be balanced or weighed against *one another*, once costs are brought into the picture. Allow me to more fully explain each of these questions before resolving them.

Consider one central clause in the Categorical-Instrumental Imperative, which is then rephrased in new terms in its Moral Original Position Formulation: the clause that whether an action is 'relevant' – whether it is one that we should try reach a universal agreement on with all of our possible future selves – is itself a higher-order question that we rationally ought to settle with our future selves through a higher-order universal agreement. We saw in Chapter 3 that it is far from obvious that all of our actions should be considered 'relevant' (or more precisely, now that we have seen the Categorical-Instrumental Imperative to be a moral principle, morally relevant). For as we saw in Chapter 3, it may actually turn out in certain cases where we confront the problem of possible future selves – wanting to know our future selves' interests – that some of the future selves we might turn out to be have interests in us not encountering the problem, due to the costs that our confronting and solving it might have on them. For instance, consider again Stocker's case of visiting a sick friend in the hospital. Suppose, unlike most people – who simply rush off to the hospital to see the sick friend – I pause to consider whether rushing off to the hospital would satisfy my future self (that is, I want to know whether going to the hospital will satisfy my future self's interest). My doing this very thing – pausing to question whether I should go to the hospital (because I feel uncertain about what my future self will want) – may itself impose costs on my future self that he does not want to face. First, my future self may be disappointed in me: in the fact that I am the kind of person who would even pause to think about whether I should rush to the hospital. Second, suppose my friend is gravely ill, and the few moments I spend contemplating whether going to the hospital would satisfy my future self cause me to get to the hospital when it is too late, just minutes after my friend has passed away. This might cause my future self immense regret. Consequently, given the character of our arguments so far – the fact that the Principles of Negative and Positive Fairness have been derived by setting all costs aside – we cannot validly assume that these principles should in fact motivate us in all cases. We need to arrive at a universal agreement from the Moral Original Position on the higher-order question of when, and to what extent, these two principles should motivate us at all, costs included. In other words, we need to arrive at a universal agreement on which actions are morally relevant – that is, to which actions the Principles of Negative and Positive Fairness apply, given the costs of being motivated by those principles. Thus, on my account, morality comprises a higher-order regulative ideal of using the Moral Original Position to determine which of our actions we should subject to first-order moral deliberation and moral ideals.

Second, insofar as our arguments for the Principles of Negative and Positive Fairness set all costs aside, we presently have no analysis of how these two regulative ideals should be balanced or weighed against one another or costs when cases *are* morally relevant. For instance, the Principles of Negative and Positive Fairness may conflict with one another in such a way that it is impossible to pursue one without imposing costs vis-à-vis the other. For instance, it may turn out that that the best way to assist people or nonhuman sentient beings (in line with the Principle of Positive Fairness) is to coerce individuals. An example here may be universal, government-funded health care. If many citizens cannot afford health care for themselves and want assistance in being able to afford it, and the best method to provide these citizens with health care is to coercively tax all citizens in order to provide it to them, the Principles of Negative and Positive Fairness come into a kind of conflict. The Principle of Negative Fairness says we should aim to reduce coercion in the world, setting all costs aside, yet the Principle of Positive Fairness says we should aim to assist others (in a certain way), setting all costs aside. In this case, however, we cannot do either without some cost to the other: if we fail to coerce people (through taxation), we fail to assist others (those who desire government-funded health care); yet if we do assist others, we coerce people (those who wish not to be taxed). Because pursuing either principle in this case imposes costs on people vis-à-vis the other, we need an analysis of whether, and how, to pursue the principles – balancing or weighing them against each other – given such conflicts and the costs of resolving such conflicts one way rather than another.

Let us examine, then, how the parties to the Moral Original Position should deliberate about costs. As we saw in Chapter 3, there are several possible types of costs that human and nonhuman sentient beings can have. First, involuntary interests generate possible costs: if I find myself angry at someone, wanting to lash out at them and say mean-spirited things, then not allowing myself to indulge my anger is a cost to me – one that, if my aim is thwarted, I cannot avoid or mitigate (I may find myself frustrated). Second, involuntary interests also generate a different type of cost: costs that can be mitigated. For instance, if I find myself angry and wanting to lash out at someone but actively work to control my anger, making myself less angry and wanting to lash out at them less than before, not allowing myself to lash out will still impose a cost on me, but a lesser one – due to my own choice to control my anger (within the constraints allowed by my psychology) – than in the involuntary case. Finally, there are costs with respect to fully voluntary interests, ones we first-personally experience when we ourselves make choices. If I choose not to want to help pay for other people's health care – if I judge to myself, 'I ought not to have to pay for other people's health,' and will myself to act on this judgment – then, if I am forced to do what I do not want, I face a cost: a cost that is the partial result of that particular voluntary choice.

Recall, as we saw in Chapter 2, that although typical adult human beings often (if not always) appear to have all three types of interests, other types of beings – nonhuman animals, psychopaths, and children – are arguably incapable of the same full range of interests. Most animals, in particular, do not appear to share our first-personal capacities for voluntary choice: the capacity to experience oneself as choosing to act on a normative judgment ('I ought to tell the truth'). Instead, most (if not all) animals appear to be impelled by involuntary and perhaps semi-voluntary motivations. If the dog wants to go outside, he will sit by the door; if he wants to come inside, he will sit outside looking in – but it does not appear that he ever thinks about whether he should want to go out or come in.

Since the Moral Original Position requires us to treat ourselves – moral agents – as though we could turn out to have the interests of any human being(s) and any nonhuman sentient being(s), our deliberations concerning costs should be sensitive to these differences. Insofar as the Moral Original Position's veil of ignorance requires the parties to it (you, me, and any other moral agent) to treat ourselves as though they could 'turn out to be anyone,' including nonmoral agents (such as animals), it is instrumentally rational for any universal agreement on which actions are 'morally relevant' given costs – and how the Principles of Negative and Positive Fairness should be weighed or balanced given costs – to be based on the assumption that (1) involuntary interests of human and nonhuman sentient beings entail given costs (costs which automatically and unavoidably accrue given certain states of affairs, particularly those that are contrary to the involuntary interest in question), (2) semivoluntary interests entail partially modifiable costs (costs that can be altered within some given psychological bounds), and (3) fully voluntary interests entail fully modifiable costs (costs determined by the agent's own choices).

Therefore, although some of our actions involve beings (animals) who may only have involuntary interests, insofar as we are moral agents engaging in actions that have effects on them, all of our actions involve at least some beings (namely, we who are acting) who are capable of semivoluntary interests and voluntary interests. In other words, all of our actions that fall under the Moral Original Position involve some beings (us) for whom the costs of their actions may not be fully given before acting: we can make voluntary and semivoluntary choices concerning what comprises costs for us, and how costly we experience different actions and events. For instance, if one initially wants some number of cookies from a box, one can nevertheless choose to give more to another person, *deciding* not to consider it such a big sacrifice. Similarly, if someone does something to make one angry, one typically has some amount of (semivoluntary) control over how angry one gets. One can let one's anger rage out of control, increasing the costs of the person's behavior on oneself, or one can work to control one's anger, controlling how much the person's behavior upsets you (thus mitigating, at least to some extent, the extent to which one suffers from their actions).

For reasons just given, the parties to the Moral Original Position – moral agents such as you and I, considering how to treat ourselves and other possible moral and nonmoral agents (agents whose interests our possible future selves could identify as their own) – cannot assume, in attempting to reach a universal agreement on how to treat costs, that costs for many of the possible agents they could be (agents with voluntary and semivoluntary interests) are necessarily fixed prior to those agents' actions. Interestingly, this also means that the parties to the Moral Original Position cannot treat the costs that nonmoral agents (animals) may experience due to only having involuntary interests as settled either: for the costs that an agent with only involuntary interests (an animal) experience depends on the actions of moral agents who do have voluntary and semivoluntary control over their own interests. For instance, although the chicken or cow may both have involuntary interests in living, and living without suffering – interests they cannot choose not to have – we may choose not to impose certain costs on them at some cost to ourselves, choosing not to kill or harm them, given our recognition of their involuntary interests. As such, the parties to the Moral Original Position – moral agents deliberating to principles of how to treat other moral and nonmoral agents – cannot regard the costs that anyone (moral or nonmoral agents alike) will face as a result of their actions as necessarily settled in advance, prior to anyone acting voluntarily or modifying their semivoluntary interests.

This has a very important implication. Given that we experience our voluntary and semivoluntary interests as unsettled prior to our acting, the parties to the Moral Original Position cannot agree to any distributive principle to decide – '*a priori*' as it were – which costs moral agents should take to determine whether an action is 'morally relevant' (vis-à-vis the Categorical-Instrumental Imperative or Principles of Negative and Positive Fairness), nor which costs should pertain to the application of the Principles of Negative and Positive Fairness in cases that are morally relevant. The parties to the Moral Original Position cannot rationally agree, for instance, that the costs of determining which actions are 'morally relevant' or the costs of weighing the Principles of Negative and Positive Fairness should be spread equally across human and nonhuman sentient beings, or unequally but to the maximum advantage of the worst off individuals (as in Rawls' theory of justice), and so on. Again, this is for the simple reason that many of the individuals the parties to the Moral Original Position could turn out to be – moral agents with semivoluntary and fully voluntary interests – may have interests in how costs are distributed which, because they are semivoluntary and voluntary, are not decided before their choices have been made. One cannot agree to any particular distribution of costs if, given one's deliberative situation, there is no fact of the matter of how the individuals you are reasoning about would like those costs to be distributed. It could well turn out that every individual with voluntary interests would want the costs to be distributed equally. However, it could also turn out (in principle) that they would all like costs to be distributed in some or indeed any other possible way (to the maximum advantage of those facing the most costs, to the advantage of the rich, and so on).

There is a simpler way to put this. Insofar as we (moral agents) have voluntary and semivoluntary capacities – capacities to choose which costs we have an interest in facing (voluntary interests), or to modify the costs we are willing to face (semivoluntary interests) – and, by definition, have motivational interests in exercising these capacities (to make choices is to be motivated to make choices), the parties to the Moral Original Position have instrumentally rational grounds to agree to a Principle of Fair Negotiation. Such a principle enables moral agents to negotiate with one another, and (in a manner of speaking) with nonmoral agents (more on this shortly), the costs they have interests in facing for the sake of defining 'morally relevant actions,' and – in cases of actions deemed morally relevant – weighing the Principles of Negative and Positive Fairness against one another. Furthermore, note that the parties to the Moral Original Position have no clear grounds for favoring any being(s) over others in such a negotiation: the parties must treat themselves as though they could turn out to be 'anyone,' and the very question of whether anyone's interests in costs should be favored over anyone else's is something that they can negotiate. The parties to the Moral Original Position therefore have instrumentally rational grounds for wanting every individual they could turn out to be to have equal bargaining power over the negotiation, so that they have an 'equal shot' of realizing their favored distribution of costs, whatever interests they may turn out to have (even interests in distributing costs one way rather than another).

Of course, in the real-world, organic negotiations over costs that afford all parties equal bargaining power are profoundly difficult – if not impossible – to achieve. Even in small groups, some parties to negotiations typically have greater bargaining power than others (due to things like intimidation, confidence, money, and so on). The parties to the Moral Original Position should surely know that potentially unequal negotiating power is a fact of life to be grappled with. Since the parties cannot rationally agree to any particular distribution of costs (given our interests in exercising our voluntary and semivoluntary interests), and should rationally favor a process of negotiation (one that enables us to exercise our voluntary and semivoluntary interests concerning the costs we are willing to take on in our actions, given their effects on other human and nonhuman sentient beings), the parties should agree that such a negotiation process should aim to approximate one that affords equal bargaining power to all those affected, as far as it is possible to do so. This is of course an 'imperfect' solution – but I hold that it is the only one the parties to the Moral Original Position can rationally agree to, given their situation and knowledge that fully equal bargaining power is difficult (and often impossible) to achieve. And though admittedly imperfect, I believe that it comports well with commonsense moral convictions about how negotiations should be. For instance, it sits well with the conviction – common in liberal-democracies today – that although democracy is far from perfect, the more equal people's negotiating power is in a democracy (the less, say, the rich determine policy or who is elected, and the more the people do), the morally better it is. Given that we prefer negotiations to be fair, the best that the parties to the Moral Original Position can do in light of real-world differences in negotiating power is to aim to approximate as fair of a negotiation process as possible.

Next, the parties to the Moral Original Position should know that some affected by our actions – some 'parties to the negotiation' in terms of experiencing costs – cannot actually negotiate. Nonhuman animals, for instance, cannot in general negotiate solutions with us: we can only 'include them' in the negotiations by proxy (by attempting to discern their interests and give their interests equal bargaining power in the process). Since the parties to the Moral Original Position are concerned with these types of beings (the interests of nonhuman animals can turn out to be our own interests, even if it is unlikely), the parties should agree upon a Principle of Fair Negotiation that affords these beings' interests equal bargaining power in the process as well.

Finally, as we will see in more detail in Section 1.4, there is another principle the parties to the Moral Original Position should want to incorporate in their negotiation: a Principle of Virtues of Fairness, which requires developing and expressing dispositions that facilitate pursuit of the Principles of Negative and Positive Fairness, and the Principle of Fair Negotiation, in the process of negotiation itself. For it is only to the extent that such a negotiation process is based on dispositions consistent with the principles it embodies – the Principles of Negative and Positive Fairness, and the Principle of Fair Negotiation – that the entire negotiation process is truly motivated by the principles it is intended to be motivated by.

For these reasons, it is rational for the parties to the Moral Original Position to agree to the following principle:

The Principle of Fair Negotiation: whether an action is morally relevant, and how the Principles of Negative and Positive Fairness and Virtues of Fairness (see below) should be applied factoring in costs, should be settled through an actual process of fair negotiation guided by the Principles of Negative Fairness, Positive Fairness, and Virtues of Fairness, where all human and nonhuman sentient beings affected by the action are afforded equal bargaining power to the extent that such a process can be approximated, and to the extent that cannot be, through a hypothetical process approximating the same, for its own sake.

1.4 The Principle of Virtues of Fairness

There is a fourth and straightforward principle that is rational for the parties in the Moral Original Position to agree upon. Given that it is rational to agree to the Principles of Negative and Positive Fairness and the Principle of Fair Negotiation in the Moral Original Position, it is also rational to develop and express stable character traits – or psychobehavioral dispositions – to apply and act in conformity with the first three principles of fairness. After all, such traits are simply dispositions to be motivated to apply and act in accordance with three principles of fairness – which, as we have just seen, are rational to agree upon from the standpoint of the Moral Original Position. It is therefore, by definition, instrumentally rational to prefer oneself to be disposed to apply and act according to the principles that one should be motivated by. Thus, we have:

> **The Principle of Virtues of Fairness:** all of our morally relevant actions should aim to develop and express stable character traits to act in accordance with and on the outcomes generated by the first three principles of fairness, for its own sake.

This principle enables us to resolve a question that I suspect has been in the back of many readers' minds for some time. In developing the problem of possible future selves in Chapter 2 – the problem I later argued is solved by the Categorical-Instrumental Imperative – I began with the observation that we arguably only encounter the problem on some, but not all, occasions. I held that in some cases, we simply act without thinking, and it may only be in cases of uncertainty about the future (including moral uncertainty) that we encounter the problem at all (which, again, is wanting to know our future selves' interests). One thing that may have troubled readers about this argument, and my contention that the Categorical-Instrumental Imperative is a solution to the problem, is that it makes morality seem arbitrary in a certain sense: that moral questions only arise, and moral principles only apply, when we in fact encounter the problem of possible future selves. What if, one may ask, one encounters that problem only rarely, or in different instances than other individuals? Does this not make morality itself completely relative regarding whether, and when, each individual encounters the problem of possible future selves?

The Principle of Virtues of Fairness enables us to resolve this concern in an intuitive fashion. Insofar as we all encounter the problem of possible future selves at least sometimes in our lives (as Chapter 2 argued), the Four Principles of Fairness entail that we should apply the four principles in those cases – negotiating what is fair with others – in ways that lead us to develop dispositions to behave fairly in other cases in the future. In other words, the Four Principles of Fairness require us, in all of our actions, to develop dispositions to be fair to our present and future selves and others, encountering the problem of possible future selves, and solving it, *when, and only when, it is fair to ourselves and others to do so*. But this is a commonsense idea. It simply means that morality it itself a matter of negotiating with others what kind of people we should become, and which of our actions we should consider to be morally relevant – which, I would argue, is exactly what we do in relationships, in the workplace, and in society at large.

Consider, for instance, changing social mores concerning sensitivity. Several decades ago, certain uses of language and ways of speaking – use of racially insensitive language (referring to people of certain racial/ethnic backgrounds as 'colored'), gender stereotypical language (using 'he' as a default pronoun in written language), and casual use of crude language concerning the physically and mentally disabled (words such as 'retarded') were not considered moral issues, and a person who engaged in these types of behaviors was not considered to lack moral virtue. This was almost certainly because, given social inequalities at the time, members of the affected populations (those who find the above language hurtful or demeaning) had not yet negotiated standards of language sensitivity with the rest of society. Insofar as the Principle of Virtues of Fairness draws on the first three principles – including the Principle of Fair Negotiation – it enables us to understand moral virtue and moral relevance (the kinds of cases we should be disposed to apply the first principles to) as being determined in an ongoing, organic fashion by social negotiation: something which is intuitive, since it is in fact what we do.

Finally, the Principle of Virtues of Fairness enables us to explain how and why moral relevance and virtue can be context sensitive, and indeed relative to individuals and relationships within certain bounds. Since my spouse is directly affected by my household habits and other actions concerning her – and we both bear different costs as a result of different types of behavior on the part of the other (she desires me to do certain things that I may find irksome and vice versa) – the first three principles of Rightness as Fairness, and by extension the Principle of Virtues of Fairness, entail that moral virtue and moral relevance in our relationship are to be defined by us in fair negotiation with one another.

Rightness as Fairness thus enables us to make sense of the widely (if only tacitly) recognized fact that what is 'morally relevant' or virtuous in one relationship may not be so in another.

2 Rightness as Fairness: a unified standard of right and wrong

Given that it is instrumentally rational for the parties to the Moral Original Position (you, me, and every other moral agent) to universally agree to the Four Principles of Fairness, it is instrumentally rational for the parties to universally agree to analyze moral rightness in terms of their conjunction:

> **Rightness as Fairness:** an action is morally right if and only if it satisfies the Four Principles of Fairness, that is, if and only if it is (A) is morally relevant, (B) has coercion-avoidance and minimization, assisting human and nonhuman sentient beings to achieve interests they cannot best achieve on their own and want assistance in achieving, and the development and expression of settled dispositions to have these ends, as at least tacit ideals, and (C) is in conformity with the outcome of an actual process of fair negotiation approximating all human and sentient beings affected by the action being motivated by the above ideals and having equal bargaining power over how those ideals should be applied factoring in costs, or, if such a process is impossible, the outcome of a hypothetical process approximating the same, where moral relevance is determined recursively, by applying (B) and (C) to the question of whether the action is morally relevant.

We can then define other deontic notions – such as moral wrongness, permissibility, indeterminacy, and the supererogatory – in a similar fashion. An action is morally wrong if and only if it is morally relevant but violates conditions (B) and/or (C) above. An action is morally permissible – that is, neither morally required nor forbidden – if and only if it is not 'morally relevant' (since morally irrelevant actions are neither required nor prohibited by morality) or is morally relevant but negotiated to be not required. An action is supererogatory (or 'above and beyond what it is required') if and only if it is morally right to perform at some cost to oneself (whatever costs are negotiated *qua* Rightness as Fairness), but one performs it at *greater* cost to oneself than required. Finally, an action has indeterminate moral status – there is no fact of the matter of its being right, wrong, or permissible – if and only if negotiation about its moral relevance and/or costs has not occurred, and there are multiple possible, conflicting outcomes of fair negotiation consistent with the ideals of negative and positive fairness.

Before applying Rightness as Fairness to several cases to illustrate its analysis of moral rightness and moral problem-solving, I want to pause to reflect on some of its unique features.

First, Rightness as Fairness is unique in holding that morality itself is partly a matter of negotiating with other people and nonhuman sentient beings which of our actions are morally relevant. I believe this to be a very important implication, as there are several related concerns that modern moral philosophy 'overmoralizes' life, wrongly turning all of our actions in moral issues. First, Michael Stocker, Bernard Williams, and others have argued that modern moral philosophy requires 'one thought too many,' requiring us to always act (at least implicitly) for moral reasons when, intuitively, many of our actions should be motivated by nothing more than love, friendship, or sympathy.[6–9] A second, related, critique is that modern moral theories require us to subsume all of our life projects to morality, requiring us to be 'moral saints,' concerned with morality above all else.[6,9–10] As Susan Wolf writes, 'One attractive ideal of love would prohibit the lover not only from thinking about morality all the time, but also from being unconditionally committed to acting according to morality all the time.'[11] A third, related critique – raised typically in relation to utilitarianism, but arguably applicable to other theories as well – is that modern moral philosophy requires too much of us, demanding extreme forms of impartial concern for others.[6,9–13] For instance, classical act-utilitarianism holds that morality requires all of our actions to maximize happiness in the aggregate, rule-utilitarianism holds that all of our actions should conform to rules that maximize happiness, and so on.[14] Yet, as many utilitarians (such as Peter Singer) have argued, maximizing happiness – either by act or by rule – may require an incredible amount of us, including giving up most of our wealth to alleviate world poverty or killing handicapped infants.[15–16] Similarly, traditional Kantian ethics requires us to always act on maxims we could will to be universal laws of nature. Yet, as Stocker points out, visiting a loved one in the hospital 'because it can be willed as a universal law of nature' seems like an overly moralized reason for acting: one should visit loved ones in the hospital simply because one loves them.[6]

While utilitarians,[17] Kantians,[18–19] and moral philosophers of other persuasions[20] have responded to these types of concerns, I believe Rightness as Fairness provides a more intuitive solution, holding that morality itself is fundamentally a matter of negotiating with others, in a manner guided by moral principles (the Principles of Negative and Positive Fairness), which of our actions are morally relevant, and as such, how 'demanding' morality is. This is a compelling implication for a couple of related reasons. First, real-life moral practice strongly suggests that this is exactly what we do: we negotiate, in relationships, in society, and the world more broadly, which things count as moral issues, and how demanding morality is. For instance, in marriages, one typically 'works out' with one's spouse a mutual understanding of which actions are moral issues in the context of the marriage. For instance, whereas neither my spouse nor I regards what time we eat lunch as a moral issue in the marriage – neither of us has much of an interest in what the other does – we have negotiated other things as moral issues, such as what time we go to bed. This became a moral issue for us because going to bed early is important to me and going to bed later is important for her (my wife is a night owl and prefers to work late), and we found that we disturbed each other's sleep when we went to bed and woke up at different times. We thus experienced a conflict of interests, and came to see bedtime as a question of what is fair between us. Second, insofar as morality has costs (as we have already seen) – as far as helping you (in line with the Principle of Positive Fairness) may impose costs upon me – Rightness as Fairness provides an elegant explanation for something that has puzzled moral philosophers. The puzzle is this: why, although we commonly recognize that there may be some sense in which we 'should' be moral saints (putting morality first, in a 'Christ-like' manner), there is also a sense in which most of us are content (morally speaking) with not being moral saints. As Eric Schwitzgabel puts it, 'it's generally true that we aim for [moral] goodness only by relative, rather than absolute standards' – that we aim, as it were, for only a grade of 'B+ on the great moral curve' rather than the 'A' grade of the moral saint (such as Buddha, Gandhi, Jesus Christ, and so on).[21] So, should we be 'moral saints,' or not? Rightness as Fairness provides a nuanced answer. Insofar as the Principles of Negative and Positive Fairness affirm certain ideals – coercion-minimization and assisting people who would benefit from and desire help – as moral ideals to be pursued all costs aside, Rightness as Fairness entails that it may be right for someone to be a 'moral saint' such as Buddha, Gandhi, or Christ. If someone is willing to endure immense personal costs for the above ideals, then provided they are also sensitive to and fairly negotiate with others the costs of their doing so, it can be *right* for them to be moral saints. However, Rightness as Fairness also entails that those of us who are not willing to endure the costs of moral sainthood have every right to negotiate with others the costs that *we* should have to face in pursuing the same moral ideals – and, if we fairly negotiate 'less saintly' moral standards, Rightness as Fairness entails that it is fair and right for us not to be moral saints. But this is precisely what critics of existing moral theories have long suggested: that what is 'right for the moral saint' need not be right for everyone. We will see the attractiveness of this line of thought in greater detail in Section 3, when we apply Rightness as Fairness to specific cases.

Second, Rightness as Fairness introduces a novel method of moral problem-solving that requires us to at least partially abandon a common and seductive, but (I believe) problematic conception of how to approach applied moral issues. Many people (including philosophers) are naturally drawn to the notion that moral issues can be properly addressed through thought and debate: that we can 'think through' sound answers to applied moral questions. To illustrate, there are countless books and articles arguing for and against the notion that it is morally right for the rights or interests of the many to outweigh the rights or interests of the few (and if so, when),[22-25] whether it is right to direct a trolley to kill one person in order to save five others,[25-27] whether it can ever be right to torture a person,[28-33] and so on. At the same time, however, the idea that applied moral issues can be settled through thought and debate is problematic. First, as we see in the applied ethics literature on the topics just listed, people on different sides of the issues find different argumentative premises attractive, and different moral theories often lead to quite different conclusions (what produces the most utility, *qua* utilitarianism, may not respect human autonomy, *qua* Kantianism, and so on). Consequently, 'principled debate' all too often results in argumentative 'standoffs': situations in which people fundamentally differ on the premises they find attractive and arguments they find compelling. We see this in the debates mentioned above. When it comes to whether, and when, the rights or interests of the many outweigh the few – of whether it is morally permissible to push a person in front of a trolley to save more lives, or torture suspected terrorists to protect large numbers of people from possible terrorist attacks – there are usually plausible arguments on multiple sides of the issue. And though some arguments may be better than others, the issue of disputed premises often remains. Whereas some people may find utilitarian analyses of the moral permissibility of torture attractive, others may be staunchly Kantian in outlook, finding utilitarian premises flawed (and vice versa). This is a deep problem indeed. For when people disagree over premises, it is unclear how a productive argument can proceed (if you and I cannot even agree on 'moral starting points,' how can either of us say anything likely to convince the other?).[34] Second, this problem often becomes particularly acute in public debate. When it comes to just about any contentious moral issue – abortion, gay marriage, and so on – there is often a pronounced unwillingness of opposing sides to engage in 'debate' with the opposing side, precisely because of apparent 'fundamental differences' over premises. This is not only a practical problem: it is arguably a moral one, as an unwillingness of people to listen to one another often (if not always) seems to result in greater conflict, fomenting divisiveness rather than leading to productive resolution of the relevant issues.

According to Rightness as Fairness, the idea that applied moral issues can be soundly addressed through principled thought and debate alone is fundamentally in error. Although Rightness as Fairness stipulates that morality is partly a principled affair (specifically, that we can and should debate which sorts of actions or policies are most in line with moral ideals of coercion-avoidance and minimization, as well as helping others), it maintains that morality is also something that cannot be wholly settled 'on principle' or through mere debate. Instead, Rightness as Fairness holds that morality is fundamentally a matter of negotiating with others the costs that we, and they, should face for the sake of the aforementioned ideals. Rightness as Fairness thus entails that while there is indeed value in debating whether abortion, the use of torture in the 'war on terror,' and gun control are more consistent with the ideals of negative and positive fairness than their opposite, the ultimate answer to these questions cannot be settled on principled grounds alone. Rather, since whichever 'answer' we arrive at will impose costs on people – pro- and anti- abortion, gun control, and torture policies all impose different costs on people – Rightness as Fairness holds that morality requires us to negotiate those costs with one another: negotiate, that is, a fair balance of moral ideals against the costs of pursuing them in one way rather than another. Therefore, once we have debated ideals – which sorts of policies are the most consistent with the moral ideals expressed by the Principles of Negative and Positive Fairness – there can be no 'principled answer' as to what the right moral answer is in the case at hand (abortion policy, gun control, torture, and so on) is. Rather, Rightness as Fairness holds that the right answer must be *created* by fair negotiation: by an actual, organic process that enables all affected to weigh moral ideals (negative and positive fairness) against the costs of different modes of implementation.

In one respect, this is entirely intuitive. When we have conflicts, say, during a project at work – where not everyone can 'get their way' – we tend to think that there is no 'principled answer' as to the 'right way' to resolve the conflict. Rather, we typically think it is right to resolve the conflict through a process that gives everyone a fair chance to speak and vote for their favored solution. Indeed, this very notion seems to underlie the project of modern democracies: namely, that when we (legitimately) disagree over 'what's right' (and I will say more about how to understand 'legitimacy' here shortly) – when opposing parties both have legitimate (in their view) principles in mind, but disagree over how they should be balanced against each other, and against costs – the answer is to forge a fair solution, where citizens negotiate on an ongoing basis the right answer to the issue. Rightness as Fairness entails that this democratic notion is a fundamental part of morality itself: that morality is not a matter of 'finding out' what maximizes utility, or respects human autonomy – things that can be written in books or articles, or debated in words – but rather a matter of real, live people affected by actions on moral issues (people whose lives are at issue when it comes to abortion, torture, and so on) (1) being motivated by certain ideals (the Principles of Negative and Positive Fairness), (2) negotiating the proper balance of those ideals, and balance against costs, with others who are similarly affected and motivated, and (3) forging fair resolutions together not through mere words or debate, but through negotiation, or fair bargaining. I believe this is intuitive, since it is commonsense that 'conflicts require fair resolutions.' Furthermore, only Rightness as Fairness puts this notion center-stage, holding that morality is fundamentally a matter of negotiating how certain ideals (the Principles of Negative and Positive Fairness) should be applied to cases given costs and conflicts thereof. I therefore believe that Rightness as Fairness promises a new, more productive vision of how to relate to each other than many moral debates presuppose. For although people have a certain tendency to 'stand on principle,' both in philosophy and in real-life – asserting, for instance, that abortion or torture is 'right' or 'wrong,' *simpliciter*, without any willingness to negotiate – Rightness as Fairness holds that an unwillingness to negotiate is itself morally wrong among people who share the Principles of Negative and Positive Fairness as ideals (since it is contrary to the Principle of Fair Negotiation). Rightness as Fairness holds that there is only one situation in which it is morally right to stand on principle: cases of morally *illegitimate* disagreement, where one's moral 'opponent' is motivated by incorrect moral ideals (such as the slave owner or racist, who are unwilling to extend the Principles of Negative and Positive Fairness, or fair negotiation, to entire classes of people).

184 *Rightness as Fairness*

A third (and related) notable feature of Rightness as Fairness is that it merges the insights of several leading moral frameworks – deontology, consequentialism, virtue ethics, and contractualism. The Categorical-Instrumental Imperative is broadly deontological, requiring all of our morally relevant actions to conform to a universal agreement with all of our possible selves for its own sake. The Principles of Negative and Positive Fairness, which we are to pursue for their own sake, are broadly consequentialist in content, requiring us to aim to bring about certain consequences (all things being equal, setting costs aside): namely, coercion avoidance and minimization (negative fairness), and assisting human and nonhuman beings to achieve their ends under certain conditions (positive fairness). Next, the Principle of Fair Negotiation is heavily contractualist, holding that we must apply the first two principles via fair negotiation with others. And finally, the Principle of Virtues of Fairness is virtue ethical in nature, requiring us to develop and express certain stable character traits.

A final important property of Rightness as Fairness is that it provides a unique and (I believe) compelling analysis of why it is rational to obey moral norms – an analysis that, insofar as it engages with our motivational interests, can actually motivate people to behave morally. As we saw in Chapter 3, Rightness as Fairness is based on concerns that we all have about our future from time to time – concerns that require us to be fair to all of our possible future selves. Furthermore, as we have seen, many empirical results appear to broadly confirm this account, strongly linking imprudent and immoral behavior to failure to be concerned for one's future,[35-38] and improved moral and prudential behavior to stimulation of concern for one's future self.[39-41]

I believe that all of these are compelling features in favor of Rightness as Fairness, and we can see their practical usefulness by briefly applying the theory to some controversial moral issues.

3 Rightness as Fairness in practice: principled fair negotiation

As we saw in Chapter 1, a compelling theory should be fruitful, solving theoretical and practical problems better than alternatives.

Existing moral theories, by and large, arguably run into one of two problems. On the one hand, 'monistic' moral theories – such as utilitarianism or Kantianism – are often criticized for the fact that they attempt to reduce morality to a simple 'formula': a formula of maximizing utility, respecting autonomy, and so on. For instance, ordinary act-utilitarianism is often alleged to entail overly simplistic, implausible analyses of applied cases, requiring us to simply 'add up' utility and pursue whichever action produces the best consequences.[42] Conversely, Kant's moral theory entails that morality is fundamentally a matter of determining which of one's maxims are 'universalizable' or 'respect humanity' – something which, at least according to Kant, has nothing to do with an action's consequences.[43] Yet theories that attempt to reduce all of morality to 'one thing,' such as consequences (per utilitarianism) or principled intentions (per Kant's theory), seem too simplistic. In real-life we tend to think that morality is a matter of weighing competing considerations against one another – that consequences should matter in some cases, but perhaps not in others. Indeed, many alternative moral frameworks – W.D. Ross' theory of *prima facie* moral duties,[44] virtue ethics,[45] moral particularism,[46] and so on – have been developed to avoid charges of 'oversimplifying' the moral domain. Yet these types of theories have been alleged to run into the exact opposite problem: that of not providing enough moral guidance. In Ross' case, it is unclear how we should weigh different duties against one another (something Ross concedes when he writes that we can never know what we morally ought to do, all things considered, but can only form 'probable opinions'[47]). There is a similar concern about virtue ethics. While it may be clear what the honest, kind, or helpful thing to do is, in cases where honesty, kindness, or helpfulness conflict with one another virtue ethics struggles to provide clear guidance, besides invoking vague (and perhaps circular) notions of 'practical wisdom' or 'what the fully virtuous agent would do' – thus providing no clear analysis on how to weigh or compare the virtues.[48-49] Lastly, moral particularism provides no general principles for moral deliberation, merely instructing us to reason about particular situations on a case-by-case basis. Although proponents of these theories have come to their defense, typically arguing that their theories are appropriately action-guiding,[50-52] these worries have not gone away.

Rightness as Fairness, I believe, provides an attractive level of action-guidance. On the one hand, it holds that morality is a matter of pursuing specific principles as ideals – the Principles of Negative and Positive Fairness. On the other hand, the Principle of Fair Negotiation entails that the correct application of these ideals, costs and all, must be settled through organic processes of fair negotiation – or, failing that (if fair negotiation processes are unavailable), by approximating such a process through hypothetical reflection. And as we will now see, this is a picture that fits well with moral practice.

3.1 Kant's four cases

In his *Groundwork of the Metaphysics of Morals*, Kant uses both the universal law and humanity formulations of his categorical imperative to argue that it is wrong to make false promises for one's own advantage, commit suicide, never help those in need, and neglect to develop one's natural talents.[53] Because these are four famous examples – ones that Kant's arguments in the *Groundwork* appear to run into famous problems with,[54] and which ordinary people have differing pre-theoretic intuitions about (some think it is always wrong to lie, others that there are exceptions, and so on) – I believe may be useful to examine them using Rightness as Fairness.

Let us begin with the case of telling a lie (or intentionally 'making a false promise') for one's own advantage. Rightness as Fairness entails that such an action is generally wrong, since lies tend to coerce people (contrary to the Principle of Negative Fairness). However, Rightness as Fairness also holds that precisely when lying is right, wrong, or permissible is something that we need to negotiate with other people, since sometimes lying for one's own advantage can have important benefits for oneself and others. And this is something that we in fact think and do. Consider, for instance, the social practice (in many cultures or, even more contextually, in certain relationships) of 'making excuses' to avoid uttering an impolite truth, such as saying one 'cannot' meet a friend who invites one to lunch (because one is 'ill' or 'has an appointment') even though the real reason is simply that one does not want to go. We have arrived at such norms – in some cases culturally, and in other cases within specific relationships (each relationship, we say, involves its 'own expectations') – because we recognize that in some cases it is fair to lie, given the costs and benefits to everyone involved. We lie to our friend, for instance, because we do not think it is fair to ourselves or to our friend to tell the truth that we don't feel like getting off the couch to see them.

Now consider suicide. Although many of us are unwilling to side with Kant that suicide is always wrong, there are intuitively two dangers with suicide: unfairness to oneself and unfairness to others. On the one hand, if someone commits suicide when their future self might wish they hadn't (if they were to live), then their committing suicide seems unfair to themselves. This, intuitively, is why many people think it is morally permissible to commit suicide only in cases of a terminal disease or some other form of unmitigated suffering which has no reasonable prospect of resolving itself. Further, even in cases where ending one's life might be 'fair to oneself' – if, that is, a person's life contains such little prospect for happiness that their (profoundly unhappy) future self would want them to die – many of us are uncomfortable with suicide on the grounds that it is 'unfair to others': namely, family and friends left behind to suffer the aftermath of the person's act. Here, as with lying, Rightness as Fairness provides a nuanced analysis. Because suicide both runs the risk of depriving a person's future self of a potentially enjoyable future, and also runs the risk of imposing immense costs on family members and others, Rightness as Fairness entails that whether it is permissible or right for a person to commit suicide should be determined through some manner of fair negotiation among all those affected: for instance, by (A) the person informing their family and friends of their thoughts of suicide, (B) allowing them to reason with the suicidal person (giving the family and friends a fair opportunity to convince the person not to go through with it), and finally (C) pursuing counseling for a time, as such counseling might enable the person to more clearly see whether it is possible that they would be better off continuing to live. And these are things we already tend to think are appropriate when people are suicidal. We tend to think our family members or friends should 'come to us' before going through with such an irreversible act, giving us a fair shot to convince them otherwise, not just for our sake, but because we are also concerned about them being fair to themselves.

Finally, consider Kant's final two cases: the cases of helping people in need and developing one's natural talents. On the one hand, the Principle of Positive Fairness holds that helping people is presumptively right – but the Principle of Fair Negotiation holds that we need to negotiate with others when, to what extent, and at what costs (to ourselves and them), we should help them. Similarly, the Principles of Negative and Positive Fairness both hold that morality requires developing one's talents, as failing to do so is unfair to oneself, putting one's future self in a worse position to successfully pursue their interests (this, broadly speaking, is why we think people 'owe it to themselves' to work hard, study hard, and so on). However, since developing one's talents has costs (as when we say, 'All work and no play makes for a dull life'), Rightness as Fairness holds that we must negotiate a fair balance, with ourselves and others, on the costs we (and they) should bear for developing our talents. This is commonsense as well. We often say that people who never stop to enjoy life are unfair to themselves, and that people who work so hard that they neglect their family, friends, or children are unfair to them.

In sum, Rightness as Fairness coheres with our commonsense beliefs and practices concerning Kant's four examples. It provides nuanced explanations of when, and why, lying and suicide are wrong and when they are not wrong, and when, and to what extent, we have duties to help others and develop our talents.

3.2 How numbers should count: trolleys, torture, and organ donors

One of the most longstanding problems in all of moral philosophy is whether 'numbers should count' – that is, whether the interests or autonomy of many people should outweigh those of the few – and if so, how.[22-27]

Here is a famous example: a doctor on a transplant ward can save five patients dying from organ failure, but only by covertly killing one innocent, relatively healthy patient.[42] If the doctor could accomplish this action without getting caught, the doctor would save more lives and produce more happiness in the aggregate than by not doing it. Yet although the doctor would save more lives and produce more happiness this way, almost everyone seems to agree that it would be wrong. Doctors, we say, should not kill patients, even to save a larger number of people. In this case, most of us want to say that 'numbers should not count.'

In other cases, however, many of us are inclined to say that numbers should count. Consider so-called 'trolley cases.'[25-27] In one version of the case ('Pull the Switch'), we are to imagine that there is a trolley hurtling down a track, which will run over and kill five innocent people unless a switch is pulled to divert it to a second track, where it will kill only one other innocent person. However, in a second version ('Push the Man'), we are to imagine that instead of pulling a switch that will kill one innocent person to save five, the only way to save the five lives is to push a single innocent person in front of the trolley, killing them. Although the numbers in these two cases are exactly the same – either one innocent person will die, or five will die – many of us judge it to be morally right or permissible to pull the switch, but morally wrong to push a person their death.[55]

Finally, consider another, very pressing ethical issue regarding 'whether numbers should count': whether it is ethical to torture suspected terrorists to potentially prevent future terrorist attacks. While some philosophers argue that torture is always morally wrong,[28-29] many people argue that it depends on whether torture is likely to save innocent lives, how many lives it is likely to save, and so on.[30-32]

When applied to these types of cases, existing moral theories tend to experience the two problems discussed earlier. On the one hand, some theories seem to give overly simplistic answers. Act-utilitarianism, for instance, entails that torture is ethical if and only if it maximizes utility. Although there is of course debate about whether, and if so when, torture does this,[30-32] the relevant point is that act-utilitarianism requires the issue to be settled through the mere calculation of utility. Similarly, Kantianism has been used to argue that torture is wrong because the tortured individual is treated as a mere means for the good of others, thus (once again) reducing the question to a single issue (does torture 'respect humanity' in a Kantian sense, or not?).[28-29,33] Conversely, when it comes to 'numbers cases' such as torture, other theories appear to provide too little guidance. For instance, Ross' theory of *prima facie* duties includes a duty to promote a maximum of aggregate good[56] as well as a duty of nonmaleficence, or duty not to harm.[57] Since torture is harmful but might produce maximum aggregate good, Ross' theory provides no clear guidance. Similarly, while virtue-theoretic analyses of right action broadly instruct one to act as the virtuous individual would act,[51,58] there seem to be plausible virtue ethical arguments both in favor of torture (it is the responsible, virtuous thing to do in response to modern terrorism) and against it (it is cruel and unnecessary). And so on.

I believe that Rightness as Fairness provides a balanced and more nuanced analysis. Since all of the cases just discussed (the organ donor case, trolley cases, and torture) involve coercion and assistance, the Principle of Fair Negotiation entails that they are cases in which the Principles of Negative and Positive Fairness apply. Next, the Principle of Negative Fairness tells us that we should aim to minimize coercion in the world, setting costs aside, and the Principle of Positive Fairness instructs us to assist others in achieving ends in which assistance is helpful and desired, (once again) setting costs aside. Thus, in 'numbers' cases, setting all costs aside, we should aim to minimize the number of people coerced and assist as many as we can who would benefit from and desire assistance. However, in order to determine whether these principles apply, and if so, how they are to be weighed against one another and against costs, Rightness as Fairness holds that we must do so through the Principle of Fair Negotiation. Therefore, let us do so, working through some of the cases summarized above.

Begin with the organ donor case. In order to properly apply the Principle of Fair Negotiation, we need to specify who is to be included in the negotiation – as the principle states that 'all beings affected' should be included. Here, however, we face a problem: one that I believe illuminates much of what is wrong with thought-experiments such as the organ donor case. Traditionally, philosophers who present such cases suggest that by considering the case in isolation – stipulating who will be affected by action, and how – we can 'isolate the case's morally relevant features.' One problem, however, is that it is unclear whether considering the cases as formulated actually does this. Rather, considering the cases in isolation may abstract away from morally relevant facts, such as the broader social effects of actions in similar real-world cases. Indeed, as we will now see, I believe this concern is brought to light by using Rightness as Fairness to analyze abstract versus real-world cases.

Consider first the classic organ donor case in isolation, where one knows for certain that one can kill one healthy person to save five lives, with no further effects beyond the case at hand. If we apply Rightness as Fairness to this case so stated, it may at first appear right to kill the person for their organs. After all, if we imagine everyone involved motivated by the Principles of Negative and Positive Fairness as ideals, and then give everyone equal bargaining power in how to apply these principles in light of costs involved, as required by the Principle of Fair Negotiation, then it might seem as though the one person will be out-bargained by the many in favor of the conclusion that they should be killed for their organs. However, this is too quick of a conclusion in the real-world. The Principle of Virtues of Fairness holds that we should have stable dispositions to conform our actions to the Principles of Negative and Positive Fairness, and the Principle of Fair Negotiation – dispositions that we should have cultivated prior to facing such a situation, given real-world living. And when we consider the real-world, Rightness as Fairness instructs us to develop dispositions to apply the principles of fairness in a manner that supports *not* killing the one person for their organs. Here is how. In the real-world, neither physicians, patients, patients' families, nor people in society more broadly are all-knowing. In particular, we cannot typically know in advance – in a specific 'numbers' case – precisely who our actions will affect, and in what way. What we do know, however, is that a moral norm permitting doctors to kill one person to save five would create fear among patients – giving doctors immense power over life and death – and incite outrage in society among the victims of such behavior. Further, given such fear, many people would likely avoid medical treatment unless absolutely necessary, potentially leading to disastrous results (individuals dying from preventable injuries or illnesses, failing to detect health problems until they are critical, performing poorly at home and at work due to having an ongoing, untreated illness, and so on). We therefore could reasonably judge that the costs incurred by the practice of harvesting organs from a healthy individual in order to save a greater number of sick individuals would be greater than the costs of not doing so. Consequently, guided (at least implicitly) by the Principles of Negative and Positive Fairness (medical ethics is, after all, guided by the principles of 'doing no harm' and beneficence[59]), we have negotiated together laws and norms against killing healthy people to save the sick (in line with the Principle of Fair Negotiation). As such, according to Rightness as Fairness, killing one healthy patient to save five is wrong in the real-world. Moreover, because Rightness as Fairness requires us to develop stable dispositions to conform to the above principles, it follows that if any of us were to find ourselves in the situation (the 'isolated' organ donor case), we should be disposed to apply the principles in the same way. In other words, if we were a physician in such an isolated case, we should be strongly disposed not to want to kill one to save the five. Similarly, if we were one of the five dying patients, we should be disposed to think it would be wrong – contrary to fair standards of medical ethics – for one healthy person to be killed for their sake. And so, if people had the dispositions Rightness as Fairness entails they should have, then even in the isolated case, a fair procedure of negotiation should still lead to the conclusion that the one should not be sacrificed for the many.

As such, Rightness as Fairness gives an intuitive analysis of the organ donor case. When we think of such a case, we intuitively think those involved should find the prospect of killing one person to save five abhorrent. And we have such strong visceral reactions to the case – strong dispositions to favor the one healthy person over the many – for more or less the reasons I have outlined. In the real-world, unless doctors, patients, and people in society more broadly found killing patients abhorrent, our lives would be clouded by fear and outrage: fear of our own lives or the lives of those we care about being sacrificed for others, and outrage in response to such cases occurring. Because this is how we, real-life human beings, respond to such cases in the real-world – and because we have negotiated standards of medical ethics against it – we consider killing one person to save five wrong, just as Rightness as Fairness does.

Now let us consider the trolley cases. Rightness as Fairness also has compelling implications here as well. In particular, it explains why many of our intuitions differ for different trolley cases, and suggests that there is no determinate answer as to what is right in those cases. Allow me to explain. Rightness as Fairness holds, once again, that we should approach applied cases motivated by virtues of fairness: that is, through settled dispositions to apply the Principles of Negative Fairness, Positive Fairness, and Principle of Fair Negotiation. On the one hand, the Principle of Negative Fairness holds that we should aim to minimize coercion in the world, setting costs aside – which supports killing one person in a trolley case to save the many. On the other hand, however, as we have just seen, Rightness as Fairness requires us in other cases (in medical ethics) to develop dispositions against sacrificing the few for the many. Consequently, Rightness as Fairness holds that when we encounter trolley cases – cases which we virtually never encounter, unlike medical ethics cases, which physicians and patients do face at times – we should be pulled in two directions (the Principle of Negative Fairness pulling us in the direction of killing one to save many, virtues of fairness pulling us in the direction of not doing so). And indeed, notice that this is how we encounter such cases. We are pulled in two directions, wanting to minimize the number of people killed while at the same time feeling an aversion to doing so. Consequently, when we imagine trolley cases, it is unclear how a fair negotiation (in conformity with the Principle of Fair Negotiation) might go. Since, on the one hand, a negotiation in such an awful situation might lead to five people 'outvoting' the one in favor of their lives, Rightness as Fairness allows that killing one to save five could be right. At the same time, however, since such a negotiation has not occurred – since society has never negotiated clear norms about what to do in such cases – Rightness as Fairness implies that the opposite could be true as well. As such, Rightness as Fairness generates an indeterminate result for trolley cases: it does not give a firm answer as to whether killing one person to save five is right in a trolley case, because this is not something human beings have negotiated. Finally, Rightness as Fairness explains why our intuitions are more strongly against killing one person in the 'Push the Man' case than in the 'Pull the Switch' case. Because physically assaulting people has a distinct tendency to be unfair (assaulting people rarely minimizes coercion in the real world), human beings have negotiated norms against assault, and should internalize those norms as virtues of fairness, according to Rightness as Fairness. Consequently, when we imagine the 'Push the Man' case, Rightness as Fairness entails that we should be more opposed to it than the 'Pull the Switch' case – while still holding that it is indeterminate whether one should push the man (since again, clear norms for this case have never been negotiated).

As such, Rightness as Fairness provides an analysis of the trolley cases that coheres with our initial reactions to them (namely, that there doesn't appear to be a good option in either case, but that pushing the man in front of the trolley seems particularly abhorrent). In addition to holding that it is presently morally indeterminate what should be done in such cases (which, again, sits well with our present judgments), Rightness as Fairness also provides a method for potentially resolving such cases. It entails that if we want to know what is right in various trolley cases, we need to collectively negotiate norms for them, much as how we have done in medical ethics and other areas of law. We need to settle and codify norms through a fair procedure if we want a determinate answer to the trolley cases. Importantly, however, Rightness as Fairness allows that it may be right for us never to actually negotiate this. Since the trolley cases are virtually never encountered, and collectively deliberating to codified norms would be costly (requiring us to spend time, energy, and other resources to deliberate and reach an agreement), Rightness as Fairness allows us to collectively negotiate never settling trolley cases and leaving their moral status indeterminate – which, essentially, is what we have done (we are uncertain about trolley cases because we have never negotiated norms for them, and we have never negotiated norms because they are so rare). Of course, this would not be the case if real-world circumstances were to arise that (Heaven forbid) made encountering trolley cases more likely.

Finally, consider the case of torture. Rightness as Fairness produces compelling results here as well. Much of the applied ethics literature on torture focuses on 'ticking bomb' cases, where the likely costs and benefits of torture are clear (in the standard case, the only way to prevent a bombing is to torture the would-be bomber), and in which the long-term costs in the world are completely abstracted away from. In such highly artificial cases, where just about all costs are set aside beyond the immediate results of the action, Rightness as Fairness provides no determinate result, but rather allows that we should be pulled in two directions: in the direction of torture (vis-à-vis the Principle of Negative Fairness, which would have us minimize the total amount of coercion in the world, which torture might do), and against torture (vis-à-vis the Principle of Virtues of Fairness, since according to this principle we should develop standing dispositions against being unfair to people, which assaulting them usually does). Further, Rightness as Fairness entails that we cannot simply 'read off' whether torture is right in real-world conditions by counting up costs and benefits. Rather, it holds that in order to settle whether torture is ever right in the real-world, we must negotiate an answer to the question through a fair procedure involving all those affected (namely, all people in the world as a whole, since the costs and benefits of torture are vast and wide-reaching), and then obey

194 *Rightness as Fairness*

the results of those negotiations, whatever they may be. But this is not only an intuitively compelling answer: it is the kind of answer the world has already pursued, albeit very imperfectly. We have set up international lawmaking organizations, such as the United Nations, in order to represent citizens around the world and negotiate standards of international laws and norms, including norms concerning torture. Now, of course, two caveats are necessary here. First, international institutions are proxy methods through which we can only approximate fair negotiation between all individuals in the world. Recall that Rightness as Fairness requires us to approximate fair negotiation as closely as we can. Since it is impossible to give every person in the world equal bargaining power over international norms for torture, we can only attempt to come as close to that as possible – which is what international institutions (at least ideally) aim to do. Second, I am not suggesting that institutions such as the United Nations are, as they currently exist, come anywhere close to being fair and equitably responsible to all – and for this very reason, Rightness as Fairness would suggest that we should be wary of simply accepting UN norms. At the same time, given that the UN is arguably the fairest available international lawmaking mechanism in place, Rightness as Fairness suggests that we should provisionally accept its norms and attempt to make the organization fairer in the future. But these too are intuitively compelling results. Many, if not all, of us think UN norms should be provisionally accepted and obeyed for these kinds of reasons, and that the UN should be made as fairer, and indeed, as fair as possible.

3.3 World poverty

Rightness as Fairness also provides a persuasive account of how we should think about world poverty. In his famous article, 'Famine, Affluence, and Morality,' Peter Singer argued that each of us in wealthy, developed nations has a duty to give up our luxuries – luxurious food, large houses, nice cars, etc. – to alleviate world poverty. Singer's argument is based on a general moral principle that he develops through a simple thought-experiment. The thought-experiment is this: you are walking by a shallow pond and witness a person drowning – a person whose life you could save at little cost to yourself. Singer contends that it is obvious that you have a moral duty to help: that this simply reflects the intuitive moral principle that if one can stop something very bad from happening without sacrificing anything of 'comparable moral significance,' one morally ought to do so.[60] Next, Singer contends that this principle establishes (1) that distance does not matter, so it does not matter if the harm one could prevent is nearby or halfway across the world, and also (2) that if other people do not do their fair share to stop something very bad from happening, one has a duty to do more than one's fair share.[61] Finally, Singer argues that since world poverty is very bad, we have the power to take action to prevent at least of some of it, and giving up our luxuries is not of comparable moral significance to the lives we might save, we all have a duty to give up our luxuries to alleviate world poverty.

Many philosophers have resisted Singer's argument on various grounds, two of which Rightness as Fairness verifies. First, some have objected to Singer's notion of 'comparative moral significance.' For although Singer might not think that giving up most of our luxuries is of comparable moral significance to alleviating world poverty, this does not seem obvious to critics. In particular, it seems to many that our ability to simply live our lives – our ability to enjoy the fruits of our hard work, among other things – is of great moral significance, perhaps even more than saving people from world poverty, since our perspective of being entitled to the money and luxuries we earn arguably plays a critical role in incentivizing economic production: the very kind of production that has given us wealth to give to charity.[62] Second, some have argued that Singer's argument involves a pernicious form of 'rampant moralism' – assuming, very implausibly, that we have a duty to prevent bad things from happening regardless of context (Kekes, for instance, argues that moral commonsense strongly suggests that context is critical: it matters whether people are responsible for their bad situations, whether they can take action to alleviate their own misfortunes, whether they want outside assistance, and so on – none of which Singer addresses[63]).

Rightness as Fairness corroborates both critiques. According to Rightness as Fairness, we cannot determine whether we have obligations to alleviate world poverty – and, if so, what the scope of those obligations are – through mere reflection on what is 'of comparable moral significance.' Indeed, Rightness as Fairness holds that Singer errs, just as trolley case theorists err, precisely by focusing on isolated 'test cases' (namely, what we should do when walking by a person drowning in a shallow pond). First, whereas a person drowning in a shallow pond presumably wants help, it is not at all clear that members of impoverished nations want help from outsiders (particularly given that outside 'help' may change their lives in ways they do not want, resulting in significant changes such as moving them from rural farms into urban environments – which may be serious costs[64]). Second, whereas the costs of helping someone from a pond are simple and limited (getting one's clothes wet, or being late for an appointment) the total costs of attempting to alleviate world poverty are uncertain, and may involve creating even more poverty, political corruption, and other negative outcomes.[65] Rightness as Fairness thus holds that in order to determine whether and to what extent we have duties to alleviate world poverty, we must engage in fair negotiation taking into account the real costs and benefits of alleviating poverty in order to arrive at an answer as to whether the costs of giving up most of our wealth to alleviate world poverty are 'comparable' to the costs of not taking action. In other words, according to Rightness as Fairness, whether a cost is 'comparable' is not something that can be settled 'from on high' by a philosopher. It is something that must be fairly negotiated by real people, in the real-world, given their actual lives and the costs as they encounter them.

This, I submit, is a convincing analysis. Rightness as Fairness does not give us a 'pat' answer as to whether and to what extent we should seek to alleviate world poverty. Rather, it presents a method for determining what our duties are, and at what cost. The method, specifically, is to set up international negotiating institutions and procedures that approximate a fair method for (A) determining the best methods for helping people if they indeed want to be helped (in line with the Principle of Positive Fairness), and for (B) distributing costs. And although the world is currently doing this in a very imperfect way – through international institutions and organizations negotiating 'fair trade' agreements, and so on – the fact we are attempting to address issues of poverty and economic inequality in such a manner sits well with Rightness as Fairness. Moral rightness is about negotiating our duties in the real-world, with real people, through as fair of a process as possible.

3.4 Distribution of scarce medical resources

Rightness as Fairness has similarly convincing implications for cases in biomedical ethics – for instance, the issue of how to distribute scarce medical resources such as hospital beds or transplantable organs.

Biomedical ethicists have formulated and defended many different answers to how scarce resources should be distributed, including:[66]

1. Scarce resources should be given to those 'first in line.'
2. Scarce resources should be utilized in whichever manner maximizes average Quality-of-Life-Years (QALYs), or patients most likely to use the resources best.
3. Scarce resources should be diverted to those most in need (most serious cases).

4. Scarce resources should be diverted to those most deserving of them (those who have made good life choices and/or have the greatest social value, viz. 'VIPs,' parents, etc.).

All of these answers, however, seem to have problems. For instance, if a scarce resource (e.g., a transplantable organ) is given to those first in line, people in greater need may die (a person first in line may be able to live three years without the organ, whereas a person later in line may only be able to live until next week). Similarly, if scarce resources are utilized to maximize QALYs, such a policy would seem to wrongly discriminate against the elderly and unhealthy, since younger, healthier patients can be expected to benefit more from scarce resources. Giving to those most in need, however – the elderly and most unhealthy – would seem to waste important resources (diverting organs to people who are likely to die relatively soon anyway, possibly leaving patients who are more likely to live without the organs necessary to survive). Finally, of course, diverting scarce resources to the 'more deserving' – to parents over non-parents, wealthy or powerful 'VIPs' over the poor – seems wrongly discriminatory.

Rightness as Fairness provides a telling and nuanced answer. According to Rightness as Fairness, there (once again) is no simple answer: instead, morality requires us to settle the issue through a fair deliberative process that treats all stakeholders equitably. Notice that this is how we already aim to resolve such dilemmas in practice. In addition to having ethics committees with representatives of stakeholders that deliberate on how scarce resources are to be utilized, we also have a broadly fair democratic process for arriving at legislation to govern the use of scarce resources. Although ethics committees and the democratic process are far from perfectly fair in practice, Rightness as Fairness directs us to aim to make them fairer, and to then abide by the results of their deliberations. Finally, insofar as all of the aforementioned answers to the scarce resources issue single out particular stakeholders to the detriment of others ('first in line' is to the maximum advantage of those first in line, 'maximize QALYs' is to the maximum advantage of those who stand to make the best use of scarce resources, etc.), Rightness as Fairness plausibly entails a fair compromise between all of these options. Specifically, it suggests:

1. Setting aside some resources (viz. X number of vital organs) for those 'first in line.'
2. Setting aside some resources to maximize QALYs.
3. Setting aside some resources for those most in need.

4. Setting aside some resources for those that are the 'most deserving.'
5. Etc.
6. Where the amount of resources distributed to each class of persons is negotiated broadly in proportion to the number of individuals in each stakeholder group and the relative strength of their interests (because people tend to have much stronger interests in avoiding death than other things – including 'being first in line' or 'deserving' organs – such negotiations should presumably prioritize saving lives to some extent over these other considerations).

A fair compromise between all of these answers is intuitively fair and right. We commonly recognize, for instance, that some people – the President of the United States, parents of young children – have a unique sort of claim to scarce medical resources in light of their responsibilities and accomplishments. However, we also commonly recognize that medical resources should not merely be directed to the most deserving, and indeed, that even people who have made poor life choices – smokers, drug-users, alcohol abusers – have lives worth saving, and should therefore have some claim to scarce resources (though Rightness as Fairness allows that a fair process of public deliberation may see fit to divert smaller amounts of scarce resources to such people, on account of their poor life decisions), etc.

As such, Rightness as Fairness provides an illuminating answer to applied ethical issues regarding scarce resources. First, it entails – in line with commonsense – that there is no simple, one size fits all answer to the question of what ought to be done in cases of scarce resources. Second, it requires us to arrive at an answer to specific issues (how to distribute organs, hospital beds, etc.) through fair deliberative processes (e.g., ethics committees comprised by stakeholder representatives). Third, it entails that such a fair process should result in a substantially fair conclusion – a fair compromise between existing answers, given that each such answer (first in line, maximize QALYs, etc.) favors some stakeholders over others. I believe that all of these implications are clearly plausible, and indeed, commonsense.

3.5 The ethical treatment of animals

Finally, let us consider the ethical treatment of nonhuman animals. Although Rightness as Fairness once again holds that there are no simple answers, it does lend support to two answers – responsible, compassionate animal husbandry and conservation efforts – over others, including vegetarianism, veganism, and current factory farming practices. Allow me to explain.

On the one hand, animals in nature face all kinds of coercive horrors, such as starvation and disease. According to the Principle of Negative Fairness, these natural horrors are a moral issue: we should care about the coercive horrors that animals experience in nature. Simply leaving animals alone in nature – however much animal advocates may like to romanticize it – is, on Rightness as Fairness, not fair to animals. Just as there is nothing fair about leaving fellow human beings to suffer or die from starvation or disease, so too is there nothing fair about leaving animals to suffer and die from such things in nature. On the other hand, prevailing 'factory farming' methods – methods which treat animals cruelly, allowing them to live only short, miserable lives – are also unfair to animals, as animal rights advocates point out. Such methods simply ignore animals' lives and well-being, and use them merely for our own purposes (for cheap consumption). Finally, although it might be nice if human beings had the time, energy, and resources to save every diseased or starving animal from the horrors of nature, this would be unfair to us: it would require us to spend our lives – day and night – being dedicated to 'saving animals from nature,' regardless of the costs we might have to thereby incur.

How, then, does Rightness as Fairness entail that we morally ought to treat animals? The answer is that we have a duty to deliberate in a manner that is fair to us and to animals about how to advance their welfare and our own. On the one hand, human beings tend to enjoy consuming animal products; such consumption is deeply embedded in many cultures and traditions around the world (I say this, as an aside, as someone who lived a vegetarian lifestyle for the better part of a decade). On the other hand, animals have an interest in living comfortable lives, protected from the many horrors of nature (starvation or disease). We can advance both sets of interests – treating human beings and animals fairly – by engaging in both (A) compassionate animal husbandry, giving farm animals comfortable and reasonably long lives on pastures, while ultimately consuming them for the sake of profits that not only benefit human beings but also animals (insofar as profits from animal agriculture may in turn be used to give more animals decent, comfortable lives in a humane animal agriculture industry), and (B) negotiating conservation efforts to protect wild animals and their habitats (for although we may not reasonably be able to help wild animals avoid disease, we can help them enjoy more comfortable and plentiful lives by protecting them from human encroachment and interference, and ought to do so insofar as it is fair to us). These I believe, are sound conclusions. Although Rightness as Fairness does not entail veganism or vegetarianism – as these practices, while not killing animals for human purposes, simply leave farm animals to suffer from natural sources of coercion and deprive humans of traditional and longstanding means of sustenance – it requires a compassionate approach to the treatment of animals that is, as far as possible, fair to both them and us.

4 Conclusion

This chapter argued that Four Principles of Fairness, and a general analysis of Rightness as Fairness comprised by their conjunction, emerge from the Moral Original Position, the method Chapter 5 argued specifies the Categorical-Instrumental Imperative's requirements. I have argued that morality is a matter of acting fairly in four ways: coercion-avoidance and minimization (the Principle of Negative Fairness), assisting others who would benefit from and desire our assistance (the Principle of Positive Fairness), applying these two principles by way of process of fair negotiation (the Principle of Fair Negotiation), and developing dispositions to conform to these first three principles (the Principle of Virtues of Fairness). Finally, I showed that although Rightness as Fairness does not entail *a priori* answers to many applied ethical questions, it provides compelling moral guidance, as it requires solving moral problems through a process of 'principled fair negotiation' that merges reflection on principles with actual negotiation with others. I argued that this is a compelling picture – providing uniquely attractive answers to moral questions ranging from suicide to trolley cases, torture, and the ethical treatment of animals, providing significant, nuanced guidance – which, I have argued, is precisely what we should expect of a sound moral theory. In real-life, morality is almost never as simple as merely applying some abstract moral principle(s), such as the principle of utility, the categorical imperative, Rossian *prima facie* moral rules, or even virtues of character, to a complex ethical issue. Rather, in real-life, morality is a matter of (1) having correct principles in mind (the Principles of Negative and Positive Fairness), but also (2) negotiating with other people, and other sentient beings, to arrive at fair compromises in cases of conflict, given full (or at least emerging) knowledge of psychological, social, and other empirical facts. Indeed, Rightness as Fairness explains and justifies how we actually go about settling moral problems in the real-world. We do not solve moral problems 'solipsistically,' or merely thinking about moral problems as isolated thinkers. Instead, we set up ethics boards with the aim of giving medical stakeholders a fair say over what ought to be done; we set up governments with the aim of giving citizens a fair say over what ought to be done in their nation; and we set up non-governmental, international organizations with the aim of giving humanity a fair say over moral issues (torture, war, and so on) that potentially affect all of us. Rightness as Fairness therefore provides a compelling new framework for resolving applied moral issues.

7
Libertarian Egalitarian Communitarianism

Chapter 6 argued from the Moral Original Position to the following analysis of moral rightness:

> **Rightness as Fairness:** an action is morally right if and only if it satisfies the Four Principles of Fairness, that is, if and only if it is (A) is morally relevant, (B) has coercion-avoidance and minimization, assisting human and nonhuman sentient beings to achieve interests they cannot best achieve on their own and want assistance in achieving, and the development and expression of settled dispositions to have these ends, as at least tacit ideals, and (C) is in conformity with the outcome of an actual process of fair negotiation approximating all human and sentient beings affected by the action being motivated by the above ideals and having equal bargaining power over how those ideals should be applied factoring in costs, or, if such a process is impossible, the outcome of a hypothetical process approximating the same, where moral relevance is determined recursively, by applying (B) and (C) to the question of whether the action is morally relevant.

This chapter uses this principle to reconcile three traditionally opposed views in political philosophy: libertarianism, egalitarianism, and communitarianism.

Section 1 provides a broad overview of libertarianism, egalitarianism, and communitarianism, their attractive elements, and some common critiques of each. Section 2 then argues that Rightness as Fairness reconciles their attractive elements while correcting each individual view's supposed drawbacks. Specifically, I argue that Rightness as Fairness entails 'Libertarian Egalitarian Communitarianism' – a doctrine which holds (1) that we are all morally required to have quasi-libertarian and egalitarian ideals, but are permitted to balance those ideals against one another and against communitarian considerations, and (2) that justice is a matter of actively negotiating a fair balance of all of the above considerations with others. Finally, Section 3 argues that Libertarian Egalitarian Communitarianism provides a convincing method for resolving a number of longstanding problems in social and political theory and practice: problems concerning (Section 3.1) divisiveness, (Section 3.2) the scope of justice (domestic vs. global, the workplace, family, and so on), and finally, (Section 3.3) the relationship between 'ideal' and 'nonideal theory.'

1 Libertarianism, Egalitarianism, and Communitarianism

A wide range of conceptions of political morality (that is, of what morality requires at the level of politics and governance) have been defended throughout history. We cannot, and need not, discuss them all here. Instead, I want to focus on three influential normative political perspectives, examining them at a broad level. These perspectives are:

Libertarianism: political morality requires minimally coercive political structures protecting human liberty against force and fraud, or roughly, rights to life, liberty, and property.[1]

Egalitarianism: political morality requires 'equalizing' political structures that in some sense afford people 'more equal chances in life.'[2]

Communitarianism: political morality is in some sense a matter of particular community values, not (merely) 'universal' values.[3]

None of these descriptions are intended to be fully comprehensive or exact representations of particular libertarian, egalitarian, or communitarian theories. Rather, they are intended to simply represent, at a broad and general level, the motivating normative notions of each perspective. As we will now see, this suffices for our purposes.

1.1 Libertarianism: attractions and critiques

Although libertarianism comes in many forms,[4] traditional libertarians hold that justice requires the state to (A) prevent coercion (protecting life, liberty, and property) in (B) the least coercive way possible (that is, by way of a 'minimal state'). Although different types of libertarians have different conceptions of what this involves – 'right libertarians' hold that liberty allows people to appropriate natural resources, whereas 'left libertarians' hold that natural resources are common property and appropriation of them is therefore coercive[5] – the relevant point for our purposes is simply as follows: in general, libertarianism is animated by the notion that morality requires political structures to be as 'minimally coercive' as possible.

To its proponents, libertarianism has obvious attractions. First, as Nozick argues, it coheres with one possible (though perhaps mistaken[6]) interpretation of Kant's influential notion of 'respect for humanity': insofar as coercion involves threatening people with harm unless they do something one wants, the libertarian preoccupation with coercion-avoidance can be understood as a commitment to avoid treating people as mere means (as required by Kant's humanity formulation of his categorical imperative).[7] Second, libertarianism coheres with a conception of individual responsibility than strikes many people as attractive: namely, a view that it is good for people to be self-reliant rather than reliant on the state.[8-9] Finally, libertarianism coheres with the thought – perhaps dubious to some, but one often defended nevertheless – that less coercive ways of social and political life (that is, 'free markets') produce higher levels of human happiness more reliably than more coercive ones (in part, because of government corruption and inefficiency).[10-11]

To its opponents, however, libertarianism is unacceptable. First, it is often argued that, far from respecting people in a Kantian sense, libertarianism violates Kant's categorical imperative, leaving people vulnerable to natural coercion (such as disease) and unfair exploitation.[12] Second, libertarianism is often alleged to be a 'heartless' doctrine because it arbitrarily prioritizes self-reliance over other goods, such as the good of helping others to flourish.[13] Third, many argue that libertarianism is excessively individualistic, presupposing a false, 'atomistic' conception of the self that does not, in practice, reliably produce flourishing, happy human beings, but instead results in alienation, crime, selfishness, and other social ills.[14-15]

In short, although libertarianism appears to its proponents to have strong moral attractions, it appears to its critics to wrongly 'fetishize' a certain conception of human liberty over all other things.

1.2 Egalitarianism: attractions and critiques

Like libertarianism, egalitarian political theories also come in many forms. Some egalitarians argue that justice requires a fair distribution of basic rights, liberties, opportunities, income and wealth[16]; others argue that it requires equality of resources,[17] others equality of basic capabilities,[18-19] and so on.[20]

To its proponents, egalitarianism has a number of obvious attractions. First, it is said to embody the intuitive notion – reflected in some interpretations of Kant's ethics – that to truly respect our fellow human beings, we must treat them fairly.[21] Second, it is argued to cohere with the moral intuition possessed by many (though not all) that it is wrong for people's life-prospects to depend on matters of brute luck.[22] Third, it is argued to correct for problems associated with the kind of unbridled concentrations of wealth that libertarian (and other nonegalitarian) forms of governance allow, such as economic exploitation and political instability.[23]

To its opponents, however, egalitarianism is unacceptable. On the one hand, libertarians argue that egalitarianism embodies an unfair form of 'fairness' that forces people to 'cooperate on fair terms,' thus violating each individual's right to liberty (and, by extension, the Kantian notion of respecting each individual as an 'end-in-themselves').[24] On the other hand, communitarians often argue that egalitarianism embodies a false moral universalism and atomistic conception of the self.[25] Further, communitarians often contend that by focusing on equality above all – on things like equal rights, opportunities, and fair distributions of wealth or resources – egalitarianism fails to deal properly with more personal things of value to individuals and communities, such as 'alienation from the political process, unbridled greed, loneliness, urban crime, and high divorce rates.'[26] According to communitarians, other things besides equality – for instance, community values of moral decency, family, and civic obligation – are necessary for people and societies to flourish.[26]

In short, although egalitarianism appears to its proponents to have obvious attractions, it appears to its detractors (libertarian, communitarian, and otherwise) to wrongly fetishize 'equality' above all other things.

1.3 Communitarianism: attractions and critiques

Finally, although communitarianism comes in many forms, it is generally animated by the notion that political morality cannot be properly reduced to any abstract, universal value such as liberty or equality, but must instead 'be found in forms of life and traditions of particular societies and hence can vary from context to context.'[27] Broadly speaking, communitarians hold that political morality may be 'different things in different places,' since morally valuable things like social stability, harmony, and individual flourishing, may differ from community to community, or culture to culture, as different values and ways of life can play important moral roles.

To its proponents, communitarianism's attractions once again seem clear. Many of us care deeply about certain personal and political values – for instance, 'American values' or religious values – and place greater importance on them than more abstract values such as liberty or equality. Indeed, communitarians argue, people in different societies often appear to conceive themselves as reciprocating members of a community that shares certain cultural or religious values,[28] as evinced by the fact that people in different societies often have collectively unique views about political morality (for instance, about what justice requires, what rights people should be seen to have, and so on).[27] Finally, communitarians often emphasize that such shared values and ends are the 'glue' that binds societies together – that societies modeled around nothing more than abstract notions of liberty or equality are likely to fall apart, or otherwise face instability, due to not being based on substantive, shared values beyond those abstract ones.[29]

To its critics, however, communitarianism is fundamentally – and objectionably – illiberal, failing to afford due concern for human liberty or equality.[27,30] This concern is clearly illustrated by the reaction to the communitarian Michael Walzer's sympathetic characterization of traditional Indian caste system a social and political system 'where the social meanings are integrated and hierarchical.'[31] As Bell writes, 'Not surprisingly, few readers were inspired by this example of non-liberal justice (not to mention the fact that many contemporary Indian thinkers view the caste system as an unfortunate legacy of the past that Indians should strive hard to overcome).'[27]

In short, while communitarianism arguably has some attractive elements, its critics allege that it wrongly prioritizes 'shared ends' and 'community values' over other things – specifically, liberty and/or equality – that matter more.

2 The case for Libertarian Egalitarian Communitarianism

Since Rightness as Fairness consists of the conjunction of Four Principles of Fairness (as we saw in Chapter 6), we can determine what Rightness as Fairness requires in political domains by applying each of its components to social and political questions. Let us begin, then, with:

The Principle of Negative Fairness: all of our morally relevant actions should have as a guiding ideal, setting all costs aside, avoiding and minimizing coercion in all its forms (coercion resulting from intentional acts, natural forces, false beliefs, and so on), for all human and nonhuman sentient beings, for its own sake.

This principle has a decidedly libertarian flavor. Libertarians hold that human life should be as minimally coercive as possible. Yet this is broadly what the Principle of Negative Fairness holds: namely, that all things being equal, we are all morally required to have and pursue coercion-avoidance and minimization as an ideal. Accordingly, Rightness as Fairness entails that libertarianism, broadly speaking, is founded on a correct moral ideal: we all should want the political domain to be as minimally coercive as possible. At the same time, however, the Principle of Negative Fairness also confirms a long-alleged criticism of libertarianism: that it wrongly prioritizes a certain conception of coercion-minimization (minimization of coercion by fellow human beings) above all else. First, contrary to traditional libertarianism, the Principle of Negative Fairness entails that natural coercion (coercion as a result of disease, starvation, and so on) is just as important to avoid and minimize as intentional human coercion. Because the best means for preventing natural coercion (enabling people to survive diseases, not starve, and so on) might be some amount of human coercion – namely, anti-libertarian social programs (such as state-mandated health insurance, welfare programs, and the like) – the Principle of Negative Fairness, despite its coherence with libertarianism's anti-coercion moral roots, nevertheless allows that the best overall means for advancing this very value (for 'protecting human liberty') might *not* be libertarianism. Second, recall that the Principle of Negative Fairness is only recognized in Rightness as Fairness as a single moral ideal – one that can be permissibly weighed against another ideal (the Principle of Positive Fairness) as well as against other costs (vis-à-vis the Principle of Fair Negotiation). Rightness as Fairness therefore entails that (1) although political morality requires us to all have a quasi-libertarian concern for coercion-avoidance and minimization as a moral ideal, (2) it is perfectly permissible for us to weigh this ideal against other concerns, and indeed, (3) we should negotiate a fair balance between that ideal and other concerns.

In short, Rightness as Fairness to a certain extent verifies libertarianism's moral foundation: the notion that morality requires us to have and pursue coercion-avoidance and minimization as a moral ideal. At the same, time, however, it also verifies critiques of libertarianism that allege libertarianism to wrongly prioritize the reduction of human-caused coercion above all else.

Now let us turn to Rightness as Fairness' second and third principles – principles which we will now see have a decidedly egalitarian spirit. Let us begin with:

> **The Principle of Positive Fairness:** all of our morally relevant actions should have as a guiding ideal, setting all costs aside, assisting all human and non-sentient beings in achieving interests they cannot best achieve on their own and want assistance in achieving, for its own sake.

On its own, this principle is not opposed to libertarianism. Indeed, it is perfectly consistent with the idea that we might best help others in a libertarian political setting – say, through charity rather than coercive, state-sanctioned programs (such as welfare, Social Security, and so on). Still, the Principle of Positive Fairness nevertheless is egalitarian in spirit, as it requires each of us to have and pursue, as a moral ideal, helping all other human beings and sentient creatures who would benefit from and desire our assistance. Furthermore, the Principle of Positive Fairness takes on a much stronger egalitarian flavor when conjoined with Rightness as Fairness' third principle:

> **The Principle of Fair Negotiation:** whether an action is morally relevant, and how the Principles of Negative and Positive Fairness and Virtues of Fairness should be applied factoring in costs, should be settled through an actual process of fair negotiation guided by the Principles of Negative Fairness, Positive Fairness, and Virtues of Fairness, where all human and nonhuman sentient beings affected by the action are afforded equal bargaining power to the extent that such a process can be approximated, and to the extent that cannot be, through a hypothetical process approximating the same, for its own sake.

This principle, after all, requires us to fairly negotiate how the Principles of Negative and Positive Fairness should be pursued or balanced against one another, given potential conflicts between them as well as other costs associated with pursuing them. Furthermore, the Principle of Fair Negotiation identifies fair negotiation (which we are morally required to pursue) in terms of (approximating) equal bargaining power. Let us now think about what this involves.

One of the primary motivating ideas of egalitarian theories of justice is that without fair distribution of rights, liberties, opportunities, income and wealth, capabilities, or resources, the political realm as a whole – lawmaking and the like – will be unfair, dominated by those with more of the above than others (specifically, the wealthy).[16-20] Since the Principle of Fair Negotiation requires the Principles of Negative and Positive Fairness to be applied through a fair negotiating process – and political morality just is a matter of determining which form of government and laws morally ought to exist – Rightness as Fairness entails that political morality must approximate a fair bargaining process guided by the aforementioned ideals. It entails, in other words, that politics – and governance – must aim to approximate a fair process. However, since libertarianism in principle permits unlimited concentrations of wealth, and wealth traditionally confers greater bargaining power in politics, it follows that (1) although Rightness as Fairness is predicated upon a quasi-libertarian ideal of negative fairness, it is (2) more egalitarian than libertarian on the whole (since, again, it requires politics to approximate equal bargaining power). Some might worry that if the above argument correct, Rightness as Fairness requires some form of communism, or completely equal distribution of opportunities, wealth, and other resources (since, one might suggest, it is only then that all in society might have truly equal bargaining power). However, this does not follow for two reasons. First, history strongly suggests that attempts to implement 'communism' in practice (the USSR, and so on) tend to lead to greater imbalances of bargaining power and outright violations of negative and positive fairness (such as starvation and political persecution), than liberal-democratic regimes. Second, insofar as large numbers of human beings have interests in having property of their own and 'working hard to get ahead' (earning more wealth for greater talent, effort, and so on) – interests which are consistent with negative and positive fairness – and the Principle of Fair Negotiation is a principle for negotiating costs of pursuing negative and positive fairness in terms of individuals' actual interests (costs, again, are determined relative to each individual's preferences), the most equal system of bargaining that enables people to negotiate their actual interests with others need not involve perfect equality of wealth or other resources, especially if other alternatives of equalizing political bargaining power (such as campaign finance laws, and so on) are available.

Finally, insofar as the Principle of Fair Negotiation permits the Principles of Negative and Positive Fairness to be balanced against other costs, Rightness as Fairness permits a certain amount of fair sensitivity to communitarian concerns: it permits people to negotiate how coercion-avoidance and minimization (negative fairness) and assistance to others

210 *Rightness as Fairness*

(positive fairness) are to be weighed against costs such as crime, alienation, cultural cohesion, the maintenance of shared values, and so on.

Rightness as Fairness therefore entails a doctrine we might call 'Libertarian Egalitarian Communitarianism.' According to this doctrine, people in any political domain are required to:

1. Have and pursue a quasi-libertarian preference for coercion-avoidance and minimization as a common ideal (negative fairness).
2. Have and pursue a quasi-egalitarian preference for assisting others who would benefit and desire assistance as a common ideal (positive fairness).
3. Negotiate, through social and political processes that approximate equal bargaining power, how these ideals are to be weighed against one another, and against other costs, including communitarian concerns.

While this doctrine might not satisfy traditional libertarians, egalitarians, or communitarians who are strictly committed to their views, I believe it is a compelling picture of political morality for several reasons.

First, it accounts for and explains why so many philosophers and laypeople are attracted to libertarianism, egalitarianism, or communitarianism. Indeed, consider the fact that liberal-democratic politics in much of the world – including US History – has been consistently characterized by vacillations between 'small government conservatism,' 'large government progressivism,' and 'concern for community values': a kind of 'ongoing conversation' and public negotiation over precisely how to balance 'liberty,' 'equality,' and cultural values. Nowhere is this clearer, perhaps, than the US during the Great Depression. Prior to the Depression, the small government policies of Calvin Coolidge (which made the regulatory state 'thin to the point of invisibility'[32]) enjoyed enormous popularity,[33] leading to the 'Roaring Twenties,' a period of wealth and prosperity. However, this period of immense deregulation was soon followed by the Depression – and when US President Herbert Hoover advocated for a noncoercive, 'volunteerist' approach to helping the unemployed – through charity rather than government programs[34] – the result was a highly disenchanted and dissatisfied public. Hoover's failure to take governmental action in order to assist the ailing American people directly paved the path for the election of his predecessor, Franklin Delano Roosevelt, who introduced a wide variety of government programs that have survived to the present day (such as Social Security). What we see, in other words, in American history is akin to an ongoing balancing act between 'coercion-avoidance' (small government) and 'assistance' (large government). Finally, 'community values' also often enter the political picture, both in economics (where people often argue for 'protecting local businesses') and on social issues. Indeed, debates over laws regarding subjects ranging from abortion, to gun control, and healthcare often involve appeals to all three things: freedom from coercion, assisting people who would benefit from and desire assistance, and community values. Public debate over abortion, for instance, has revolved around whether women's interests in freedom from coercion (control over their own bodies) and equal rights (an equal right to make medical decisions pertaining to their own bodies) should outweigh a developing fetus' interests in the same (continued life), as well as cultural values of personal responsibility and compassion (opponents of abortion often advocate 'a culture of respect for life'). Similarly, debates over gun control have focused on whether the liberty to own guns (a quasi-libertarian aim) should be outweighed by the rights of all to live free of gun violence (a quasi-egalitarian and/or communitarian aim). Rightness as Fairness explains why these debates occur, as it holds that political morality is a matter of fairly negotiating the proper balance between these competing ideals and costs. Rightness as Fairness thus provides a normative picture for how these debates, and political negotiation, should play out. According to Rightness as Fairness, political morality requires us to settle these kinds of issues – issues about what justice requires – subject to conditions (1) –(3): people must be mutually committed to the values of negative and positive fairness, and realize a political system that provides people with as close-to-equal bargaining power as possible for negotiating fair solutions.

Second, in addition to explaining these features of public political life, Rightness as Fairness provides an attractive method for resolving political disagreements. As we have seen, it entails that in many political debates, all sides have legitimate moral concerns (those who want to protect gun ownership, for instance, argue that gun ownership is supported on anti-coercion grounds, as guns enable people to protect themselves, whereas people who want to restrict gun ownership point to similar grounds, namely, protecting people from gun violence). Consequently, Rightness as Fairness holds that political morality – including justice – is ultimately something that no single theorist can write out in a book or political tract. Through the doctrine of Libertarian Egalitarian Communitarianism, Rightness as Fairness holds that there is no 'one size fits all' answer to what political morality or justice requires. It holds instead that these issues must be negotiated, in real time, by real people, given real costs, so long as the negotiation (public debate and political process) is (A) oriented around correct ideals (of coercion-avoidance/minimization and assistance), and (B) affords people broadly equal bargaining power. But these are commonly held ideals – ones often trumpeted by proponents of democracy, who maintain that democracy itself, provided it gives people fair bargaining power, is intrinsically fair: a method for forging just institutions and laws through democratic debate and negotiation.[35]

3 Additional advantages

I believe we can further explore the attractiveness of Libertarian Egalitarian Communitarianism by examining its implications for (Section 3.1) the morality of social and political debate, (Section 3.2) the scope of justice, and finally, (Section 3.3) 'ideal' and 'nonideal theory.'

3.1 (Qualified) fair negotiation over divisiveness

It is often remarked in popular media how divisive modern political debate has become: that is, how unwilling different sides of social and political debates often appear to be to 'talk to' or negotiate with one another. While such divisiveness has probably always been a significant part of politics, it is nevertheless distressing. When it comes to many issues – such as the size and proper role of government, abortion-rights, gun control, and so on – debates often appear to come down to matters of 'fundamental disagreement,' with each side denying the other side's moral legitimacy in ways that do not seem to permit discussion or negotiation. Indeed, political debates often seem to devolve into 'talking-points' in which each side simply reasserts their views and fails to acknowledge the other side's moral legitimacy, as when abortion opponents point to a fetal 'right to life' and pro-abortion advocates point to a 'woman's right to choose.'

These sorts of 'fundamental disagreements' – that is, flat denials the moral legitimacy of the 'other side's concerns' – do not merely occur in public political debate. They also occur in political philosophy, with different sides typically beginning from fundamentally different premises (libertarians appealing to liberty, egalitarians to equality, and so on).[36] Furthermore, to the extent such fundamental disagreements do occur, it is unclear how to productively proceed. Since philosophical arguments have to be based on premises, when two sides fundamentally disagree over premises there appears to be little that either side can do to make headway with respect to the other. For instance, if we look at contemporary debates between libertarians and egalitarians, 'in-group' debates (each group debating among its own members) appear far more common than 'cross-debates' between libertarians and egalitarians (although cross-debates certainly do occur as well).[11,37-38]

It is important to note that Libertarian Egalitarian Communitarianism does not maintain that all forms of divisiveness are wrong. Indeed, because it holds that the Principles of Negative and Positive Fairness are objectively correct moral ideals, it permits denying the legitimacy of arguments that are directly contrary to those ideals (for instance, slavery or racism). However, because Rightness as Fairness also holds (in the Principle of Fair Negotiation) that morality requires people who share ideals of negative and positive fairness to negotiate with one another, it entails that some forms of divisiveness – namely (A) unwillingness to recognize the legitimacy of arguments based on those ideals, and (B) unwillingness to negotiate fairly with people who share those ideals – are immoral. Allow me to illustrate.

Consider again debates over abortion. Both sides can plausibly point to the Principles of Negative and Positive Fairness in support of their position. Anti-abortion advocates want to protect fetuses from coercion (namely, death as a result of abortion). Pro-abortion advocates, however, argue that disallowing abortion would be coercive to women (since it would coerce them into carrying a child to term against their will). While Rightness as Fairness does not require either side to accept the other side's overall position – since, on Rightness as Fairness, 'coercion-conflicts' cannot be settled on principle – it does require both sides to (A) recognize the moral legitimacy of the values appealed to (protection of sentient fetuses and women from coercion), and (B) be willing to determine an answer through a fair political process. It allows, in other words, for moral disagreement (for both sides to keep advocating for their favored balance of negative and positive fairness against costs), while at the same time requiring both sides to accept the legitimacy of a fair political process to arrive at social policy.

I believe this feature of Libertarian Egalitarian Communitarianism to be particularly compelling. Political divisiveness is often publicly decried for more or less the reasons given by Rightness as Fairness: namely, that when two sides both have arguments founded in plausible moral ideals (of coercion-avoidance or assistance), simply denying the legitimacy of the other side's concerns amounts to a kind of unfair and counterproductive unwillingness to listen or negotiate. Although, again, Libertarian Communitarian Egalitarianism does not require people to agree on moral or social issues (such as abortion, gun control, domestic surveillance, and so on) – since it recognizes the permissibility of people negotiating in favor of different answers – it does require a mutual willingness to (A) recognize the moral legitimacy of arguments on both sides (provided the arguments are at least plausibly based on the ideals of negative and positive fairness), and (B) engage in and respect fair political processes and the answers arrived through such processes (rather than, say, physically intimidating or assaulting members of the other side). In short, although Libertarian Communitarian Egalitarianism permits disagreement, it prohibits social or political 'hard-headedness,' intimidation, and non-cooperation (at least, again, in cases where both sides are plausibly motivated by correct ideals).

3.2 Resolving the scope and requirements of justice

Through Libertarian Egalitarian Communitarianism, Rightness as Fairness also provides a compelling new method for resolving disputes about the nature and scope of justice. There are currently many ongoing debates over the 'scope' of justice. First, there are debates over domestic, international, and global justice. For instance, some argue that justice only applies within nation-states, and that there is no such thing as international or global justice.[39] Others, so-called 'cosmopolitan egalitarians,' argue instead that justice is fundamentally global: that all human interactions should be governed by principles of fairness, and that such cosmopolitan principles of justice should determine which matters of justice are properly thought of as 'domestic' issues within the purview of nation-states' governments.[40] Next, there is 'liberal nationalism,' the view – famously defended by Rawls in *The Law of Peoples* – that liberal standards of justice only hold within nation-states, and toleration for certain types of illiberal regimes is required internationally.[41] And so on. Second, there are debates over whether justice primarily concerns the 'basic structure' of society,[42] or whether it also applies to individuals,[43–45] families,[46–47] the workplace,[48] religious organizations,[49] and so on.

Perhaps the most notable thing about the major views here – aside from the fact that there is little agreement on which of the views is correct – is that all of them attempt to settle the question of 'jurisdiction' or 'scope' at the level of theory: that is, on principled terms one might settle in a book or journal article. Conversely, Libertarian Egalitarian Communitarianism holds – much more plausibly I believe – that the 'scope' or 'jurisdiction' of justice must be negotiated in an ongoing fashion by the world's people and the societies they constitute. Note that on the one hand, Libertarian Egalitarian Communitarianism stipulates that there are ideals that all people in the world should possess, setting all costs aside: ideals of coercion-minimization (in line with negative fairness) and assisting other human and nonhuman sentient creatures (in line with positive fairness). As such, it entails that social and political systems that are not plausibly motivated by these ideals – such as political systems that aim to dominate or coerce women, members of certain religions, and so on – are fundamentally immoral. On the other hand, however, Libertarian Egalitarian Communitarianism also contends that when it comes to social and political systems that are broadly inspired by ideals of negative and positive fairness – as, I would argue, many modern democratic systems are, as such forms of governance are typically defined by (i) protections against coercion (rights to free speech, association, and so on), and (ii) forms of governmental assistance (Social Security programs, and so on) – justice cannot simply be read off from abstract principles. Rather, when it comes to such systems (those broadly based on ideals of negative and positive fairness), justice is something that must be negotiated in a fair, ongoing fashion, including the extent to which justice is domestic, global, familial, work-related, and so on. In short, Rightness as Fairness entails that issues concerning the scope and nature of justice must instead be answered by real people, given the actual state of the world in which they find themselves, through ongoing negotiation.

This, I believe, is an intuitive notion. Since there are potential costs to global justice (imposing global principles on societies restricts their capacities to 'self-determine'), domestic justice (not imposing global principles on societies increases their capacities to impose costs on citizens – including minorities – that they may find oppressive), restricting justice to the basic structure of society (not extending justice to family relations can give rise to forms of domination within the family), extending principles of justice to the family (the more a family is regulated by principles not of their choosing, the more society gets to dictate how we interact with one another), and so on, Rightness as Fairness correctly entails that there is no 'pat answer' as to what exactly justice concerns. Rather, morality requires us to negotiate with others answers to these very questions. And in many respects, this is already something that people (and societies) often do. For instance, industrialized and developing nations around the world are continually negotiating – through the United Nations, human rights treaties, the World Trade Organization, and so on – whether and to what extent justice is 'global.' Rightness as Fairness simply adds that – contrary to what is often the case (since international institutions are notoriously imbalanced) – these questions should be settled *fairly*, through fair rather than unfair negotiation.

3.3 Resolving the ideal-nonideal theory distinction

Rightness as Fairness also has critical – and convincing – implications for a matter of intense debate in political philosophy: the debate over 'ideal and nonideal theory.'[50] Historically most major political theories have focused on 'ideal theory,' that is, on defining fully just or legitimate social and political systems. In Plato's *Republic*, for instance, Socrates famously defends a conception of a 'just society' ruled by philosopher kings. Similarly, in *A Theory of Justice*, John Rawls defends an egalitarian analysis of a fully fair, 'well-ordered' society: one whose members and institutions strictly comply with principles of fairness. Next, in *Anarchy, State, and Utopia*, Robert Nozick argues that only a fully just libertarian state could come about without ever violating anyone's moral rights. And so on.

Many critics, however – myself included – have argued that a focus on ideal theory alone inappropriately ignores 'nonideal theory,' or what justice requires in social-political conditions that fall short of such ideals.[51-55] As I and many others have argued, it is mistake to think that one can use an ideal theory of justice to simply 'read off' what justice requires in a nonideal world. For while an ideal theory may (or may not) describe a fully just system – and it is always open to question which ideal theory is correct, or whether any ideal theory is correct – deviations from ideals impose costs on people that are, in principle, never taken into account in ideal theory.

There have been three broad types of responses to these critiques. First, some theorists have attempted to extend ideal theories to the nonideal world.[51] Second, some have argued that ideal theory is a mistake altogether, and that political philosophy should focus on nonideal theory alone.[52-55] Third, some have suggested that there may be no coherent way to distinguish between ideal and nonideal theory – that every social system, no matter how 'ideal' it may be in some respects, must necessarily be 'nonideal' in other respects.[56]

Rightness as Fairness synthesizes all three views. First, it entails that there are moral ideals – of coercion-avoidance and minimization, and assistance – that should guide all moral and political theorizing as well as social-political institutions. Secondly, however, Rightness as Fairness holds that we cannot usefully separate these ideals from the issue of costs. In just about any realistic social or political setting, there will be conflicts between the Principles of Negative and Positive Fairness, as well as costs associated with pursuing the their ideals. For instance, coercion as a result of forces of nature – such as disease – are likely to exist in any realistic social-political system, and minimizing such coercion is likely to involve costs on people and institutions. Thus, while Rightness as Fairness affirms moral (and, by extension, political) ideals, it does not allow us to formulate a 'fully just society' that abstracts away from conflicts between these ideals. Rather, it holds that in all realistically possible situations, human beings in social and political systems must negotiate, as fairly as possible, how those costs and conflicts are to be resolved or distributed. In other words, Rightness as Fairness entails that political theory and practice must always simultaneously include ideal and nonideal elements: moral 'ideals' and negotiation of 'nonideal' costs. Rightness as Fairness thus verifies 'ideal theory' in a sense (it holds that there are two genuine ideals that should always guide social and political philosophy), while maintaining that these ideals cannot be isolated from 'nonideal theory' (or fair negotiation) as far as we are concerned with theorizing about real-world 'just institutions.' According to Rightness as Fairness, what constitutes a just institution depends partly on ideals (the Principles of Negative and Positive Fairness) and partly on nonideal costs (to be settled via the Principle of Fair Negotiation). This is, I submit, a compelling picture. The idea that we can formulate a 'perfectly just society' is a mistake. There are always 'nonideal costs' associated with social and political institutions that must be negotiated in an ongoing basis.

4 Conclusion

We saw in Chapter 6 that Rightness as Fairness comprises a compelling analysis of moral rightness. We have now seen that it has similarly illuminating implications for political philosophy by synthesizing three traditionally opposed political philosophies – libertarianism, egalitarianism, and communitarianism. Specifically, Rightness as Fairness shows how each perspective is inspired by legitimate moral ideals that are taken too far, and how morality requires us to negotiate how opposing ideals should be weighed against one another and other costs. Finally, we have seen that Rightness as Fairness provides promising and even transformative guidance for social and political debates, encouraging negotiation over divisiveness and providing a new framework for determining the proper scope of justice.

8
Evaluating Rightness as Fairness

We are now in a position to evaluate Rightness as Fairness using the seven principles of theory selection defended in Chapter 1. This chapter argues that there are general reasons to believe that Rightness as Fairness has significant advantages on these principles over other moral theories. Although I will offer broad rather than detailed comparisons (given space constraints), I believe the arguments I provide in favor of Rightness as Fairness justify serious consideration of the theory in future philosophical work.

1 Firmer foundations

Chapter 1 argued that, above all, a sound theory of morality should be based on Firm Foundations – on observations that virtually all observers recognize to be clearly, incontrovertibly true. I argued for this principle on the grounds that it is necessary for reliably distinguishing what is true from what merely 'seems true' to some but not others. I further argued for the importance of this principle by showing how it appears to be the distinguishing mark of mature, productive sciences (such as modern physics, chemistry, and so on), as compared to rudimentary or pseudo sciences (such as ancient Greek cosmology and early-twentieth century psychology), which now appear, in retrospect, to have been based on little more than speculation.

We have seen that Rightness as Fairness satisfies Firm Foundations extremely well. First, as we saw in Chapter 1, Rightness as Fairness is based on an instrumental conception of normative rationality that virtually all human beings – people of all ages, cultures, mental faculties, and moral sensibilities (even criminals and psychopaths) – recognize and accept. Second, as we saw in Chapters 2 and 3, Rightness as

Fairness is based on observable motivational interests about the past, present, and future that all paradigmatic moral agents – normal, nonpsychopathic adult human beings – possess. Further, as we saw in Chapters 2–4, Rightness as Fairness coheres with a variety of empirical observations and experiments linking moral responsibility to capacities for mental time travel and concern for one's future. Indeed, just as Rightness as Fairness predicts (since it founds the rationality of morality on our future-directed interests), failure to be concerned for one's future has been demonstrated to be a strong predictor of immoral behavior.[1-4] Thus, although the arguments I have provided for Rightness as Fairness are complex, the core of the theory satisfies Firm Foundations very well: it is based on observable facts that virtually all human observers can attest to.

In contrast, as we saw in Chapter 1, other predominant approaches to moral philosophy – moral intuitionism, reflective equilibrium, constitutivism, moral language analysis, and so on – fare less favorably on Firm Foundations, as such views tend to be based on controversial premises that are denied by their critics (particularly 'immoralists' or criminals who purport not to experience morality the way others of us do, but instead, following instrumentalism, only feel the normative pull of instrumental arguments appealing to their interests). Because my arguments that Rightness as Fairness satisfies Firm Foundations better than the above alternatives have already been given, primarily in Chapter 1 but also in Chapters 2 and 3, I will not repeat these arguments again.

What I would like to do instead is briefly compare Rightness as Fairness to another theory not yet discussed – Derek Parfit's 'Triple-Theory' of ethics[5] – on Firm Foundations. Parfit explicitly states that his theory is founded on a non-naturalist, realist conception of 'reasons fundamentalism': a metaethical doctrine that reasons (including moral reasons) cannot be reduced to any natural phenomena, such as our motivational interests or concept of instrumental normative rationality.[6] Indeed, Parfit notes on several occasions that if his conception of non-naturalism is not true, then his entire life's work will have been in vain.[7] Yet, although I think this is going too far – as Parfit's work could be of philosophical interest and prove useful in certain respects even if it has incorrect foundations (Newton's theory of physics is based on false foundations, after all, yet it is still of interest and has certain practical uses today) – Parfit's predication of his theory on a non-naturalist, realist theory of reasons is problematic vis-à-vis Firm Foundations. For although such a doctrine has enjoyed a certain amount of philosophical popularity dating back at least to T.M. Scanlon's *On What We Owe to Each Other*,[8] it simply does not satisfy Firm Foundations: it is not a foundation that human observers generally recognize as obviously, incontrovertibly true. First, as we saw in Chapter 1, whereas the conception of instrumental normative rationality Rightness as Fairness is based on is commonly appealed to in ordinary life and the history of philosophy (dating back at least to Plato's dialogues, where, again, conversant after conversant asks Plato's 'Socrates' to demonstrate the instrumental rationality of moral behavior), Scanlon and Parfit's non-naturalistic reasons fundamentalism has only been considered for the past several years, and only in philosophical work (ordinary people do not obviously have any views at all about whether 'reasons are fundamental'). Further, within philosophy, a significant number of critics argue that both normative non-naturalism and reasons fundamentalism are false.[9-11] Consequently, even if there are plausible philosophical arguments for Parfit's non-naturalist reasons fundamentalism based on premises that seem true to some philosophers (such as Parfit), the position does not satisfy Firm Foundations, at least not at present: it is not based on premises that are recognized as obviously true by virtually all observers

2 Greater internal coherence

Rightness as Fairness also has advantages over its rivals on the principle of Internal Coherence.

First, although many moral theories are arguably internally coherent as moral theories, most moral theories nevertheless entail a broader kind of normative inconsistency between morality and prudence. For most moral philosophers, morality is one thing and prudence another. That is, what one ought to do from a moral point of view might be what one ought not to do from a nonmoral or purely prudential point of view. This is true of Kantian ethics, utilitarianism, moral intuitionism, moral particularism, and moral pluralism (such as W.D. Ross' theory of *prima facie* duties). All of these theories entail that morality and prudence can normatively conflict with one another – a kind of internal incoherence in the normative domain. While such theorists can of course argue that there is no logical contradiction per se (as, they might say, moral reasons or norms should always outweigh mere reasons or norms of prudence), it is nevertheless the case, on all such views, that the normative realm contains an internal tension between 'the moral' and 'the prudent.' I have argued that Rightness as Fairness resolves this tension – that morality ultimately is a kind of prudence: prudence vis-à-vis one's future selves.

Second, Rightness as Fairness has internal coherence advantages over two kinds of theories that purport to unify prudence and morality: virtue theories and contractarian theories. First, while virtue theories typically purport to consistently unify prudence and morality – arguing that moral virtue is either a necessary means to or constitutive of human flourishing[12] – it is a contentious matter whether they do so in a way that is coherent in other respects. In particular, it seems offhand that many different virtues – virtues of honesty, kindness, and so on – can conflict (it may be kind not to be honest, and vice versa). Indeed, although some virtue theorists have defended doctrines of the so-called 'unity of the virtues' – holding that, properly speaking, the moral virtues can never conflict – this doctrine is widely rejected.[13] Similarly, while contractarian theories (such as Thomas Hobbes' and David Gauthier's) aim to render prudence and morality consistent, it is not clear that they succeed – since, on both of their accounts, the instrumental grounds that one has to agree to moral principles arguably no longer exist once *others* uphold the agreement.[14]

Third, as we saw in Chapter 4, Rightness as Fairness has advantages in internal coherence over the approach to moral theorizing it most closely resembles: Kantian ethics. For although, as we saw, Kant contends that his various formulations of the categorical imperative are consistent (and indeed, express the very same moral law), he never shows how this is the case, and it is generally believed by most Kantian scholars to be false.[15] Further, because the unity of Kant's formulas has never been convincingly demonstrated to the satisfaction of many Kant scholars, this has left Kantian ethics in a bind, having to determine which of Kant's formulations is 'correct' and should be used as a test of right and wrong (as, once again, Kant offers at least the first two formulas – the universal law and humanity formulas – as offering different tests of right and wrong).[16] In contrast, Rightness as Fairness is comprised by several formulations of the Categorical-Instrumental Imperative, all of which were shown to be identical in Chapter 4, and to entail a single, unified moral test (the Moral Original Position) in Chapter 5.

Finally, Rightness as Fairness has internal coherence advantages over Parfit's triple-theory. Parfit argues that 'the best forms' of consequentialism, Kantianism, and contractualism converge on a single moral principle: the principle that we ought to act in ways that are 'optimific, uniquely universally willable, and not reasonably rejectable.'[17] However, Parfit's arguments for this convergence have been widely repudiated.[18–23] In contrast, instead of attempting to erase the differences between these competing moral perspectives (as Parfit's theory attempts to), we saw in

Chapter 6 that Rightness as Fairness *reconciles* deontology, consequentialism, contractualism, and virtue ethics: its Four Principles of Fairness entail that morality is a matter of *balancing* and negotiating different types of (deontological, consequentialist, contractualist, and virtue ethical) moral considerations against one another.

3 Greater external coherence

Rightness as Fairness also has advantages over rival theories on the principle of External Coherence.

First, as we saw in Chapter 1, it is based on and coheres with the most universal conception of normative rationality deployed by human beings in ordinary conversation and throughout philosophical history: instrumentalism – holding that morality itself can be reduced to a form of instrumental rationality. Second, although many people (in ordinary life and philosophical history) have doubted whether morality reduces to prudence, we saw in Chapters 2 and 3 that Rightness as Fairness predicts and explains a variety of empirical facts linking morality to prudence – specifically, to a kind of prudential concern for the future. We saw in Chapter 2, just as Rightness as Fairness predicts, that beings who lack the kinds of mental time travel abilities that produce the problem of possible future selves – nonhuman animals, young children, teenagers, and psychopaths – fail to feel the normative force of morality, and in direct proportion to their lack of those abilities to care about their future.[24-35] Furthermore, we also saw in Chapter 2, just as Rightness as Fairness predicts, that (a) failure to care about one's future is among the strongest predictors of morally delinquent behavior,[1-4] and (b) prompting people to care about their future appears to improve moral *and* prudential behavior.[36-38] There is, to my knowledge, no other moral theory that explains and coheres as well with these empirical phenomena. And notice that this coherence again traces back to Rightness as Fairness' satisfaction of Firm Foundations. Unlike other moral theories, which are based on controversial philosophical judgments – judgments about 'our moral intuitions,' 'the meaning of moral language,' 'the constitutive features of practical reason,' and so on – Rightness as Fairness is based on observation of *human behavior*: observation of how we care about our past, present, and future, and how we deploy the instrumental theory of normative rationality.

Second, Rightness as Fairness coheres with many common moral beliefs and practices more strongly than other rival theories. For instance, as we saw in Chapter 6, whereas moral theories such as Kantianism, utilitarianism, and virtue ethics aim to reduce morality to 'one kind of thing' – to either acting on universalizable principles, maximizing utility, or behaving virtuously – Rightness as Fairness embodies and verifies, in its Four Principles of Fairness, the commonsense idea that morality is a matter of balancing many competing considerations. Similarly, as we also saw in Chapter 6, Rightness as Fairness coheres with the commonsense, broadly democratic notion that although morality is in some respects a matter of 'acting on principle,' it is also fundamentally a matter of negotiation, and indeed, fairly resolving costs and conflicts between moral ideals and costs associated with them. Finally, as we saw in Chapter 6, Rightness as Fairness is consistent with the fact that most people appear to be willing, and consider it morally appropriate, to only put in 'B+' moral effort.[39] Rightness as Fairness does not require us to be 'moral saints': it permits us to negotiate with others the sacrifices that we should have to make for the sake of the moral ideals of negative and positive fairness. Additionally, we saw that Rightness as Fairness coheres with and explains the notion that 'moral relevance' can change over time: that morality is a matter of negotiating with others, on an ongoing basis, what moral sensitivity requires (something which appears, in real-life, to be a truly central part of moral practice, as when we 'debate as a society' precisely what is sexist, bigoted, intolerant, and so on).

Finally, Rightness as Fairness has advantages in external coherence over Parfit's triple-theory in the above ways. First, insofar as it is not based on claims about mental time travel or concern for one's future, Parfit's theory does not predict or explain above list of empirical observations linking moral responsibility to 'mental time travel' and concern for one's future. Second, Parfit's theory does not explain or cohere with the above moral practices as well as Rightness as Fairness. For whereas Parfit's theory holds that morality involves acting in ways that are 'optimific, uniquely universally willable, and not reasonably rejectable,' Rightness as Fairness' Four Principles of Fairness were shown to cohere with several specific, widespread moral notions: (a) a moral ideal of coercion-avoidance and minimization (negative fairness), (b) a moral ideal of assistance (positive fairness), (c) a notion that morality requires fairly settling conflicts with others (fair negotiation), (d) the notion that morality is a matter of being a certain kind of person (virtues of fairness). Further, in Chapter 7, these notions which were shown to cohere with and explain several influential conceptions of political morality (libertarianism, egalitarianism, and communitarianism).

4 Greater explanatory power

Rightness as Fairness also has advantages on the principle of Explanatory Power over rival theories.

First, as we have seen in multiple chapters (Chapters 2–6), Rightness as Fairness predicts and explains a variety of empirical findings and other observations that other moral theories do not. For instance, it predicts that morality's experienced normative force (the extent to which a person finds it rational to obey moral norms) should depend, at least in part, on the extent to which the person can engage in 'mental time travel' – which is consistent with what is observed. Specifically, nonhuman animals and psychopaths, who do not experience morality's normative force, appear to lack mental time travel capacities.[25,33–35] Similarly, children and teenagers, who poorly appreciate morality's normative force, have impoverished (but developing) capacities to imagine or care about their future.[26,29] And so on. Similarly, Rightness as Fairness explains why failure to think about one's future strongly predicts immoral (and criminal) behavior,[1–4] and why stimulating concern for one's future self has been observed to improve both moral and prudential behavior.[36–38] To the best of my knowledge, Rightness as Fairness is unique in predicting these specific empirical findings. Further, although it is only an anecdotal example, Rightness as Fairness predicts and explains why the screenwriters for the *Star Trek* episode, 'By Any Other Name,' made morality's perceived normative force dependent on ignorance of the future. If you recall Chapter 2's discussion of this case, the screenwriters based the episode around an alien species, the Kelvans, who initially felt no normative force of moral norms because they (the Kelvans) knew they could satisfy their future interests with impunity. It was only when the Kelvans became unsure of that their future interests might be – of the ways they could be punished by or empathize with human beings – that they began to feel morality's force, just as Rightness as Fairness predicts they should.

Second, unlike many moral theories – such as Kantianism, utilitarianism, contractualism, or virtue ethics – which, again, aim to reduce morality to 'one thing' (respect for autonomy, promotion of utility, contractual agreement, or virtue, respectively), Rightness as Fairness provides a systematic explanation of how morality involves all of these things, and how they are related: it holds that morality is simultaneously a matter of coercion-avoidance/minimization, assistance, fair negotiation, and virtue. Further, as we saw in Chapter 7, Rightness as Fairness not only explains (and reconciles) the attractiveness of these moral frameworks, it also explains and reconciles several traditionally opposed conceptions of political morality: libertarianism, egalitarianism, and communitarianism. To the best of my knowledge, no other moral theory has purported to explain the merits of, or incorporate, this diverse array of moral-political perspectives.

Second, unlike most moral theories – which, again, typically distinguish morality and prudence – Rightness as Fairness explains morality in terms of prudence: as a certain kind of prudence necessitated by a problem (the problem of possible future selves) that we all encounter. Although again it is not the only theory that reduces morality to some form of prudence (virtue ethical theories have long sought to analyze morality as either a means to or constitutive of human happiness or flourishing,[40] and contractarians have long sought to show that morality is prudent in terms of engendering social cooperation[41]), Rightness as Fairness – in its Four Principles of Fairness – explains more than such theories. Unlike virtue ethical theories, which merely explain moral virtue, and contractarian theories, which merely purport to explain social cooperation, Rightness as Fairness explains a variety of specific empirical observations (regarding the relationship of 'mental time travel,' future-concernedness, and so on) and moral observations (the simultaneous attractiveness of competing moral and political systems) in a way that virtue ethical and contractarian theories do not.

Finally, as we have already seen, Rightness as Fairness has explanatory advantages over Parfit's triple-theory. First, whereas Parfit takes normative reasons as basic and unexplainable, Rightness as Fairness explains normativity in terms of our interests and concept of instrumental normative rationality. Second, because Parfit's theory is based on non-naturalistic claims about reasons, his theory does not predict or explain the empirical observations (concerning the relationships between moral responsibility, future-concernedness, 'mental time travel,' and so on) that Rightness as Fairness does. Third, although Parfit's theory attempts to explain how the best forms of consequentialism, Kantianism, and contractualism converge on a single moral principle, his derivation of this convergence has been widely argued to be unsuccessful.[18–23] In contrast, Rightness as Fairness does not argue that these different moral frameworks converge: it instead explains how deontological, consequentialist, contractualist, and virtue ethical norms – the Four Principles of Fairness – have a single basis (the Categorical-Instrumental Imperative), and must be reconciled with one another through negotiation. In so doing, Rightness as Fairness also uniquely explains the simultaneous attractiveness of libertarian, egalitarian, and communitarian theories of political morality.

5 Greater unity

Rightness as Fairness also has advantages on the principle of Unity over competing theories.

First, in contrast to the moral theories – such as Kantianism, utilitarianism, intuitionism, Rossian pluralism, and so on – that (as already noted) split the normative realm into two ('the moral' and 'the prudent'), Rightness as Fairness unifies morality and prudence. Specifically, it shows how a kind of prudence – fairness to one's present and future selves – is identical to fairness to others.

Second, in contrast to other existing moral theories – which do not predict or explain the empirical facts that Rightness as Fairness explains (about how 'mental time travel,' concern for one's future, and so on, have been observed to relate to moral and immoral behavior), Rightness as Fairness provides a unified explanation of those phenomena, showing how the instrumental rationality of moral behavior *emerges* from our capacities for mental time travel and caring about our future.

Finally, Rightness as Fairness unifies more moral phenomena than alternatives. It not only provides – in its Four Principles of Fairness – a unified explanation of how morality has deontological, consequentialist, contractualist, and virtue ethical elements, reconciling them into a unified whole. It also provides a unified explanation of the attractiveness of three traditionally opposed conceptions of political morality (libertarianism, egalitarianism, and communitarianism), also reconciling them into a unified whole: 'Libertarian Egalitarian Communitarianism.' In comparison, while Parfit's triple-theory of ethics attempts to unify consequentialism, Kantian-deontology, and contractualism, Parfit's attempt appears unsuccessful and does not explain (as Rightness as Fairness does) how morality fundamentally involves moral virtue (virtues of fairness), nor does it provide a unified justification (as Rightness as Fairness does) of libertarian, egalitarian, and communitarian political values.

6 Greater parsimony

Rightness as Fairness also has advantages over rival theories on the principle of Parsimony.

First, whereas 'realist' moral theories – intuitionistic theories[42], as well as Parfit's triple-theory – invoke a realm of 'non-natural moral facts,' normative facts above and beyond the empirical facts attested to by modern science, Rightness as Fairness bases morality on observable human interests and our instrumental conception of normative rationality – the latter of which, as I suggested in Chapter 1 and others have also argued[43], can reduce normativity to non-normative/empirical facts (namely, facts concerning the satisfaction conditions of our concept of instrumental rationality). Rightness as Fairness, in other words, draws upon fewer facts and entities that many other moral theories: it understands and explains morality in purely naturalistic terms, appealing to facts observable and testable by the sciences.

Second, unlike Kantian, Nietzschean, and other constitutivist approaches to moral philosophy, Rightness as Fairness does not posit any controversial 'constitutive features of agency,' such as Kantian transcendental freedom, Nietzschean drives, or Korsgaardian unified agency. Rightness as Fairness affirms nothing beyond the observations that we virtually all share a concept of instrumental normative rationality (with specific satisfaction-conditions), sometimes have interests in knowing the future (among those of us to whom morality applies), and experience ourselves, first-personally, as having three possible types of interests: voluntary, involuntary, and semivoluntary interests (again, among those of us to whom morality applies).

In short, Rightness as Fairness is a particularly parsimonious moral theory, explaining morality in terms of observable facts and properties (cohering, again, with a variety of empirical observations regarding the relationship between prudence, mental time travel, concern for the future, ignorance of the future, and so on).

7 Greater fruitfulness

Finally, Rightness as Fairness has advantages over competing moral theories on the principle of Fruitfulness.

First, unlike most existing moral theories, which do not appear to have substantial implications for improving human moral behavior, Rightness as Fairness explains recent experimental interventions that have been shown, at least in laboratory conditions, to actually prompt better moral behavior.[36-38]

Second, Rightness as Fairness provides a systematic method for resolving applied moral questions: the method of 'principled fair negotiation.' Unlike rival moral theories, such as traditional forms of Kantianism, utilitarianism, and virtue ethics – which, as we saw in Chapter 6, have been used to defend opposing conclusions on just about every issue imaginable (trolley cases, torture, world poverty, animal rights, and so on), Rightness as Fairness holds that sound answers to moral questions cannot generally be arrived at through thought or debate alone. Morality, according to Rightness as Fairness, fundamentally involves negotiating fair solutions with others, in the real-world, provided the parties to the negotiations can point to the Principles of Negative and Positive Fairness in defense of their side's conclusions. As such, as we saw in Chapters 6, Rightness as Fairness provides a fruitful way of answering moral questions – a way of resolving, in an ongoing basis, our duties to ourselves and each other on issues ranging from lying to suicide, trolley cases, torture and so on – through negotiation. It further promises, as we saw in Chapter 7, an attractive resolution to problems of moral and political divisiveness. For although Rightness as Fairness does not permit negotiating with individuals or groups whose arguments blatantly contradict the Principles of Negative and Positive Fairness (such as racists, sexists, and so on), it requires negotiation in cases where both sides' arguments are plausibly consistent with the ideals of negative and positive fairness, requiring us not to deny the legitimacy of the other side, but rather, to forge a fair solution to the disagreement.

We can see the unique fruitfulness of this conception of moral problem-solving by once again comparing Rightness as Fairness to rival theories. Consider Kantianism, utilitarianism, virtue ethics, and Parfit's triple-theory. Kantianism states that morality is a matter of respecting human autonomy – yet, as we saw in Chapter 6, there appear to be cases in which there are 'autonomy' (or coercion) conflicts. Trolley cases are a good example. Offhand, there is no way to respect the autonomy of all in trolley cases, as no matter what one does, someone will die. Utilitarianism attempts to resolve such issues in terms of utility. Yet, as utilitarianism's many critics argue, this aspect of it – the notion that morality is merely a matter of tallying up utility – seems horrifically impersonal.[44] Virtue ethicists have traditionally aimed to correct for these perceived deficiencies (of both Kantianism and utilitarianism) by appealing to virtue: virtues of honesty, compassion, friendship, and so on. Yet virtue theories struggle to provide clear answers to moral questions, typically arguing that we should 'act as the virtuous person would' in a given circumstance[40] – despite the fact that in many moral dilemmas, it often seems unclear what the virtuous person would do (indeed, that very question, according to virtue ethics' critics, is what we need a moral theory or argument for: namely, whether pushing someone in front of a trolley is virtuous, or whether giving to alleviate world poverty is virtuous, and so on[45]). Finally, contractualists have attempted to provide an interpersonal method of determining what is moral, such as Scanlon's principle of acting in ways that others 'could not reasonably reject'[46] and Parfit's triple-theory, which holds that morality requires acting in ways that are 'optimific, uniquely universally willable, and not reasonably rejectable.'[17] Yet these enjoinders in turn seem obscure. What exactly does it mean to say that an action is 'optimific' or one that another 'could not reasonably reject'? As Pogge argues[47], these notions seem hopelessly obscure.

Rightness as Fairness provides a more fruitful method for resolving applied moral problems, and indeed, explains why rival theories have had difficulties providing clear answers to real-life moral questions. For whereas Kantian, utilitarian, pluralistic, and contractualist theories hold that morality is a matter of 'thinking through' answers – determining through thought or debate 'what respects human autonomy,' what produces utility, what is beneficent, or 'what others could reasonably reject' – and virtue theories hold that morality is a matter of discovering answers through moral virtue, Rightness as Fairness holds that morality is not a matter of 'discovering' answers to moral questions at all: it is a matter of *creating* fair answers with others, through actual processes of fair negotiation, guided by sound moral ideals (of negative and positive fairness) and moral cultivation (virtues of fairness).

8 Conclusion

This book defended a new moral theory, Rightness as Fairness. Although no theory is perfect, and problems are sure to remain, there are good grounds for believing that Rightness as Fairness has systematic advantages over its competitors across seven important – indeed, truth-apt – principles of theory selection. It is, therefore, a theory worthy of serious philosophical consideration.

Notes

Introduction

1. Baird (2011): 8–13, 18–21, 39–41.
2. Oerter (2006).
3. Piotrowski (2003): 239–43, 569–74, 608–12, 755–8, 823–7, 1201–16.
4. Van Roojen (2014).
5. Shafer-Landau (2003).
6. Enoch, D. (2011).
7. Kant, I. [1785].
8. Kant, I. [1788].
9. Korsgaard (1996a).
10. Korsgaard (2008, 2009).
11. Hare (1981).
12. Kauppinen (2014).
13. Gowans (2015).
14. Harman (2000).
15. Velleman (2013).
16. Joyce (2007, 2015).
17. Mackie (1977).
18. Driver (2014).
19. Bentham [1789].
20. Mill [1861].
21. Parfit (2011): 31.
22. Korsgaard (1996b).
23. Baron (1995).
24. Herman (1993).
25. Scanlon (1998).
26. Hursthouse (1999).
27. Swanton (2001).
28. Ross [1930].
29. Mason (2015).
30. Dancy (2004, 2013).
31. Stratton-Lake (2014).
32. Timmons (2007): 27–31.
33. Vaughn (2009): 46–7.
34. Ross [1930]: 41.
35. Moore [1904]: Section 45.
36. Audi (2015): 57–77.
37. Brink (1989).
38. Dancy (1986).
39. Finlay (2007).
40. Thomson (2008a).
41. Korsgaard (2008).
42. Katsafanas (2011, 2015).
43. Van Gelder, Hershfield & Nordgren (2013).

44. Ersner-Hershfield, Wimmer & Knutson (2009).
45. Ersner-Hershfield, Garton, Ballard, Samanez-Larkin & Knutson (2009).
46. Hershfield, Goldstein, Sharpe, Fox, Yeykelis, Carstensen, et al. (2011).
47. Smith (2012).
48. Kant [1785]: 4:421, 4:428–9, 4:433–4.
49. Rawls (1999a).

1 Ethics for the Twenty-First Century

1. Piotrowski (2003): 242–3, 756–7, 1206.
2. Braibant, Giacomelli & Spurio (2011): 1.
3. Baird (2011): 9–13.
4. Wald (2010).
5. Clemence (1947).
6. Ashby (2003).
7. Will (2014).
8. Gauch (2003): 11.
9. Driver (2014).
10. Johnson (2014).
11. Kant, I. [1785].
12. Korsgaard (1996a).
13. Wood (1999, 2008).
14. Dean (2006, 2013).
15. Nyholm (2013).
16. Glasgow (2007).
17. Leiter (2015): Section 1.
18. Katsafanas (2015).
19. Anscombe (1958).
20. Greene (2010).
21. Grenberg (2009).
22. Mason (2015).
23. Ross [1930].
24. Stratton-Lake (2014).
25. Prichard [1912].
26. Moore [1904].
27. Audi (2015).
28. Lichtenberg (1994).
29. Bambrough [1979]: 104.
30. Sinnott-Armstrong (2011).
31. Joyce (2007).
32. Mackie (1977).
33. Joyce (2015).
34. Plato, *The Republic*: 338d–362.
35. Plato, *Gorgias*: 460–471d, 483e.
36. Beebe & Sackris (2015): 19.
37. Shafer-Landau (2003).
38. Enoch (2011).
39. Brink (1989).

40. Dancy (1986).
41. Finlay (2007).
42. Joyce (2005): Section 3.
43. Blackburn (1993).
44. Timmons (2007): 27–31.
45. Vaughn (2009): 46–7.
46. Barcalow (2007): 14–5.
47. Daniels (2013).
48. Olsson (2014): Section 6–7.
49. Moore [1904]: ix.
50. Vessot et al. (1980): 2081–4.
51. Glanzberg (2014).
52. Kuhn [1977]: 75, italics added.
53. Descartes [1641]: Meditation I.
54. Klein (2015).
55. Popper [1963].
56. Cover & Curd (1998): 1–82.
57. Bogen (2014).
58. Van Fraassen (1980): 16–7.
59. Kuhn [1977]: 75.
60. LaFolette (2014): 5.
61. Priest & Berto (2013).
62. Bell (1987): 172.
63. Seevinck (2010).
64. Swinburne (2009): 206–7.
65. Dyson, Eddington & Davidson (1920).
66. James-Griffiths (2007).
67. Laudan (1997).
68. Ylikoski & Kuorikoski (2010).
69. Schupbach (2011).
70. Oerter (2006).
71. Joyce (2007): 52–6.
72. Foot (1972).
73. Finlay (2008, 2011).
74. Kitcher (1981).
75. Maxwell (2004).
76. Mulnix (2011).
77. Schurz (1999).
78. Baker (2013).
79. Joyce (2015): Section 3.
80. Mackie (1977): 38.
81. Laudan (1977).
82. Van Roojen (2014).
83. Scanlon (1998).
84. Parfit (2011).
85. Katsafanas (2011).
86. Korsgaard (2008, 2009).
87. Herman (1993).
88. Thomson (2008a).

89. Kauppinen (2014).
90. Hume [1751].
91. Slote (2009).
92. Weirich (2012).
93. Aristotle, *Nichomachean Ethics*: Section 8–9.
94. Hobbes [1651]: 40.
95. Kavka [1985].
96. Gauthier (1987).
97. Aristotle, *Nichomachean Ethics*: 1098a.
98. Bedke (2010).
99. Boyd (1988).
100. Jackson (1998).
101. Cohon (2010): Section 5.
102. Parfit (2011): 324–7.
103. Dancy (2006): 122–145.
104. Fleming (2015).
105. Van Gelder et al. (2013).
106. Ersner-Hershfield, Wimmer & Knutson (2009).
107. Ersner-Hershfield, Garton, et al. (2009).
108. Hershfield et al. (2011).
109. Plato, *The Republic*: 338–44.
110. Nietzsche [1887].
111. Joyce (2007): Ch. 6.
112. Fumerton (2010).
113. Sinclair (2012).
114. Sias (2015).
115. Gibbard (1990).
116. Stevenson (1937).
117. Ayer (1936): Ch. 6.
118. Thomson (2008a): Ch. I–III.
119. Almotahari & Hosein (2015).
120. Kant [1785]: Section III.
121. Kant [1797a]: Introduction, Section III.
122. Rosati (2014).
123. Schlosser (2011).
124. Chappell (2010).
125. Hill (1995).
126. Guyer (1996): Section III.
127. Holloway (1995).
128. Wallace (2014).
129. Darwall (2006).
130. Darwall (2006): 6–8.
131. Nagel (1970): Section 8.
132. Hume [1738]: Section 3.1.2.4.
133. Strawson (1962).
134. Korsgaard (2007a).
135. Watson (2007).
136. Wallace (2007).
137. Pauer-Studer (2010).

138. Sterba (2012, 2015).
139. Russell (2013).
140. Darwall (2014).
141. Miller (2014).
142. MacIntosh (2014).
143. Joyce (2007): Ch. 3–4.
144. Prichard [1912]: 467.
145. Bedke (2009).
146. Thomson (2008a): 181–2.
147. Thomson (2008a): 182.
148. Prichard [1912]: 465–7.
149. Hursthouse (2013): Section 2.
150. Thoits & Hewitt (2001).
151. Anderson et al. (2014).
152. UnitedHealthGroup (2013).
153. Schreier, Schonert-Reichl & Chen (2013).
154. Plato, *Gorgias*: 471a–d.
155. Mughal (2009): 1254–5.
156. DiSalle (2009): Section 1.2.
157. Schwitzgebel & Rust (2009, 2012).
158. Marx [1845]: Section 11.
159. Joyce (2007): Section 3.2.
160. Sumner (1998).

2 The Problem of Possible Future Selves

1. Kant [1785]: 4:389.
2. Joyce (2007): 30–4.
3. Smith (2012).
4. Kahneman (2011): Ch. 35.
5. Kahneman (2000).
6. Kahneman, Wakker & Sarin (1997).
7. Debus (2014).
8. Smith (2013).
9. Suddendorf & Corballis (2007): Section 3.
10. Casey, Jones & Hare (2008).
11. Kennett & Matthews (2009).
12. Giedd, Blumenthal & Jeffries (1999).
13. Moffitt (1993).
14. Litton (2008).
15. Shoemaker (2011).
16. Levy (2007).
17. Hare (1999).
18. Hart & Dempster (1997).
19. Stuss, Gow & Hetherington (1992).
20. Weber et al. (2008).
21. Yang & Raine (2009).
22. Blair (2003).

23. Ersner-Hershfield, Wimmer & Knutson (2009).
24. Ersner-Hershfield et al. (2009).
25. Hershfield et al. (2011).
26. Van Gelder et al. (2013).
27. Van Gelder et al. (2013): 974.
28. Hirschi (2004).
29. Gottfredson & Hirschi (1990).
30. Wilson & Herrnstein (1985): 44–5.
31. Lichtenstein & Slovic (1971).
32. Lindman (1971).
33. Grether & Plott (1979).
34. Bazerman, Loewenstein & White (1992).
35. Kahneman (2011): Ch. 38.
36. Gilbert & Wilson (2009).
37. Wilson & Gilbert (2003).
38. Ayton, Pott & Elwakili (2007).
39. Brickman, Coates & Janoff-Bulman (1978).
40. Myers & Diener (1995): 13.
41. Argyle (1986).
42. Kahneman, Wakker & Sarin (1997).
43. Varey & Kahneman (1992).
44. Botti (2004).
45. Paul (2015a, b).
46. Experience Project (2015).
47. Facebook (2015).
48. Burris & Rempel (2012).
49. Hoefer (2015).
50. Arvan (2013a).
51. Rosati (2014): Section 3.1.
52. Tornado Hills (2015).
53. Serial Killer Calendar (2015).
54. Listverse (2015).
55. CNN (2014).
56. Kant [1785]: 4:455.
57. Kant [1785]: 4:449.
58. Kant [1785]: Section III.
59. Kant [1788]: Book one, Ch. 1, Section 1–6.
60. Kant [1797a]: Introduction, Section I–III.
61. Graybiel & Smith (2014): 42.
62. Weber et al. (2008).
63. Blair (2003).
64. Craig et al. (2009).
65. Kant [1785]: 4:407.
66. Schwitzgebel (2011).
67. Foot (1972).
68. Smith (2012): 313.
69. Williams (1995).
70. Smith (2012): 311.

3 The Categorical-Instrumental Imperative

1. Altshuler (2010, forthcoming).
2. Roskies (2012).
3. Vincent (2013).
4. Fischer & Ravizza (1998).
5. Levy (2008).
6. Hoefer (2015).
7. Stocker (1976).
8. Schumann, Zaki & Dweck (2014).
9. Shaw, Batson & Todd (1994).
10. Weirich (2012).
11. Van Gelder et al. (2013).
12. Ito, Larsen, Smith & Cacioppo (1998).
13. Baumeister et al. (2001).
14. Baumeister et al. (2001): 323.
15. Wolf (1982).
16. Elizondo (forthcoming): Section VII–VIII.
17. Plato, *The Republic*: Book IV.
18. Kant [1785]: 4:393–4, 4:397–403.
19. Kant [1788]: 5:162.
20. Kauppinen (2014): Section 2.

4 Three Unified Formulations

1. Schumann, Zaki & Dweck (2014).
2. Shaw, Batson & Todd (1994).
3. Kant [1785]: 4:421.
4. Kant [1785]: 4:429.
5. Kant [1785]: 4:434.
6. Kant [1785]: 4:433.
7. Kant [1785]: 4:428–9.
8. Kant [1785]: Section III.
9. Kant [1788]: Ch. 1.
10. Korsgaard (1996a, b).
11. Wood (1999, 2008).
12. Dean (2006, 2013).
13. Nyholm (2013, 2015).
14. Ware (2014).
15. Kant [1785]: 4:436.
16. Kant [1785]: 4:422–3, 4:429–31.
17. Johnson (2014): Section 9.
18. Kim (2004).
19. Arvan (2012).
20. Korsgaard (1985).
21. Kahn (2014).
22. Nyholm (2015).
23. Rivera-Castro (2014).

24. Timmons (1998, 2005).
25. Korsgaard (1986).
26. Nozick (1974): 28–34.
27. Cureton (2013).
28. Dean (2013).
29. Glasgow (2007).
30. Nelson (2008).
31. Pallikkathayil (2010).
32. Formosa (2014).
33. Flikschuh (2009).
34. Rawls (1999a): Section 40.
35. Kant [1797b].
36. Varden (2010).
37. Weinrib (2008).
38. Korsgaard (1996b).
39. Wood (2011).
40. Sussman (2009).
41. Mahon (2006).
42. Herman (1993).
43. Baron (1995).
44. Korsgaard (2008, 2009).
45. Schlosser (2011).
46. Chappell (2010).
47. Guyer (1996): Section III.
48. Richardson (1997).
49. Johnson (1997).
50. Johnson (2014): Section 10.
51. Grenberg (2009).
52. Greene (2010).
53. Katsafanas (2015).
54. Leiter (2015): Section 1.
55. Nietzsche [1887].
56. Van Gelder et al. (2013).
57. Ersner-Hershfield, Wimmer & Knutson (2009).
58. Ersner-Hershfield, Garton et al. (2009).
59. Hershfield et al. (2011).
60. Pereboom (1991).
61. Kohl (2014).
62. Casey et al. (2008).
63. Kennett & Matthews (2009).
64. Giedd et al. (1999).
65. Moffitt (1993).
66. Hare (1999).
67. Hart & Dempster (1997).
68. Stuss et al. (1992).
69. Weber et al. (2008).
70. Yang & Raine (2009).
71. Blair (2003).
72. Hirschi (2004).

238 *Notes*

73. Gottfredson & Hirschi (1990).
74. Wilson & Herrnstein (1985): 44–5.
75. Stocker (1976).
76. Williams (1981).
77. Wolf (2012).
78. Wolf (1982).
79. Baron (2008).
80. Schwitzgebel (2015).
81. Nowak & Vallacher (1998).
82. Dorsey (forthcoming).
83. Kant [1772–96]: 27:459.
84. Wood (1998).
85. Korsgaard (2007b).
86. Johnson (2014): Section 4.
87. Denis (2007).
88. Cholbi (2000).

5 The Moral Original Position

1. Rawls (1999a): esp. Section 1–4.
2. Rawls (1999a): 3.
3. Rawls (1999a): 6–10.
4. Rawls (1993): 40–1.
5. Rawls (1999a): 4–5, 7–8, 215–6.
6. Rawls (1999a): 7, 93, 99, 401.
7. Rawls (1999b): 11–23.
8. Rawls (1999a): Section 3.
9. Rawls (1999a): Section 4, 24.
10. Rawls (2001): 42.
11. Rawls (1999a): 53, 266.
12. Rawls (1993): 5–6.
13. Rawls (1999b): esp. 37.
14. Rawls (1999a): 1, Section 6, 160.
15. Kant [1785]: 4:429.
16. Rawls (1999a): Section 40.
17. Rawls (1999a): 222.
18. Kant [1785]: 4:421.
19. Kant [1785]: 4:433.
20. Arvan (2012).
21. Kim (2004).
22. Rawls (1999a): 18–9, 42–5, 507–8.
23. Daniels (2013).
24. Timmons (2007): 27–31.
25. Vaughn (2009): 46–7.
26. Ross [1930]: 41.
27. Rawls (1999a): 18, Section 87.
28. Rawls (1999a): Section 4, 26.

29. Rawls (1999b): Section 10.
30. Rawls (1993): xxxvii–lxii, Section 1–5, and Lecture IV.
31. Rawls (1999b): 32, 170–74.
32. Nozick (1974): 32–3, 90–5.
33. Caney (2005).
34. Moellendorf (2002).
35. Pogge (1994).
36. Nussbaum (2007).
37. Okin (1989, 1991).
38. Cohen (2008).
39. Farrelly (2007).
40. Arvan (2014).
41. Gaus (2011).
42. Quong (2011).

6 Rightness as Fairness

1. Rawls (1999a): 4–5, 7–8, 215–6.
2. Anderson (2014).
3. Farquhar (1984).
4. Bettman, Luce & Payne (1998).
5. Slovik (1995).
6. Williams (1981): 1–19.
7. Stocker (1976).
8. Annas (1984).
9. Wolf (1982).
10. Young (1998).
11. Wolf (2012): 71, italics added.
12. Baron (2008).
13. Cottingham (1983).
14. Nathanson (2015).
15. Singer (1972).
16. Kuhse & Singer (1985).
17. Murphy (2000).
18. Herman (1993): Ch. 1–2.
19. Baron (1995, 2008).
20. Annas (2008).
21. Schwitzgebel (2015).
22. Taurek (1977).
23. Sanders (1988).
24. Cohen (2014).
25. Foot (1967).
26. Thomson & Parent (1986).
27. Thomson (2008b).
28. Fiala (2005).
29. Hill (2007).
30. Allhoff (2006, 2012).

31. Steinhoff (2013).
32. Arrigo (2004).
33. Sussman (2005).
34. Arvan (2013b).
35. Van Gelder et al. (2013).
36. Hirschi (2004).
37. Gottfredson & Hirschi (1990).
38. Wilson & Herrnstein (1985): 44–5.
39. Ersner-Hershfield, Wimmer & Knutson (2009).
40. Ersner-Hershfield, Garton, et al. (2009).
41. Hershfield et al. (2011).
42. Nathanson (2015): Section 3.b.i.
43. Kant [1785]: 4:394, 4:399.
44. Skelton (2012): Section 5.
45. Hursthouse (2013): Section 3.1.
46. Dancy (2013): Section 8.
47. Ross [1930]: 19, 30, 31, 33.
48. Das (2003).
49. Svensson (2010).
50. Ross [1930]: 42.
51. Hursthouse (1999): Ch. 1.
52. Dancy (1983).
53. Kant [1785]: 4:422–3, 4:429–31.
54. Potter (1993).
55. Cushman, Young & Hauser (2006).
56. Ross [1930]: 25, 27, 30.
57. Ross [1930]: 21.
58. Zagzebski (2004).
59. Beauchamp & Childress (2009): 13.
60. Singer (1972): 874.
61. Singer (1972): 874–5.
62. Arthur [1996].
63. Kekes (2002).
64. Schmidtz (2000): 685–6.
65. Schmidtz (2000): 686–8.
66. Vaughn (2009): 620–6.

7 Libertarian Egalitarian Communitarianism

1. Vallentyne & Van der Vossen (2014).
2. Arneson (2013).
3. Bell (2013).
4. Zwolinski (2015).
5. Vallentyne & Van der Vossen (2014): Section 2.
6. Rawls (1999a): Section 40.
7. Nozick (1974): 33.
8. Badhwar & Long (2015): Section 4.

9. Zwolinski (2015): Section 5.a.
10. Zwolinski (2015): Section 3.
11. Brennan (2014).
12. Cohen (1995): 239–41.
13. Zwolinski (2015): Section 5.a.
14. Bell (2013): Section 2.
15. Taylor (1985).
16. Rawls (1993, 1999a).
17. Dworkin (2000).
18. Sen [1980], (1992).
19. Nussbaum (1992, 1999).
20. Arneson (2013): Section 2–4.
21. Rawls (1999a): Section 40.
22. Lippert-Rasmussen (2014).
23. Rawls (1999a): Section 29, Ch. VIII.
24. Nozick (1974): 160–4, 167–74.
25. Bell (2013): Section 1–2.
26. Bell (2013): Section 3.
27. Bell (2013): Section 1.
28. MacIntyre (1984).
29. Bell (2013): Section 3.
30. Barry (1995): 3.
31. Walzer (1983): 313.
32. Ferrell (1998): 72.
33. History Channel (2013).
34. Miller Center (2015).
35. Christiano (2015): Section 2.2.
36. Arvan (2013b): 155–6.
37. Cohen (2009).
38. Nozick (1974): 90–5, 183–275.
39. Nagel (2005).
40. Brock (2015): Section 2.3.
41. Rawls (1999b).
42. Rawls (1999a): 6–10, 47, 73–4.
43. Cohen (1997).
44. Hodgson (2012).
45. Macleod (2010).
46. Okin (1989, 1991).
47. Neufeld (2009).
48. Hsieh (2005).
49. Bailey (2014).
50. Valentini (2012).
51. Arvan (2008, 2014).
52. Farrelly (2007).
53. Mills (1997).
54. Sen (2009).
55. Wiens (2012).
56. Schaub (2014).

8 Evaluating Rightness as Fairness

1. Van Gelder et al. (2013): 974.
2. Hirschi (2004).
3. Gottfredson & Hirschi (1990).
4. Wilson & Herrnstein (1985): 44–5.
5. Parfit (2011).
6. Parfit (2011): 31.
7. Parfit (2011): 2, 304, 367.
8. Scanlon (1998): 20–1.
9. Smith (2015).
10. Lang (2012).
11. Thomson (2008a).
12. Hursthouse (2013).
13. Toner (2014).
14. Cudd (2013): Section 4.
15. Johnson (2014): Section 9.
16. Johnson (2015): Section 5–6.
17. Parfit (2011): Section 49.
18. Hooker (2014).
19. Nebel (2012).
20. Ross (2009).
21. Morgan (2009).
22. Otsuka (2009).
23. Chappell (2012).
24. Debus (2014).
25. Suddendorf & Corballis (2007): Section 3.
26. Casey et al. (2008).
27. Kennett & Matthews (2009).
28. Giedd et al. (1999).
29. Moffitt (1993).
30. Litton (2008).
31. Hart & Dempster (1997).
32. Stuss et al. (1992).
33. Weber et al. (2008).
34. Yang & Raine (2009).
35. Blair (2003).
36. Ersner-Hershfield, Wimmer & Knutson (2009).
37. Ersner-Hershfield, Garton, et al. (2009).
38. Hershfield et al. (2011).
39. Schwitzgebel (2015).
40. Hursthouse (2009, 2013).
41. Kavka [1985].
42. Stratton-Lake (2014).
43. Fleming (2015).
44. Sinnott-Armstrong (2014): Section 5.
45. Svensson (2010).
46. Scanlon (1998): 4, 191.
47. Pogge (2001).

Bibliography

Allhoff, F. (2012). *Terrorism, Ticking Time-Bombs, and Torture: A Philosophical Analysis* (Chicago: University of Chicago Press).
____ (2006). 'A Defense of Torture: Separation of Cases, Ticking Time-Bombs, and Moral Justification,' *International Journal of Applied Philosophy* 19(2): 243–64.
Almotahari, M., Hosein, A. (2015). 'Is Anything Just Plain Good?,' *Philosophical Studies* 172(6): 1485–1508.
Altshuler, R. (forthcoming). 'Free Will, Narrative, and Retroactive Self-Constitution,' *Phenomenology and the Cognitive Sciences*: 1–17.
____ (2010). *An Unconditioned Will: The Role of Temporality in Freedom and Agency*. Dissertation, SUNY Stony Brook, http://philpapers.org/rec/ALTAUW, accessed July 28, 2015.
Anderson, N.D, Damianakis, T., Kröger, E., Wagner, L.M., Dawson, D.R., Binns, M.A., et al. (2014). 'The Benefits Associated with Volunteering Among Seniors: A Critical Review and Recommendations for Future Research,' *Psychological Bulletin* 140(6), Nov 2014: 1505–33.
Anderson, S. (2014). 'Coercion,' in E.N. Zalta (ed.), *The Stanford Encyclopedia of Philosophy* (Spring 2014 Edition), http://plato.stanford.edu/archives/spr2014/entries/coercion/.
Annas, J. (2008). 'Virtue Ethics and the Charge of Egoism,' in P. Bloomfield (ed.), *Morality and Self-Interest* (Oxford: Oxford University Press): 205–23.
____ (1984). 'Personal Love and Kantian Ethics in Effi Briest,' *Philosophy and Literature* 8: 15–31.
Anscombe, G.E.M. (1958). 'Modern Moral Philosophy,' *Philosophy* 33(124): 1–19.
Argyle, M. (1986). *The Psychology of Happiness* (London: Methuen).
Aristotle, *Nichomachean Ethics*, T. Irwin (trans.) (1999). *Aristotle: Nicomachean Ethics*, 2nd Ed. (Indianapolis: Hackett).
Arneson, R. (2013). 'Egalitarianism,' in E.N. Zalta (ed.), *The Stanford Encyclopedia of Philosophy* (Summer 2013 Edition), http://plato.stanford.edu/archives/sum2013/entries/egalitarianism/.
Arrigo, J.M. (2004). 'A Utilitarian Argument against Torture Interrogation of Terrorists,' *Science and Engineering Ethics* 10(3): 543–72.
Arthur, J. [1996]. 'Famine Relief and the Ideal Moral Code,' reprinted in S.M. Cahn & P. Markie (eds.), *Ethics: History, Theory, and Contemporary Issues*, 5th ed. (Oxford: Oxford University Press, 2012): 881–92.
Arvan, M. (2014). 'First Steps Toward a Nonideal Theory of Justice." *Ethics & Global Politics* 7(3): 95–117.
____ (2013a). 'A New Theory of Free Will,' *Philosophical Forum* 44(1): 1–48.
____ (2013b). 'Groundwork for a New Moral Epistemology,' *Klesis* 23: 155–190.
____ (2012). 'Unifying the Categorical Imperative,' *Southwest Philosophy Review* 28(1): 217–225.
____ (2008). 'A Non-Ideal Theory of Justice,' PhD Dissertation, University of Arizona, http://citeseerx.ist.psu.edu/viewdoc/download?doi=10.1.1.357.3720&rep=rep1&type=pdf, accessed July 25, 2015.

Bibliography

Ashby, N. (2003). 'Relativity in the Global Positioning System,' *Living Reviews in Relativity* 6: 1–42.
Audi, R. (2015). 'Intuition and Its Place in Ethics,' *Journal of the American Philosophical Association* 1(1): 57–77.
Ayer, A.J. (1936). *Language, Truth, and Logic* (New York: Viking Penguin Inc.).
Ayton, P., Pott, A., Elwakili, N. (2007). 'Affective Forecasting: Why Can't People Predict Their Emotions?' *Thinking & Reasoning* 13(1): 62–80.
Badhwar, N.K., Long, R.T. (2015). 'Ayn Rand,' in E.N. Zalta (ed.), *The Stanford Encyclopedia of Philosophy* (Spring 2015 Edition), http://plato.stanford.edu/archives/spr2015/entries/ayn-rand/.
Bailey, A.D. (2014). 'Anti-Discrimination Law, Religious Organizations, and Justice,' *New Blackfriars* 95(1060): 727–38.
Baird, F.E. (2011). *Ancient Philosophy: Volume 1*, 6th ed. (Upper Saddle River: Prentice Hall).
Baker, A. (2013). 'Simplicity,' in E.N. Zalta (ed.), *The Stanford Encyclopedia of Philosophy* (Fall 2013 Edition), http://plato.stanford.edu/archives/fall2013/entries/simplicity/.
Barcalow, E. (2007). *Moral Philosophy: Theories and Issues*, 4th ed. (Belmont, CA: Thomson Wadsworth).
Baron, M. (2008). 'Virtue Ethics, Kantian Ethics, and the "One Thought too Many" Objection,' in M. Betzler (ed.) *Kant's Ethics of Virtue* (Berlin: Walter de Gruyter): 245–77.
____ (1995). *Kantian Ethics Almost Without Apology* (Ithaca: Cornell University Press).
Barry, B. (1995). *Justice as Impartiality* (Oxford: Clarendon Press).
Baumeister, R.F., Bratslavsky, E., Finkenauer, C., Vohs, K.D. (2001). 'Bad is Stronger than Good,' *Review of General Psychology* 5(4): 323–70.
Bazerman, M.H., Loewenstein, G.F., White, S.B. (1992). 'Reversals of Preference in Allocation Decisions: Judging Alternatives Versus Judging Among Alternatives,' *Administrative Science Quarterly* 37: 220–40.
Beauchamp, T.L., Childress, J.F. (2009). *Principles of Biomedical Ethics*, 6th ed. (Oxford: Oxford University Press).
Bedke, M.S. (2010). 'Might All Normativity Be Queer?,' *Australasian Journal of Philosophy* 88(1): 41–58.
Bedke, M.S. (2009). 'The Iffiest Oughts: A Guise of Reasons Account of End-Given Conditionals,' *Ethics* 119(4): 672–98.
Beebe, J.R., Sackris, D. (2015). 'Moral Objectivism Across the Lifespan,' http://www.acsu.buffalo.edu/~jbeebe2/Beebe%20Sackris%20MOAL.pdf, accessed July 16, 2015.
Bell, D. (2013). 'Communitarianism,' in E.N. Zalta (ed.), *The Stanford Encyclopedia of Philosophy* (Fall 2013 Edition), http://plato.stanford.edu/archives/fall2013/entries/communitarianism/.
Bell, J.S. (1987). *Speakable and Unspeakable in Quantum Mechanics* (Cambridge: Cambridge University Press).
Bentham, J. [1789]. *An Introduction to the Principles of Morals and Legislation* (Oxford: Clarendon Press, 1907).
Bettman, J.R., Luce, M.F, Payne, J.W. (1998). 'Constructive consumer choice processes,' *Journal of Consumer Research* 25: 187–217.
Blackburn, S. (1993). *Essays in Quasi-Realism* (Oxford: Oxford University Press).

Blair, R.J.R. (2003). 'Neurobiological Basis of Psychopathy,' *The British Journal of Psychiatry* 182(1): 5–7.
Bogen, J. (2014). 'Theory and Observation in Science,' in E.N. Zalta (ed.), *The Stanford Encyclopedia of Philosophy* (Summer 2014 Edition), http://plato.stanford.edu/archives/sum2014/entries/science-theory-observation/.
Botti, S. (2004). 'The Psychological Pleasure and Pain of Choosing: When People Prefer Choosing at the Cost of Subsequent Outcome Satisfaction,' *Journal of Personality and Social Psychology* 87(3): 312–26.
Boyd, R. (1988). 'How to be a Moral Realist,' in G Sayre-McCord (ed.), *Essays on Moral Realism* (Ithaca: Cornell University Press): 187–228.
Braibant, S., Giacomelli, G., Spurio, M. (2011). *Particles and Fundamental Interactions: An Introduction to Particle Physics* (Dordrecht: Springer Science & Business Media).
Bambrough, R. [1979]. 'Proof,' in R. Shafer-Landau (ed.) *Ethical Theory: An Anthology* (Malden: Blackwell, 2007): 103–10.
Brennan, J. (2014). *Why Not Capitalism?* (New York: Routledge).
Brickman, P., Coates, D., Janoff-Bulman, R. (1978). 'Lottery Winners and Accident Victims: Is Happiness Relative?' *Journal of Personality and Social Psychology* 36(8): 917–27.
Brink, D. (1989). *Moral Realism and the Foundations of Ethics* (Cambridge: Cambridge University Press).
Brock, G. (2015). 'Global Justice,' in E.N. Zalta (ed.), *The Stanford Encyclopedia of Philosophy* (Spring 2015 Edition), http://plato.stanford.edu/archives/spr2015/entries/justice-global/.
Burris, C.T., Rempel, J.K. (2012). 'The Crystal Globe: Emotional Empathy and the Transformation of Self,' *Consciousness and Cognition* 21(3): 1526–32.
Caney, S. (2005). *Justice Beyond Borders: A Global Political Theory*. (Oxford: Oxford: University Press).
Casey, B.J., Jones, R.M., Hare, T.A. (2008). 'The Adolescent Brain,' *Annals of the New York Academy of Sciences* 1124: 111–26.
Chappell, T. (2012). 'Climbing Which Mountain? A Critical Study of Derek Parfit, On What Matters,' *Philosophical Investigations* 35(2): 167–1.
____ (2010). 'Book Review. Self-Constitution: Agency, Identity, and Integrity. By Christine Korsgaard,' *Philosophy* 85(3): 425–32.
Cholbi, M. (2000). 'Kant and the Irrationality of Suicide,' *History of Philosophy Quarterly* 17(2): 159–76.
Clemence, G.M. (1947). 'The Relativity Effect in Planetary Motions,' *Reviews of Modern Physics* 19(4): 361–4.
CNN (2014). 'Secret Lives presents the Green River Killer,' http://transcripts.cnn.com/TRANSCRIPTS/1401/10/ijvm.01.html, accessed July 27, 2015.
Cohen, G.A. (2009). *Why Not Socialism?* (Princeton: Princeton University Press).
____ (2008). *Rescuing Justice and Equality* (Cambridge, MA: Harvard University Press).
____ (1997). 'Where the Action Is: On the Site of Distributive Justice,' *Philosophy & Public Affairs* 26(1): 3–30.
____ (1995). *Self-Ownership, Freedom, and Equality* (Cambridge: Cambridge University Press).
Cohen, Y. (2014). 'Don't Count on Taurek: Vindicating the Case for the Numbers Counting,' *Res Publica* 20(3): 245–61.

Cohon, R. (2010). 'Hume's Moral Philosophy,' in E.N. Zalta (ed.), *The Stanford Encyclopedia of Philosophy* (Fall 2010 Edition), http://plato.stanford.edu/archives/fall2010/entries/hume-moral/.

Cottingham, J. (1983). 'Ethics and Impartiality,' *Philosophical Studies* 43(1): 83–99.

Cover, J.A., Curd, M. (1998). *Philosophy of Science: The Central Issues* (New York: W.W. Norton & Company).

Craig, M.C., Catani, M., Deeley, Q., Latham, R., Daly, E., Kanaan, R., Murphy, D.G. (2009). 'Altered Connections on the Road to Psychopathy,' *Molecular Psychiatry* 14(10): 946–53.

Cudd, A. (2013). 'Contractarianism,' in E.N. Zalta (ed.), *The Stanford Encyclopedia of Philosophy* (Winter 2013 Edition), http://plato.stanford.edu/archives/win2013/entries/contractarianism/.

Cureton, A. (2013). 'A Contractualist Reading of Kant's Proof of the Formula of Humanity,' *Kantian Review* 18(3): 363–86.

Cushman, F., Young, L., Hauser, M. (2006). 'The Role of Conscious Reasoning and Intuition in Moral Judgment Testing Three Principles of Harm,' *Psychological Science* 17(12): 1082–9.

Dancy, J. (2013). 'Moral Particularism,' in E.N. Zalta (ed.), *The Stanford Encyclopedia of Philosophy* (Fall 2013 Edition), http://plato.stanford.edu/archives/fall2013/entries/moral-particularism/.

___ (2006). 'Non-naturalism'. In D. Copp (ed.), *The Oxford Handbook of Ethical Theory* (Oxford: Oxford University Press): 122–45.

___ (2004). *Ethics Without Principles* (Oxford: Oxford University Press).

___ (1986). 'Two Conceptions of Moral Realism,' *Proceedings of the Aristotelian Society, Supplementary Volume* 60: 167–87.

___ (1983). 'Ethical Particularism and Morally Relevant Properties,' *Mind* 92(368): 530–47.

Daniels, N. (2013). 'Reflective Equilibrium,' in E.N. Zalta (ed.), *The Stanford Encyclopedia of Philosophy* (Winter 2013 Edition), http://plato.stanford.edu/archives/win2013/entries/reflective-equilibrium/.

Darwall, S.L. (2014). 'On Sterba's Argument from Rationality to Morality,' *Journal of Ethics* 18: 243–52.

___ (2006). *The Second-Person Standpoint: Morality, Respect, and Accountability* (Cambridge: Harvard University Press).

Das, R. (2003). 'Virtue Ethics and Right Action,' *Australasian Journal of Philosophy*, 81(3): 324–39.

Dean, R. (2013). 'Humanity as an Idea, as an Ideal, and as an End in Itself,' *Kantian Review* 18(2): 171–95.

___ (2006). *The Value of Humanity in Kant's Moral Theory* (Oxford: Clarendon Press).

Debus, D. (2014). '"Mental Time Travel": Remembering the Past, Imagining the Future, and the Particularity of Events,' *Review of Philosophy and Psychology* 5(3): 333–50.

Denis, L. (2007). 'Abortion and Kant's Formula of Universal Law,' *Canadian Journal of Philosophy* 37(4): 547–80.

Descartes, R. [1641]. *Meditations on First Philosophy*, in D.A. Cress (trans.), *Discourse on Method and Meditations on First Philosophy*, 4th ed. (Indianapolis: Hackett): 47–99.

DiSalle, R. (2009). 'Space and Time: Inertial Frames,' in E.N. Zalta (ed.), *The Stanford Encyclopedia of Philosophy* (Winter 2009 Edition), http://plato.stanford.edu/archives/win2009/entries/spacetime-iframes/.
Dorsey, D. (forthcoming). 'Amorality,' *Ethical Theory and Moral Practice*, http://philpapers.org/rec/DORA-4, accessed July 28, 2015.
Driver, J. (2014). 'The History of Utilitarianism,' in E.N. Zalta (ed.), *The Stanford Encyclopedia of Philosophy* (Winter 2014 Edition), http://plato.stanford.edu/archives/win2014/entries/utilitarianism-history/.
Dworkin, R. (2000). *Sovereign Virtue* (Cambridge, MA: Harvard University Press).
Dyson, F.W., Eddington, A.S., Davidson, C. (1920). 'A Determination of the Deflection of Light by the Sun's Gravitational Field, from Observations Made at the Total Eclipse of 29 May 1919,' *Philosophical Transactions of the Royal Society* 220A: 291–315.
Elizondo, S.E. (forthcoming). 'Morality is its own Reward,' *Kantian Review*, available at http://philpapers.org/rec/ELIMII, accessed July 28, 2015.
Enoch, D. (2011). *Taking Morality Seriously: A Defense of Robust Realism* (Oxford: Oxford University Press).
Ersner-Hershfield, H., Garton, M.T., Ballard, K., Samanez-Larkin, G.R., Knutson, B. (2009). 'Don't Stop Thinking About Tomorrow: Individual Differences in Future Self-continuity Account for Saving,' *Judgment and Decision Making* 4: 280–6.
___, Wimmer, G. E., Knutson, B. (2009). 'Saving for the Future Self: Neural Measures of Future Self-Continuity Predict Temporal Discounting,' *Social Cognitive and Affective Neuroscience*, 4(1): 85–92.
Experiment Project (2015). 'I Wish I'd Never Had Children,' http://www.experienceproject.com/groups/Wish-Id-Never-Had-Children/219469, accessed July 27, 2015.
Fabienne, P. (2014). 'Political Legitimacy,' in E.N. Zalta (ed.), *The Stanford Encyclopedia of Philosophy* (Winter 2014 Edition), http://plato.stanford.edu/archives/win2014/entries/legitimacy/.
Facebook (2015). 'I Regret Having Children,' https://www.facebook.com/IRegretHavingChildren, accessed July 27, 2015.
Farquhar, P.H. (1984). 'Utility-assessment Methods,' *Management Science* 30(11): 1283–1300.
Farrelly, C. (2007). 'Justice in Ideal Theory: A Refutation,' *Political Studies* 55(4): 844–64.
Fiala, A. (2005). 'A Critique of Exceptions: Torture, Terrorism, and the Lesser Evil Argument,' *International Journal of Applied Philosophy* 20(1): 127–42.
Finlay, S. (2011). 'Errors Upon Errors: A Reply to Joyce,' *Australasian Journal of Philosophy* 89(3): 535–47.
___ (2008). 'The Error in the Error Theory,' *Australasian Journal of Philosophy* 86(3): 347–69.
___ (2007). 'Four Faces of Moral Realism,' *Philosophy Compass* 2: 820–49.
Fischer, J.M., Ravizza, M. (1998). *Responsibility and Control: A Theory of Moral Responsibility* (Cambridge: Cambridge University Press).
Fleming, P. (2015). 'The Normativity Objection to Normative Reduction,' *Acta Analytica*, available online at: http://link.springer.com/article/10.1007%2Fs12136-015-0255-y.

Flikschuh, K. (2009). 'Kant's Kingdom of Ends: Metaphysical, Not Political,' in Jens Timmermann (ed.), *Kant's Groundwork of the Metaphysics of Morals: A Critical Guide* (Cambridge: Cambridge University Press): 119–39.
Foot, P. (1972). 'Morality as a System of Hypothetical Imperatives,' *Philosophical Review* 81, reprinted in R. Shafer-Landau (ed.), *Ethical Theory: An Anthology* (Malden, MA: Blackwell): 153–9.
___ (1967). 'The Problem of Abortion and the Doctrine of Double Effect,' *Oxford Review* 5: 5–15.
Formosa, P. (2014). 'Dignity and Respect: How to Apply Kant's Formula of Humanity,' *The Philosophical Forum* 45(1): 49–68.
Fumerton, R. (2010). 'Foundationalist Theories of Epistemic Justification,' in E.N. Zalta (ed.), *The Stanford Encyclopedia of Philosophy* (Summer 2010 Edition), http://plato.stanford.edu/archives/sum2010/entries/justep-foundational/.
Gauch, H.G. (2003). *Scientific Method in Practice* (Cambridge: Cambridge University Press).
Gaus, G. (2011). *The Order of Public Reason: A Theory of Freedom and Morality in a Diverse and Bounded World* (Cambridge: Cambridge University Press).
Gauthier, D. (1987). *Morals by Agreement* (Oxford: Oxford University Press).
Gibbard, A. (1990). *Wise Choices, Apt Feelings* (Cambridge: Harvard University Press).
Giedd, J.N., Blumenthal, J., Jeffries, N.O. (1999). 'Brain Development During Childhood and Adolesence: A Longitudinal MRI Study,' *Nature Neuroscience* 2(10): 861–3.
Gilbert, D.T., Wilson, T.D. (2009). 'Why the Brain Talks to Itself: Sources of Error in Emotional Prediction,' *Philosophical Transactions of the Royal Society B* 364: 1335–41.
Glanzberg, M. (2014). 'Truth,' in E.N. Zalta (ed.), *The Stanford Encyclopedia of Philosophy* (Fall 2014 Edition), http://plato.stanford.edu/archives/fall2014/entries/truth/.
Glasgow, J. (2007). 'Kant's Conception of Humanity,' *Journal of the History of Philosophy* 45(2): 291–308.
Gottfredson, M.R., Hirschi, T. (1990). *A General Theory of Crime* (Stanford, CA: Stanford University Press).
Gowans, C. (2015). "Moral Relativism", in E.N. Zalta (ed.), *The Stanford Encyclopedia of Philosophy* (Summer 2015 Edition), http://plato.stanford.edu/archives/sum2015/entries/moral-relativism/.
Graybiel, A.M., Smith, K.S. (2014). 'Good Habits, Bad Habits,' *Scientific American*, June 2014: 39–43.
Greene, J.D. (2010). 'The Secret Joke of Kant's Soul,' in T. Nadelhoffer, E. Nahmias, and S. Nichols (eds.), *Moral Psychology: Historical and Contemporary Readings* (New York: Wiley-Blackwell): 359–72.
Grenberg, J.M. (2009). 'The Phenomenological Failure of *Groundwork III*.' *Inquiry* 52(4): 335–6.
Grether, D.M., Plott, C.R. (1979). 'Economic Theory of Choice and the Preference Reversal Phenomenon,' *The American Economic Review* 69(4): 623–38.
Guyer, P. (1996). 'The Value of Agency: The Practice of Moral Judgment. Barbara Herman.' *Ethics* 106(2): 404–23.
Hare, R.D. (1999). 'The Hare Psychopathy Checklist-Revised: PLC-R' (Toronto: Multi-Health Systems).

Hare, R.M. (1981). *Moral Thinking: Its Levels, Method and Point* (Oxford: Oxford University Press).
Harman, G. (2000). 'Moral Relativism Defended,' in G. Harman, *Explaining Value: And Other Essays in Moral Philosophy* (Oxford: Clarendon Press): 3–19.
Hart, S.D., Dempster, R.J. (1997). 'Impulsivity and Psychopathy,' in C.D. Webster & M.A. Jackson (eds.), *Impulsivity: Theory, Assessment, and Treatment* (New York: The Guilford Press): 212–32.
Herman, B. (1993). *The Practice of Moral Judgment* (Cambridge, MA: Harvard University Press).
Hershfield, H.E., Goldstein, D.G., Sharpe, W.F., Fox, J., Yeykelis, L., Carstensen, LL, et al. (2011). 'Increasing Saving Behavior Through Age-Progressed Renderings of the Future Self,' *Journal of Marketing Research: November* 2011, 48, No. SPL: S23–S37.
Hill, D.J. (2007). 'Ticking Bombs, Torture, and the Analogy with Self-Defense,' *American Philosophical Quarterly* 44(4): 395–404.
Hill Jr, T.E. (1995). '*The Practice of Moral Judgment* by Barbara Herman.' *Journal of Philosophy* 92(1): 47–51.
Hirschi, T. (2004). 'Self-control and Crime,' In R.F. Baumeister & K.D. Vohs (eds.), *Handbook of Self-Regulation: Research, Theory, and Applications* (New York, NY: Guilford Press): 537–52.
Hobbes, T. [1651]. *Leviathan*, in Sir W. Molesworth (ed.), *The English Works of Thomas Hobbes: Now First Collected and Edited* (London: John Bohn, 1839–45), 11 vols, Vol 3: ix–714.
Hodgson, L. (2012). 'Why the Basic Structure?,' *Canadian Journal of Philosophy* 42(3–4): 303–34.
Hoefer, C. (2015). 'Causal Determinism,' in E.N. Zalta (ed.), *The Stanford Encyclopedia of Philosophy* (Fall 2015 Edition), http://plato.stanford.edu/archives/fall2015/entries/determinism-causal/.
Holloway, M. (1995). 'The Practice of Moral Judgment.' *Review of Metaphysics* 48(3): 658–9.
Hooker, B. (2014). 'Must Kantian Contractualism and Rule-Consequentialism Converge?,' *Oxford Studies in Normative Ethics* 4: 34–52.
Hsieh, N. (2005). 'Rawlsian Justice and Workplace Republicanism,' *Social Theory and Practice* 31(1): 115–42.
Hume, D. [1751]. *An Enquiry Concerning the Principles of Morals* (Indianapolis: Hackett Publishing Company, 1983).
____ [1738]. *A Treatise of Human Nature*, reprinted in D.F. Norton and M.J. Norton, editors (Oxford: Clarendon Press, 2000).
Hursthouse, R. (2013). 'Virtue Ethics,' in E.N. Zalta (ed.) *The Stanford Encyclopedia of Philosophy* (Fall 2013 Edition), http://plato.stanford.edu/archives/fall2013/entries/ethics-virtue/.
____ (1999). *On Virtue Ethics* (Oxford: Oxford University Press).
Ito, T.A., Larsen, J.T., Smith, N.K., Cacioppo, J.T. (1998). 'Negative Information Weighs More Heavily on the Brain: The Negativity Bias in Evaluative Categorizations,' *Journal of Personality and Social Psychology* 75(4): 887–900.
Jackson, F. (1998). *From Metaphysics to Ethics: A Defence of Conceptual Analysis* (Oxford: Clarendon).
James-Griffiths, P. (2007). 'Creation Days and Orthodox Jewish Tradition,' *Creation Ministries International*, http://creation.mobi/creation-days-and-orthodox-jewish-tradition, accessed June 12, 2015.

Johnson, R.N. (2014). 'Kant's Moral Philosophy,' in E.N. Zalta (ed.), *The Stanford Encyclopedia of Philosophy* (Summer 2014 Edition), http://plato.stanford.edu/archives/sum2014/entries/kant-moral/.
____ (1997). 'Kantian Ethics Almost Without Apology,' *Philosophical Review* 106(4): 594–5.
Joyce, R. (2015). 'Moral Anti-Realism,' in E.N. Zalta (ed.), *The Stanford Encyclopedia of Philosophy* (Summer 2015 Edition), http://plato.stanford.edu/archives/sum2015/entries/moral-anti-realism/.
____ (2007). *The Myth of Morality* (Cambridge, UK: Cambridge University Press).
Kahn, S. (2014). 'Can Positive Duties be Derived from Kant's Formula of Universal Law?,' *Kantian Review* 19(1): 93–108.
Kahneman, D. (2011). *Thinking Fast and Slow* (New York: Farrar, Straus, and Giroux).
____ (2000). 'Evaluation by Moments: Past and Future,' in D. Kahneman & A. Tversky (eds.), *Choices, Values and Frames* (Cambridge: Cambridge University Press, 2000): Ch. 38.
____, Frederickson, B.L., Schreiber, C.A., Redelmeier, A. (1993). 'When More Pain is Preferred to Less: Adding a Better End,' *Psychological Science* 4: 401–5.
____, Wakker, P. P. & Sarin, R. (1997). 'Back to Bentham? Explorations of Experienced Utility,' *The Quarterly Journal of Economics* 112(2): 375–406.
Kant, I. [1797a]. *The Metaphysics of Morals*, in M.J. Gregor (ed.), *The Cambridge Edition of the Works of Immanuel Kant: Practical Philosophy* (Cambridge: Cambridge University Press, 1996): 363–603.
____ [1797b]. 'On a Supposed Right to Lie from Philanthropy,' in M.J. Gregor (ed.), *The Cambridge Edition of the Works of Immanuel Kant: Practical Philosophy* (Cambridge: Cambridge University Press, 1996): 605–16.
____ [1788]. *Critique of Practical Reason*, in M.J. Gregor (ed.), *Immanuel Kant: Practical Philosophy* (Cambridge: Cambridge University Press, 1996): 133–271.
____ [1785]. *Groundwork of the Metaphysics of Morals*, in M.J. Gregor (ed.), *The Cambridge Edition of the Works of Immanuel Kant: Practical Philosophy* (Cambridge: Cambridge University Press, 1996): 38–108.
____ [1772–96] *Lectures on Anthropology*, A.W. Wood and R.B. Louden (trs.) (Cambridge: Cambridge University Press, 2012).
Katsafanas, P. (2015). 'Nietzsche and Kant on the Will: Two Models of Reflective Agency,' *Philosophy and Phenomenological Research* 89(1): 185216.
____ (2011). 'Deriving Ethics from Action: A Nietzschean Version of Constitutivism,' *Philosophy and Phenomenological Research* 83(3): 620–60.
Kauppinen, A. (2014). "Moral Sentimentalism", in E.N. Zalta (ed.), *The Stanford Encyclopedia of Philosophy* (Spring 2014 Edition), http://plato.stanford.edu/archives/spr2014/entries/moral-sentimentalism/.
Kavka, G.S. [1985]. 'The Reconciliation Project,' in R. Shafer-Landau (ed.) *Ethical Theory: An Anthology* (Malden: Blackwell, 2007): 160–73.
Kekes, J. (2002). 'On the Supposed Obligation to Relieve Famine,' *Philosophy* 77(4): 503–17.
Kennett, J., Matthews, S. (2009). 'Mental Timetravel, Agency and Responsibility,' in M. Broome and L. Bortolotti (eds.), *Psychiatry as Cognitive Neuroscience: Philosophical Perspectives* (Oxford: Oxford University Press): 327–50.
Kim, H. (2004). 'The Unity of Kant's Categorical Imperative,' *Southwest Philosophy Review* 20(1): 75–82.

Kitcher, P. (1981). 'Explanatory Unification,' *Philosophy of Science* 48: 507–31.
Klein, P. (2015). 'Skepticism,' in E.N. Zalta (ed.) *The Stanford Encyclopedia of Philosophy* (Summer 2015 Edition), http://plato.stanford.edu/archives/sum2015/entries/skepticism/.
Kohl, M. (2014). 'Transcendental and Practical Freedom in the Critique of Pure Reason,' *Kant-Studien* 105(3): 313–35.
Korsgaard, C.M. (2009). *Self-Constitution: Agency, Identity, and Integrity* (Oxford: Oxford University Press).
____ (2008). *The Constitution of Agency* (Oxford: Oxford University Press).
____ (2007a). 'Autonomy and the second person within: A commentary on Stephen Darwall's the second-person standpoint,' *Ethics* 118 (1): 8–23.
____ (2007b). 'Facing the Animal You See in the Mirror,' *Harvard Review of Philosophy* 16: 2–7.
____ (1996a). *The Sources of Normativity* (New York: Cambridge University Press).
____ (1996b). *Creating the Kingdom of Ends* (New York: Cambridge University Press).
____ (1986). 'Kant's Formula of Humanity,' *Kant-Studien*, 77: 183–202.
____ (1985). 'Kant's Formula of Universal Law,' *Pacific Philosophical Quarterly* 66(1–2): 24–47.
Kuhn, T.S. [1977]. 'Objectivity, Value Judgment, and Theory Choice,' in A. Bird and J. Ladyman (eds.), *Arguing About Science* (New York: Routledge, 2013): 74–86.
Kuhse, H., Singer, P. (1985). *Should the Baby Live?: The Problem of Handicapped Infants* (Oxford: Oxford University Press).
LaFolette, H. (ed.) (2014). *Ethics in Practice: An Anthology*, 4th ed. (Malden: Wiley-Blackwell).
Lang, G. (2012). 'What's the Matter? Review of Derek Parfit, On What Matters,' *Utilitas* 24(2): 300–12.
Laudan, L. (1997). 'What About Bust? Factoring Explanatory Power Back into Theory Evaluation,' *Philosophy of Science* 64(2), June 1997: 306–16.
____ (1977). *Progress and Its Problems: Towards a Theory of Scientific Growth* (London: University of California Press).
Leiter, B. (2015). 'Nietzsche's Moral and Political Philosophy,' in E.N. Zalta (ed.), *The Stanford Encyclopedia of Philosophy* (Spring 2015 Edition), http://plato.stanford.edu/archives/spr2015/entries/nietzsche-moral-political/.
Levy, N. (2008). 'Counterfactual Intervention and Agents' Capacities,' *The Journal of Philosophy* 105(5): 223–39.
____ (2007). 'The Responsibility of the Psychopath Revisited,' *Philosophy, Psychiatry, and Psychology* 14(2): 129–38.
Lichtenberg, K. (1994). 'Moral Certainty' *Philosophy* 69(268): 181–204.
Lichtenstein, S., Slovic, P. (1971). 'Reversals of Preference Between Bids and Choices in Gambling Decisions,' *Journal of Experimental Psychology* 89: 46–55.
Lindman, H. (1971). 'Inconsistent Preferences Among Gambles,' *Journal of Experimental Psychology* 89: 390–7.
Lippert-Rasmussen, K. (2014). 'Justice and Bad Luck,' in E.N. Zalta (ed.), *The Stanford Encyclopedia of Philosophy* (Summer 2014 Edition), http://plato.stanford.edu/archives/sum2014/entries/justice-bad-luck/.
Listverse (2015). 'Top 10 Serial Killer Quotes,' http://listverse.com/2012/09/04/top-10-serial-killer-quotes/, accessed July 27, 2015.

Litton, P. (2008). 'Responsibility Status of the Psychopath: On Moral Reasoning and Rational Self-Governance,' *Rutgers Law Journal* 39(349): 350–92.

MacIntosh, D. (2014). 'Sterba's Argument from Non-Question-Beggingness for the Rationality of Morality,' *International Journal of Applied Philosophy* 28(1): 171–89.

MacIntyre, A. (1984). *After Virtue*, 2nd ed. (Notre-Dame: University of Notre Dame Press).

Mackie, J.L. (1977). *Ethics: Inventing Right and Wrong* (London: Penguin UK).

Macleod, A.M. (2010). 'G. A. Cohen on the Rawlsian Doctrine of the Basic Structure as Subject,' *Social Philosophy Today* 26: 153–163.

Mahon, J.E. (2006). 'Kant and the Perfect Duty to Others Not to Lie,' *British Journal for the History of Philosophy* 14(4): 653–85.

Marx, K. [1845]. *Theses on Feuerbach*, available online at https://www.marxists.org/marx/works/1845/theses/index.htm, accessed July 27, 2015.

Mason, E. (2015). 'Value Pluralism,' in E.N. Zalta (ed.), *The Stanford Encyclopedia of Philosophy* (Summer 2015 Edition), http://plato.stanford.edu/archives/sum2015/entries/value-pluralism/.

Maxwell, N. (2004). 'Non-Empirical Requirements Scientific Theories Must Satisfy: Simplicity, Unification, Explanation, Beauty.' *PhilSci Archive*, http://philsci-archive.pitt.edu/1759/, accessed July 27, 2015.

Mill, J.S. [1861]. *Utilitarianism*, Roger Crisp, ed. (Oxford: Oxford University Press, 1998).

Miller, R.W. (2014). 'From Rationality to Equality: Three Stages of Doubt,' *Journal of Ethics* 18: 253–264.

Mills, C. (1997). *The Racial Contract* (Ithaca: Cornell University Press).

Moellendorf, D. (2002). *Cosmopolitan Justice* (Oxford: Oxford University Press).

Moffitt, T. E. (1993). 'Adolescence-limited and Life-course Persistent Antisocial Behavior: A Developmental Taxonomy,' *Psychological Review* 100: 674–701.

Moore, G.E. [1904]. *Principia Ethica* (London: Cambridge University Press, 1960).

Morgan, S. (2009). 'Can there be a Kantian Consequentialism?,' *Ratio* 22(1): 19–40.

Mughal, M.A.Z. (2009). 'Time, Absolute,' in B.H. James (ed.), *Encyclopedia of Time: Science, Philosophy, Theology, and Culture*, Vol 3 (Thousand Oaks, CA: Sage): 1254–5.

Mulnix, J.W. (2011). 'Explanatory Unification and Scientific Understanding,' *Acta Philosophica* 20(2): 383–404.

Murphy, L.B. (2000). *Moral Demands in Nonideal Theory* (Oxford: Oxford University Press).

Myers, D. G., Diener, E. (1995). 'Who is Happy?,' *Psychological Science*, 6(1): 10–19.

Nagel, T. (2005). 'The Problem of Global Justice,' *Philosophy and Public Affairs* 33(2): 113–47.

____ (1970). *The Possibility of Altruism* (Princeton: Princeton University Press).

Nathanson, S. (2015). 'Act and Rule Utilitarianism,' *Internet Encyclopedia of Philosophy*, available at: http://www.iep.utm.edu/util-a-r/, accessed July 28, 2015.

Nebel, J. (2012). 'A Counterexample to Parfit's Rule Consequentialism,' *Journal of Ethics and Social Philosophy*: 1–10.

Nelson, W. (2008). 'Kant's Formula of Humanity,' *Mind* 117(465): 85–106.

Neufeld, B. (2009). 'Coercion, the Basic Structure, and the Family,' *Journal of Social Philosophy* 40(1): 37–54.
Nietzsche, F.W. [1887]. *On the Genealogy of Morals* (Oxford: Oxford Paperbacks, 2009).
Nowak A., Vallacher, R.R. (1998). *Dynamical Social Psychology* (New York: Guilford).
Nozick, R. (1974). *Anarchy, State, and Utopia* (New York: Basic Books):
Nussbaum, M. (2007). *Frontiers of Justice: Disability, Nationality, Species Membership* (Cambridge: Harvard University Press).
____ (1999). *Sex and Social Justice* (New York: Oxford University Press).
____ (1992). 'Human Functioning and Social Justice: In Defense of Aristotelian Essentialism,' *Political Theory* 20: 202–46.
Nyholm, S. (2015). 'Kant's Universal Law Formula Revisited,' *Metaphilosophy* 46(2): 280–299.
____ (2013). 'On Kant's Idea of Humanity as an End in Itself,' *European Journal of Philosophy*. doi: 10.1111/ejop.12057
Oerter, R. (2006). *The Theory of Almost Everything: The Standard Model, the Unsung Triumph of Modern Physics* (New York: Plume).
Okin, S.M. (1991). 'Justice, Gender, and the Family,' *Philosophy and Public Affairs* 20(1): 77–97.
____ (1989). *Justice, Gender, and the Family* (New York: Basic Books).
Olsson, E. (2014). 'Coherentist Theories of Epistemic Justification,' in E.N. Zalta (ed.), *The Stanford Encyclopedia of Philosophy* (Spring 2014 Edition), http://plato.stanford.edu/archives/spr2014/entries/justep-coherence/.
Otsuka, M. (2009). 'The Kantian Argument for Consequentialism,' *Ratio* 22(1): 41–58.
Pallikkathayil, J. (2010). 'Deriving Morality from Politics: Rethinking the Formula of Humanity,' *Ethics* 121(1): 116–47.
Parfit, D. (2011). *On What Matters*, Vols. 1&2 (Oxford: Oxford University Press).
Pauer-Studer, H. (2010). 'The Moral Standpoint: First or Second Personal?,' *European Journal of Philosophy* 18(2): 296–310.
Paul, L.A. (2015a). 'What You Can't Expect When You're Expecting,' *Res Philosophica* 92(2): 1–23.
____ (2015b). *Transformative Experience* (Oxford: Oxford University Press).
Pereboom, D. (1991). 'Is Kant's Transcendental Philosophy Inconsistent?,' *History of Philosophy Quarterly* 8(4): 357–72.
Piotrowski, N.A. (ed.) (2003). *Magill's Encyclopedia of Social Science: Psychology*, Vols. 1–4 (Pasadena: Salem Press).
Plato, *Complete Works*, J.M. Cooper (ed.), (Indianapolis: Hackett, 1997).
Pogge, T.W. (2001). 'What We Can Reasonably Reject,' *Noûs* 35(s1): 118–147.
____ (1994). 'An Egalitarian Law of Peoples,' *Philosophy and Public Affairs* 23(3): 195–224.
Popper, K. [1963]. *Conjectures and Refutations: The Growth of Scientific Knowledge*, 2nd edition (New York: Routledge, 2002).
Potter, Nelson (1993). 'What Is Wrong with Kant's Four Examples,' *Journal of Philosophical Research* 18: 213–29.
Prichard, H.A. [1912]. 'Does Moral Philosophy Rest on a Mistake?,' *Mind* 21: 21–37, reprinted in S.M. Cahn and P. Markie (eds.), *Ethics: History, Theory, and Contemporary Issues*, 5th edition (Oxford: Oxford University Press): 465–75.

Priest, G., Berto, F. (2013). 'Dialetheism,' in E.N. Zalta (ed.), *The Stanford Encyclopedia of Philosophy* (Summer 2013 Edition), http://plato.stanford.edu/archives/sum2013/entries/dialetheism/.

Quong, J. (2011). *Liberalism without Perfection* (Oxford: Oxford University Press).

Rawls, J. (2001). *Justice as Fairness: A Restatement*, E. Kelly (ed.) (Cambridge: Harvard University Press).

____ (1999a). *A Theory of Justice: Revised Edition* (Cambridge, MA: The Belknap Press of Harvard University Press).

____ (1999b). *The Law of Peoples, with 'The Idea of Public Reason Revisited'* (Cambridge, MA: Harvard University Press).

____ (1993). *Political Liberalism* (New York: Columbia University Press).

Richardson, H.S. (1997). 'Book Review: Kantian Ethics Almost Without Apology. Marcia W. Baron,' *Ethics* 107(4): 746–9.

Rivera-Castro, F. (2014). 'Kant's Formula of the Universal Law of Nature Reconsidered: A Critique of the Practical Interpretation,' *Journal of Moral Philosophy* 11(2): 185–208.

Rosati, C. (2014). 'Moral Motivation,' in E.N. Zalta (ed.), *The Stanford Encyclopedia of Philosophy* (Spring 2014 Edition), http://plato.stanford.edu/archives/spr2014/entries/moral-motivation/.

Roskies, A.L. (2012). 'Don't Panic: Self-Authorship Without Obscure Metaphysics,' *Philosophical Perspectives* 26(1): 323–42.

Ross, J. (2009). 'Should Kantians be Consequentialists?,' *Ratio* 22(1): 126–35.

Ross, W.D. [1930]. *The Right and the Good* (Oxford: Oxford University Press, 2002).

Russell, B. (2013). 'James P. Sterba, *From Rationality to Equality*,' *Notre Dame Philosophical Reviews*, https://ndpr.nd.edu/news/44599-from-rationality-to-equality/.

Sanders, J.T. (1988). 'Why the Numbers Should Sometimes Count,' *Philosophy and Public Affairs* 17(1): 3–14.

Scanlon, T.M. (1998). *What We Owe to Each Other* (Cambridge, MA: Harvard University Press).

Schafer, K. (forthcoming). 'Realism and Constructivism in Kantian Metaethics,' *Philosophy Compass*, available at: http://www.pitt.edu/~schaferk/ConstructivismCompass_bib.docx, accessed July 29, 2015.

Schaub, J. (2014). 'The Incompleteness of Ideal Theory,' *Res Publica* 20(4): 413–39.

Schlosser, M.E. (2011). 'Review of *Self-Constitution: Agency, Identity, and Integrity*, by Christine M. Korsgaard, 2009.' *Philosophical Quarterly* 61(242): 212–14.

Schmidtz, D. (2000). 'Islands in a Sea of Obligation: Limits of the Duty to Rescue,' *Law and Philosophy* 19(6): 683–705.

Schreier, H. M., Schonert-Reichl, K. A., Chen, E. (2013). 'Effect of Volunteering on Risk Factors for Cardiovascular Disease in Adolescents: A Randomized Controlled Trial,' *JAMA Pediatrics*, 167(4): 327–32.

Schumann, K., Zaki, J., Dweck, C. S. (2014). 'Addressing the Empathy Deficit: Beliefs about the Malleability of Empathy Predict Effortful Responses when Empathy is Challenging,' *Journal of Personality and Social Psychology* 107(3): 475–93.

Schupbach, J.N. (2011). *Studies in the Logic of Explanatory Power*. Dissertation, University of Pittsburgh, http://d-scholarship.pitt.edu/7885/, accessed July 27, 2015.

Schurz, G. (1999). 'Explanation as Unification,' *Synthese* 120(1): 95–114.
Schwitzgebel, E. (2015). 'Cheeseburger Ethics,' *Aeon*, http://aeon.co/magazine/philosophy/how-often-do-ethics-professors-call-their-mothers/, accessed July 15, 2015.
____ (2011). *Perplexities of Consciousness* (Cambridge: MIT Press).
____, Rust, J. (2012). 'The Moral Behavior of Ethics Professors: Relationships Among Self-Reported Behavior, Expressed Normative Attitude, and Directly Observed Behavior,' *Philosophical Psychology* (3): 1–35.
____, Rust, J. (2009). 'The Moral Behavior of Ethicists: Peer Opinion,' *Mind* 118(472): 1043–59.
Seevinck, M.P. (2010). 'Can quantum theory and special relativity peacefully coexist?' [preprint], http://philsci-archive.pitt.edu/8359/, accessed July 29, 2015.
Sen, A. (2009). *The Idea of Justice* (Cambridge, MA: The Belknap Press of Harvard University Press).
____ (1992). *Inequality Reexamined* (Cambridge: Harvard University Press).
____ [1980]. 'Equality of What?,' in S. McMurrin (ed.), *The Tanner Lectures on Human Values*, vol. 1, 1980 (Salt Lake City: University of Utah Press), reprinted in A. Sen, *Choice, Welfare and Measurement* (Cambridge: MIT Press, 1982): 353–69.
Serial Killer Calendar (2015). 'Serial Killer Quotes,' http://www.serialkillercalendar.com/Serial-Kilelr-quotes.html, accessed July 27, 2015.
Shafer-Landau, R. (2003). *Moral Realism: A Defense* (Oxford: Oxford University Press).
Shaw, L.L., Batson, C.D., Todd, R.M. (1994). 'Empathy avoidance: Forestalling Feeling for Another in Order to Escape the Motivational Consequences,' *Journal of Personality and Social Psychology* 67(5): 879–87.
Shoemaker, D.W. (2011). 'Psychopathy, Responsibility, and the Moral/Conventional Distinction,' *Southern Journal of Philosophy*, 49(s1): 99–124.
Sias, J. (2015). 'Ethical Expressivism,' *Internet Encyclopedia of Philosophy*, http://www.iep.utm.edu/eth-expr/, accessed July 27, 2015.
Sinclair, N. (2012). 'Moral Realism, Face-Values and Presumptions,' *Analytic Philosophy* 53(2): 158–79.
Singer, P. (1972). 'Famine, Affluence, and Morality,' *Philosophy and Public Affairs* 1(3): 229–43.
Sinnott-Armstrong W. (2014). 'Consequentialism,' in E.N. Zalta (ed.), *The Stanford Encyclopedia of philosophy* (Spring 2014 Edition), http://plato.stanford.edu/archives/spr2014/entries/consequentialism/.
____ (2011). 'Moral Skepticism,' in E.N. Zalta (ed.), *The Stanford Encyclopedia of Philosophy* (Fall 2011 Edition), http://plato.stanford.edu/archives/fall2011/entries/skepticism-moral/.
Skelton, A. (2012). 'William David Ross,' in E.N. Zalta (ed.), *The Stanford Encyclopedia of Philosophy* (Summer 2012 Edition), http://plato.stanford.edu/archives/sum2012/entries/william-david-ross/:
Slote, M. (2009). *Moral Sentimentalism* (Oxford: Oxford University Press).
Slovik, P. (1995). 'The Construction of Preference,' *American Psychologist* 50(5): 364–71.
Smith, M. (2015). 'Parfit's Mistaken Metaethics,' available at http://www.princeton.edu/~msmith/mypapers/ParfitsMistakenMetaethics.pdf, accessed July 22, 2015.

____ (2013). 'A Constitutivist Theory of Reasons: Its Promise and Parts.' *LEAP: Law, Ethics, and Philosophy*, 1: 9–30.

____ (2012). 'Agents and Patients, or: What We Learn About Reasons for Action by Reflecting on Our Choices in Process-of-Thought Cases,' *Proceedings of the Aristotelian Society*, Vol. CXII, Part 3: 309–31.

Steinhoff, U. (2013). *On the Ethics of Torture* (Albany: State University of New York Press).

Sterba, J.P. (2013). *From Rationality to Equality* (Oxford: Oxford University Press).

____ (2012). *Morality: The Why and the What of It* (Boulder, CO: Westview Press).

Stevenson, C.L. (1937). 'The Emotive Meaning of Ethical Terms,' *Mind* 46: 14–31.

Stocker, M. (1976). 'The Schizophrenia of Modern Ethical Theories,' *The Journal of Philosophy* 73(14): 453–66.

Stratton-Lake, P. (2014). 'Intuitionism in Ethics,' in E.N. Zalta (ed.), *The Stanford Encyclopedia of Philosophy* (Winter 2014 Edition), http://plato.stanford.edu/archives/win2014/entries/intuitionism-ethics/

Strawson, P.F. (1962). 'Freedom and Resentment,' *Proceedings of the British Academy* 48: 1–25.

Stuss D.T., Gow, C.A., Hetherington, C.R. (1992). '"No Longer Gage": Frontal Lobe Dysfunction and Emotional Changes,' *Journal of Consulting and Clinical Psychology* 60(3): 349–59.

Suddendorf, T., Corballis M.C. (2007). 'The Evolution of Foresight: What is Mental Time Travel, and is it Unique to Humans?,' *Behavioral and Brain Sciences* 30(3): 299–313.

Sumner, L.W. (1998). 'Is Virtue Its Own Reward?,' *Social Philosophy and Policy*, 15(01): 18–36.

Sussman, D. (2009). 'On the Supposed Duty of Truthfulness: Kant on Lying in Self-Defense,' in C.W. Martin (ed.), *The Philosophy of Deception* (Oxford: Oxford University Press): 225–43.

____ (2005). 'What's Wrong with Torture?,' *Philosophy & Public Affairs* 33(1): 1–33.

Svensson, F. (2010). 'Virtue Ethics and the Search for an Account of Right Action,' *Ethical Theory and Moral Practice* 13(3): 255–71.

Swanton, C. (2001). 'A Virtue Ethical Account of Right Action,' *Ethics* 112(1): 32–52.

Swinburne, R. (2009). 'What Makes a Scientific Theory Probably True,' in M.Y. Stewart (ed.), *Science and Religion in Dialogue* (Malden: Blackwell): 205–12.

Taurek, J.M. (1977). 'Should the Numbers Count?,' *Philosophy and Public Affairs* 6(4): 293–316.

Taylor, C. (1985). *Philosophy and the Human Sciences: Philosophical Papers 2* (Cambridge: Cambridge University Press).

Thoits, P. A., Hewitt, L. N. (2001). 'Volunteer Work and Well-Being,' *Journal of Health and Social Behavior* 42: 115–31.

Thomson, J.J. (2008a). *Normativity* (Chicago: Open Court).

____ (2008b). 'Turning the Trolley,' *Philosophy & Public Affairs* 36(4): 359–74.

____, Parent, W. (1986). *Killing, Letting Die, and the Trolley Problem* (Cambridge: Harvard University Press).

Timmons, M. (2007). *Disputed Moral Issues: A Reader* (New York: Oxford University Press).

____ (2005). 'The Practical and Philosophical Significance of Kant's Universality Formulations of the Categorical Imperative,' In B. Sharon Byrd & Jan C. Joerdan (eds.), *Jahrbuch für Recht Und Ethik*. Duncker & Humblot): 313–33.

____ (1998). 'Decision Procedures, Moral Criteria, and the Problem of Relevant Descriptions in Kant's Ethics,' In B. Sharon Byrd, J. Hruschka & J.C. Joerdan (eds.), *Jahrbuch für Recht Und Ethik*. (Berlin: Duncker & Humblot): 389–17.

Toner, C. (2014). 'The Full Unity of the Virtues,' *Journal of Ethics* 18(3): 207–27.

Tornado Hills (2015). 'Dahmer Quotes,' http://www.tornadohills.com/dahmer/quotes.htm, accessed July 20, 2015.

UnitedHealthGroup (2013). 'Doing Good is Good for You: 2013 Health and Volunteering Survey,' http://www.unitedhealthgroup.com/Newsroom/Articles/Feed/UnitedHealth%20Group/2013/0619StudyHealthVolunteering.aspx, accessed July 22, 2015.

Valentini, L. (2012). 'Ideal vs. Nonideal Theory: A Conceptual Map,' *Philosophy Compass* 7(9): 554–64.

Vallentyne, P., Van der Vossen, B. (2014). 'Libertarianism,' in E.N. Zalta (ed.), *The Stanford Encyclopedia of Philosophy* (Fall 2014 Edition), http://plato.stanford.edu/archives/fall2014/entries/libertarianism/.

Van Gelder, J.L., Hershfield, H.E., Nordgren, L.F. (2013). 'Vividness of the Future Self Predicts Delinquency,' *Psychological Science* 24(6): 974–80.

Van Fraassen, B.C. (1980). *The Scientific Image* (Oxford: Clarendon Press):

Van Roojen, M. (2014). 'Moral Cognitivism vs. Non-Cognitivism,' in E.N. Zalta (ed.), *The Stanford Encyclopedia of Philosophy* (Fall 2014 Edition), http://plato.stanford.edu/archives/fall2014/entries/moral-cognitivism/.

Varden, H. (2010). 'Kant and Lying to the Murder at the Door...One More Time: Kant's Legal Philosophy and Lies to Murderers and Nazis,' *Journal of Social Philosophy* 41(4): 403–21.

Varey, C., Kahneman, D. (1992). 'Experiences Extended Across Time: Evaluation of Moments and Episodes,' *Journal of Behavioral Decision Making* 5(3): 169–85.

Vaughn, L. (2009). *Bioethics: Principles, Issues, and Cases* (Oxford: Oxford University Press).

Velleman, J.D. (2013). *Foundations for Moral Relativism* (Cambridge, UK: Open Book Publishers).

Vessot, R.F.C., Levine, M.W., Mattison, E.M., Blomberg, E.L, Hoffman, T.E., Nystrom, G.U., et al. (1980). 'Test of Relativistic Gravitation with a Space-Borne Hydrogen Maser,' *Physical Review Letters* 45(26): 2081–4.

Vincent, N.A. (2013). 'Blame, Desert and Compatibilist Capacity: A Diachronic Account of Moderateness in Regards to Reasons-Responsiveness,' *Philosophical Explorations* 16(2): 1–17.

Wald, R.M (2010). *General Relativity* (Chicago: University of Chicago Press).

Wallace, R.J. (2014). 'Practical Reason,' in E.N. Zalta (ed.), *The Stanford Encyclopedia of Philosophy* (Summer 2014 Edition), http://plato.stanford.edu/archives/sum2014/entries/practical-reason/.

____ (2007). 'Reasons, Relations, and Commands: Reflections on Darwall,' *Ethics* 118: 24–36.

Walzer, M. (1983). *Spheres of Justice* (Oxford: Blackwell).

Ware, O. (2014). 'Rethinking Kant's Fact of Reason,' *Philosophers' Imprint* 14(32): 1–21.

Watson, G. (2007). 'Morality as Equal Accountability: Comments on Stephen Darwall's *The Second-Person Standpoint*,' *Ethics* 118(1): 37–51.

Weber, S., Habel, U., Amunts, K., Schnieder, F. (2008). 'Structural Brain Abnormalities in Psychopaths – A Review,' *Behavioral Sciences & the Law* 26(1): 7–28.

Weinrib, J. (2008). 'The Juridical Significance of Kant's "Supposed Right to Lie",' *Kantian Review* 13(1): 141–70.

Weirich, P. (2012). 'Causal Decision Theory,' in E.N. Zalta (ed.), *The Stanford Encyclopedia of Philosophy* (Winter 2012 Edition), http://plato.stanford.edu/archives/win2012/entries/decision-causal/.

Wiens, D. (2012). 'Prescribing Institutions Without Ideal Theory,' *Journal of Political Philosophy* 20(1): 45–70.

Will, C. M. (2014). 'The Confrontation between General Relativity and Experiment,' *arXiv:1403.7377v1*.

Williams, B. (1995). 'Internal Reasons and the Obscurity of Blame,' in B. Williams, *Making Sense of Humanity* (Cambridge. Cambridge University Press): 33–45.

____ (1981). 'Persons, Character, and Morality,' in B. Williams, *Moral Luck* (Cambridge: Cambridge University Press): 1–19.

Wilson, J.Q., Herrnstein, R.J. (1985). *Crime & Human Nature: The Definitive Study of the Causes of Crime* (New York, NY: Free Press).

Wilson, T.D., Gilbert, D.T. (2003). 'Affective Forecasting' *Advances in Experimental Social Psychology* 35: 345–411.

Wolf, S. (2012). 'One Thought Too Many': Love, Morality, and the Ordering of Luck, Value, and Commitment,' in U. Heuer & G. Lang (eds.), *Themes From the Ethics of Bernard Williams* (Oxford: Oxford University Press): Ch. 3.

____ (1982). 'Moral Saints,' *Journal of Philosophy* 79(8): 419–39.

Wood, A.W. (2011). 'Kant and the Right to Lie. Reviewed Essay: on a Supposed Right to Lie from Philanthropy, by Inmanuel Kant (1797),' *Eidos: Revista de Filosofía de la Universidad Del Norte* 15: 96–117.

____ (2008). *Kantian Ethics* (Cambridge: Cambridge University Press).

____ (1999). *Kant's Ethical Thought* (Cambridge: Cambridge University Press).

____ (1998). 'Kant on Duties Regarding Nonrational Nature,' *Proceedings of the Aristotelian Society Supplement*, LXXII: 189–210.

Yang, Y., Raine, A. (2009). 'Prefrontal Structural and Functional Brain Imaging Findings in Antisocial, Violent, and Psychopathic Individuals: a Meta-analysis,' *Psychiatry Research* 174(2): 81–8.

Ylikoski, P., Kuorikoski, J. (2010). 'Dissecting Explanatory Power,' *Philosophical Studies* 148(2): 201–19.

Young, W.E. (1998). 'Resentment and Impartiality,' *Southern Journal of Philosophy* 36(1): 103–30.

Zagzebski, L. (2004). *Divine Motivation Theory* (Cambridge: Cambridge University Press).

Zwolinski, M. (2015). 'Libertarianism,' *The Internet Encyclopedia of Philosophy*, available at: http://www.iep.utm.edu/libertar/#H3, accessed July 28, 2015.

Index

abortion, *see* applied ethics
Absolute Veil of Ignorance, *see* veil of ignorance
abstract
  moral reasoning, 134–5, 138, 190
  principles, 136, 200, 215
  values, 205–6
abstracting
  away from human and sentient ends, 5–6, 117, 128–30, 140, 145, 146–9, 155–7
  away from relevant facts, wrongly, 85, 190–3, 217
  away from particular ends; in Kant's ethics, 130, 143, 149; in Rawls' original position, 142–3
action-guidance,
  ideal amount of in Rightness as Fairness, 184–200, 227–9
  problems of, with existing moral theories, 184–5, 227–9
adolescents
  failure to care for future consequences, 46–7, 95, 134, 222, 224
  impulsivity in, 46–7, 95
  and mental time travel, 46–7, 134
  see also agents
affective forecasting, 54
agency
  causal basis of, 57–8, 62, 63, 81–2
  moral, nature of according to Rightness as Fairness, 46–7, 78, 155, 219
  See also deliberation; mental time travel
agents
  moral, 46, 147, 162, 171–4, 178, 219
    definition of, 155
  nonmoral, 46, 171, 172
  'questionable' moral, 46

agreement
  between one's present and future selves, 4–5, 76–9, 81–5, 92, 102, 107, 109, 111, 114
  based on mutual recognition of problem of possible future selves, 4, 5, 76–7, 80, 82, 83, 92–3, 104, 109, 116–8, 128–9
  higher-order, to determine moral relevance, 4–7, 76, 77, 83–5, 92–3, 116–7, 127–30, 140, 146, 148–9, 153–4, 163, 168–71, 173–80, 184, 202, 206, 208, 223
  universal, with all of one's possible future selves, 4–5, 76, 92–3, 102, 107, 111, 114, 116–7, 127–9, 138–9, 140, 146–8, 156, 167, 172, 184
  see also Categorical-Instrumental Imperative; original position; relevance
AI: Artificial Intelligence (2001), 126–7
Altruism, 34–5, 41
Altshuler, Roman, 78
Anarchy, State, and Utopia (Nozick), 216
animal behavior, 58–9, 165–6
animals
  actual negotiation with, 165–6
  capacities of, 46–7, 58–9, 95, 134, 165–6, 171, 222, 224
  interests of, 119–20, 124–6, 136, 155–7, 161, 165–6, 171–2, 175, 199–200
  negotiation with by proxy, 157, 175
  see also beings, sentient
antirealism, moral, 1–2, 12, 22, 31–32
applied ethics
  abortion, 138, 182–3, 211–3
  animals, ethical treatment of, 55, 126, 136, 145, 147–8, 151, 155–7, 161, 165–6, 171–2, 175, 198–200

applied ethics – *continued*
  development of natural talents, 186–7
  health care, 167–8, 170–1
  helping those in need, 186–9, 195–6
  gun control, 182, 211–3
  false promises, 186
  Kant's four cases, 7, 155, 186–8
  lying, 131, 186–8, 228
  organ transplantation, 7, 188–91, 196–8
  scarce medical resources, 7, 196–8
  suicide, 138, 186–8, 200, 228
  torture, 7, 12, 30, 181–3, 188–9, 193–4, 200–1, 228
  trolley cases, 181, 188–9, 191–4, 195, 200, 228
  world poverty, 89, 123, 179, 194–6, 228
Aristotle, 26
artificial intelligence, *see* beings
assistance
  ideal of, *see* Rightness as Fairness
  interests in, 163, 167–8, 180, 195–6, 199–200
  see also applied ethics; poverty
astronomy, 23
attitudes, reactive, 34
attributivism, 32
autonomy, 138, 142, 149, 181, 183, 184, 188, 224, 228–9

Bambrough, Renford, 12
bargaining, *see* negotiation, principled fair
basic structure, 214–5
Baumeister, Roy, 104
Bedke, Matt, 36–37, 40
beings
  affected by one's actions, 6–8, 147, 154, 174–5, 177–8, 182–3, 187, 189–90, 192–3
  human, 5–7, 39, 42–46, 53–70, 86–91, 94–6, 108, 110–11, 120–6, 132–3, 141, 145, 147, 149, 155–78, 191–2, 199, 204–5, 207–9, 217–9, 222, 224
  nonhuman sentient, 5–7, 39, 116–20, 124–30, 137, 140, 146–50, 153, 160–80

beliefs
  false, 6, 153, 163,
  self-evident moral, 2, 12, 30
  common moral, 20, 31–2, 135, 143, 188, 222
  considered, 2, 13, 20, 24
  role in action, 58–9, 61–4, 69
  see also face-value; equilibrium, reflective
'By Any Other Name' (1968), 69–70, 135, 224

capacities, *see* adolescents; animals; children; humans; psychopaths
categorical
  nature of morality
    a common assumption, 20–21, 36, 38–39, 43–4, 67–70, 136
    reasons to doubt, 39–40, 43–4, 68–70, 136–7
    and transcendental freedom, 70
  normative judgments, 132
  see also categorical imperative; imperatives
categorical imperative, the
  advantages of Rightness as Fairness over, 130–8, *see also* applied ethics
  and animals, 136
  applications of, *see* Kant's four cases; applied ethics
  arguments for obeying, 130–3
  formulations of
    humanity, 129–30, 138, 144, 204
    kingdom of ends, 129–30, 138
    universal law, 129–30, 138, 142
    unity of, 131, 133, 221
  interpretive challenges, 130–1, 138
  and Rawls' original position, 142–3, 144
  unverifiable by empirical science, 133–4
  see also imperatives, categorical
Categorical-Instrumental Imperative, The
  advantages on principles of theory-selection, 131–9, 218–29
  as equilibrium point, 104

Categorical-Instrumental Imperative, The – *continued*
  argument for
    background premises, 76–7, 79–91
    decision-theoretic, 94–103
    intuitive, 77, 91–97, 104–115
    not dependent on transcendental freedom, 81–2
    recursive aspects of, 95–6, 100, 108–9, 121, 169, 173, 176–7
    role of conscience in, 78, 110–11
    satisfies Firm Foundations, 79
  coherence with empirical research, 29–30, 44–7, 56, 103–4, 123, 133–6, 219, 222–7
  consequentialist features of, 138, 184, 222, 225–6
  contingency of, 67–70, 81, 135
  contractualist features of, 138, 184, 222, 225–6
  and costs, 6, 85, 87, 88, 90–1, 94, 103–4, 113, 157–9, 162–75, 177, 178–96, 199, 207–13, 215–7, 223
  deontological features of, 138, 184, 222, 225–6
  expected value of acting upon, infinite, 76, 78, 101–110, 114–115
  explains human behavior, 135, 138
  formulations of
    Humanity and Sentience, 5, 117–29
    Kingdom of Human and Sentient Ends, 5–6, 117, 128–9, 140, 146
    Moral Original Position, 129, 149, 153
    primary, 4, 76, 92–3, 116, 120, 124, 126–8, 129–30
    unity of, 117–30, 133, 147
  implications for political philosophy, 149–151
  intuitive nature of, 78, 104–8
  and mental time travel, 79
  reconciliation of opposing moral frameworks, 2, 7, 111, 152, 155–84, 224–6
  reconciliation of opposing political frameworks, 8, 111, 136, 206–12, 224–6
  recursive definition of moral relevance in, 4–6, 95–6, 100, 108–9, 121, 169, 173, 176–80, 184
  as (partial) solution to the problem of possible selves, 4–5, 75–8, 91–109, 111–5, 176–7
  satisfaction-conditions of, 6–7, 141, 147, 153, 155, 158, 200
    see also Moral Original Position; Absolute Veil of Ignorance
  unity of formulas, 5, 118–30, 139, 221
  virtue-ethical features of, 176–8, 184
  see also Rightness as Fairness; Four Principles of Fairness
Catfish (2015), 119–120
cheating
  infidelity, 119, 121
  on an exam, 48–54, 58, 61, 65–66, 82, 89, 93–6, 98, 100–2, 105, 109, 119, 121–3
children, 36; *see also* adolescents
choices
  free, 56–64, 72, 75, 80–2, 86, 88–90, 108–10, 123, 127, 130, 136, 145, 155, 164, 171–3, 197–8
  possible, 56–64
  see interests, dominant motivational
closed society, 141, 148
coercion
  defining, 162
  from false beliefs, 6, 161
  higher-order interest in avoiding, 160–4, 166
  ideal of avoidance and minimization, 6–7, 153–4, 223; *see* negative fairness
  indeterminate prior to making a decision, 163–4
  natural, 6, 160, 163
  by others, 160–1
  relevant sense of, 160–2
  self, 160–1
cognitivism, 1
coherence
  of one's possible ends, interest in, 159
  external, *see* theory selection

coherence – *continued*
  internal, *see* theory selection
  see diachronic
  see justification
  see Moral Original Position
coherentism, 24; *see also* reflective equilibrium
common observation, *see* observation
commonsense, moral
  appeals to in moral philosophy, 19–20, 24, 30–32, 67
  skepticism regarding, 30, 32, 34
communitarianism, 2, 8
compliance
  empirical research on, 136
  strict, 141, 145, 148, 149, 156
compromise, 34–35
conscience
  absence of, 35, 46, 93, 109
  fear of punishment in, 76, 78
  role in argument for the Categorical-Instrumental Imperative, 110–11
  role in argument for the Humanity and Sentience Formulation, 122
  as worry about future, 48, 62
consequences,
  capacities to appreciate, 46–7
  concerns for in the Moral Original Position, 184
  external, 53, 69, 76, 78, 120–1, 166
  future, 46, 61, 65, 90, 95, 109, 115, 122
  internal, 35, 46, 48, 50, 53, 65–6, 69, 89, 93–110, 118–27
  long-term, 50, 104, 122
  possible, 69, 78, 97
consequentialism, 2, 7, 82, 111, 135, 137, 154, 179, 181, 184–5, 189, 220–8
  see also interests; utilitarianism
conservatism, 210–11
consistency, diachronic motivational, 72–4, 159
constitutive
  elements of human flourishing, 26, 41, 221, 225
  elements of ideal rationality, 72

  see constitutivism
constitutivism, 33, 219, 227
constructed preference theory, 164
contingency of morality, potential, 67–70, 81, 135
contractarianism, 26, 40, 221, 225
contractualism, 2, 7, 221, 223, 229
Coolidge, Calvin, 210
cooperation,
  between one's present and future selves, 4, 67–70, 72, 78–85, 91–109
  non-cooperation, 214
  social, 148, 150, 225
cosmology, ancient Greek, 1, 10–11, 15
cosmopolitanism, 145–6, 150, 214
costs
  of diachronic motivational consistency, 72–74, 158, 162–3
  legitimately weighed against negative and positive fairness, 169–74, 182, 185, 189, 207, 210–11, 217,
  potentially indeterminate prior to negotiation, 163–7
  see also applied ethics
creationism, 15
Critique of Practical Reason (Kant), 106–7

Darwall, Stephen, 33
decision theory, *see* theory
deliberation
  moral, 76, 78, 134–5, 155–201
  practical, 2, 22, 33, 58–64, 87, 131–3
  Humean Model, 58–9, 62–3
  Hybrid Model, 62–64, 132, 155
  Kantian Model, 61–64, 132
demandingness
  over-, 179
  of morality, in Rightness as Fairness, 136, 179–81; *see also* relevance
deontology, 2, 7, 111, 135–7, 154, 184, 222, 226
Depression, The Great, 210
Descartes, René, 14

desires
  role in deliberation, *see* Humean Model; Hybrid Model; Kantian Model
  role in morality
    see Categorical-Instrumental Imperative
  see also interests
determinism, 57, 70, 81–2
development of one's natural talents, *see* applied ethics
diachronic
  cooperation with oneself, *see* cooperation; consistency, motivational
  see also agreement
dialecticalism, Sterba's, 33–34
dignity, 105, 108, 114, 130
disability, 145, 151, 165, 177
disagreement, moral
  legitimate, 183, 211
  illegitimate, 183
disappointment, potential
  aim of avoiding, *see* interests, in knowing the future; in not 'betting' on probable futures
  always possible, 102–3, 114
  minimized by Categorical-Instrumental Imperative, 103–9
divisiveness, 182, 212–3, 217
dominant motivational interests, *see* interests

education, moral, 43, 95, 104–5, 166
egoism, 34–35
élan vital, 22
Elizondo, Sonny, 106
emotional reactions, *see* interests, voluntary; semivoluntary
emotivism, 1, 13
empathy
  experiences of, 56, 78, 110, 120, 123, 125–7
  malleability of, 89, 125–6
  transformative, 55
empirical studies
  of ethicists, 39
  of human flourishing, 37, 41
  of mental time travel, 46–7, 133
  of ordinary moral judgments, 12, 30, 136
  of relationship between morality and prudence, 47, 56, 134, 222
egalitarianism, 2, 8, 141, 143–4, 202–6, 208–17; *see also* Libertarian Egalitarian Communitarianism
equality, 8, 142–3, 145–6, 205–6, 209–10, 212
equilibrium, reflective, *see* reflective equilibrium
end-in-itself, 130
epistemically responsible theorizing, 11–17; *see also* theory-selection
eudaimonism, 26, 37, 40–1, 221, 225
evolution, 11, 18, 31, 68, 127
experience
  first-personal, 34, 56–64, 77, 82, 88, 90, 132, 155, 171, 227
  second-personal, 33
  third-personal, 33–4, 58
  transformative, 54–6, 98, 123, 125
explanation, *see* theory-selection
expressivism, 1, 12–13, 32
external coherence, *see* theory selection

face-value, of moral language, 2, 12, 32
factory farming, *see* applied ethics
facts
  incontrovertible, 3, 14–16, 31
  moral, 1–2, 12, 22, 31–2, 226
  normative, 26–8
fair negotiation, *see* negotiation; Rightness as Fairness
fairness
  to oneself, 5, 40, 43, 67, 76, 78, 100, 105, 116, 186–7, 226
  to others, 40, 43, 67, 105, 115–6, 186–7, 226
  see justice; negotiation; Four Principles of Fairness; Rightness as Fairness
false promises, *see* applied ethics
family, 48, 52, 55–6, 112–5, 118–9, 124, 187, 205, 215

Index

Firm Foundations, *see* theory selection
first-personal perspective, *see* experience
flourishing, see *eudaimonism*; empirical studies
free will, 57, 61, 64, 70
friends, 13, 55, 84, 93, 112–3, 115, 120, 124, 169, 186–7
friendship, 164, 179, 228
Firm Foundations, *see* theory-selection
foundationalism, 31
Four Principles of Fairness
  applications of, 179–200, 206–17
  combined into analysis of rightness, 17, 154, 178–201, 206–17
  listed, 6–7, 153–4
  Principle of Fair Negotiation, 6, 154, 168–77, 183–92, 200, 207–9, 213, 217
  Principle of Negative Fairness, 6, 153–166, 170, 175, 184, 186, 189, 192–3, 199–200, 206–15, 223
  Principle of Positive Fairness, 166–168, 169–71, 173–6, 179–80, 182–5, 187, 189–92, 196, 200, 207–211, 213–7, 223, 228–9
  Principle of Virtues of Fairness, 6–7, 109, 154, 175, 176–8, 184, 190–3, 200, 208, 223, 226, 229
  see also Rightness as Fairness
fruitfulness, *See* theory-selection
future, possible
  events, 43, 44, 46, 51–3, 56, 64, 83
  psychologies, 43, 53–6
  choices, 43, 56–64
  See also selves; experience

Gauthier, David, 26, 40, 221
gender, 141, 145, 146, 151, 177
goals, motivational, *see* interests
good will, 106
Gorgias (Plato), 26, 37, 40
Groundwork of the Metaphysics of Morals (Kant), 7, 61, 186–8
gun control, *see* applied ethics
guilt, *see* conscience

happiness, see *eudaimonism*; empirical studies
health care, *see* applied ethics
helping those in need, *see* applied ethics
Herman, Barbara, 33, 132
higher-order interests
  in avoiding coercion, 158–62
  in determining moral relevance, 77, 83, 148
  in receiving assistance when in need and desired, 166–8
  in the Moral Original Position, 158–62. 166
Hobbes, Thomas, 26, 40, 221
home, purchasing a, 47–523, 57, 64, 71, 79–80, 83, 96, 158–9, 190
hospital, visiting a friend, 84, 169, 179
human rights, 143, 215
humanity
  Kantian conception of respect for, 12, 129–32, 134, 138, 142–5, 149–50, 185–6, 189, 204
  see also categorical imperative; Categorical-Instrumental Imperative
Humanity and Sentience Formulation, *see* Categorical-Instrumental Imperative
Hume, David, 33
Humean
  Model of deliberation, 58–9, 62–3
  reduction, 28–29
Hybrid Model of deliberation, 62–64, 132, 155

ideal theory, 141, 145, 203, 216–7
ideals, *see* Four Principles of Fairness
ignorance
  of the future as condition for morality, *see* omniscient evil being
  See also veil of ignorance
immoralist, 26, 32, 34–35, 40, 105, 219
immorality
  explanation of apparent rationality of, 77, 93–4, 108
  explanation of irrationality of, 77, 94–110

impartiality, 39, 179
imperatives, 38, 137
'impulsive being', 68–69
impulsivity, 46, 48, 63, 68–9
inclinations, 45, 47, 69, 80, 86–9, 95, 124
  see also interests, involuntary; and interests, semivoluntary
indeterminate moral status, 178–9, 192–3
infinite expected value of acting on the Categorical-Instrumental Imperative, 76, 100–110, 114–115
instrumental rationality, 3–4, 10, 24–41, 42, 45, 49–50, 61, 65–85, 87, 90, 93–115, 117–8, 129–30, 133, 137, 146–7, 155–67, 171, 174, 176, 178, 218–22, 225–7; *see also* instrumentalism
instrumentalism, principle of
  stated, 3, 10, 42, 75
  virtual universal acceptance of, 10, 24–27, 68, 218–20, 227
intentional action, *see* deliberation
interests
  conflict between present and future, 50–51, 72–74
  dominant motivational, 56–7, 64, 80–1, 87, 123, 126
  extrinsic, 108
  future, 4–6, 43–44, 50–7, 64–5, 67–8, 70–1, 74–7, 79–80, 82–4, 91, 93, 95–7, 99, 101, 107–8, 110–1, 116–7, 128, 132, 135, 140, 224
  higher-order, *see* higher-order interests
  in knowing one's future, 4, 42, 44, 48–53, 64, 74, 75, 85, 96–7, 99, 110
  in not betting on probable outcomes, 43, 49–53, 65, 71–72, 99
  in ordering one's present and future interests, 43, 50–51, 53, 64, 66–67, 74, 79, 83, 85, 91, 110
  intrinsic, 76–7, 82–5, 92, 97, 102
  involuntary, 4, 57, 76–7, 81, 85–93

  motivational, 3–5, 21, 22, 24, 28, 31, 35, 44–6, 54, 56–64, 66, 68, 72–3, 75–7, 80–1, 86–92, 116–18, 123–6, 159–61, 168, 173, 184, 219
  possible nonhuman-animal-regarding, 124–6
  possible other-human-regarding, 121–4
  possible sentient-being-regarding, 126–7
  present, 5, 44–53, 66, 71, 76, 78, 92, 94–5, 116
  prospective, regarding one's future, 2, 4–6, 30, 42, 44–53, 65–67, 96–7, 99, 110
  retrospective, regarding one's past, 4, 42, 44–52, 55; *see also* preference reversals
  semivoluntary, 4, 76–7, 79–81, 85, 88–93, 103, 107, 109, 111, 118, 123–5, 129, 133, 137, 147, 157–9, 162, 167, 171–4, 227
  shared, between present and future selves, 75, 77, 79, 81–2, 92, 97, 127, 129–30, 148, 167
  voluntary, 4, 57, 76, 79–85, 90–2, 97, 102, 123, 158–60, 171–3
internal coherence, *see* theory selection
intrinsic value, 12
introspection, unreliability of, 63
intuitionism, 13, 30–1, 219
is-ought gap, 28–29

Joyce, Richard, 40, 68
justice
  as fairness, 141–4
    Rawls' principles of, 142
  domestic, 141, 143, 144–5, 150–1, 213–5
  international/global, 145, 150–1, 214–5
  and animals, 145, 148, 151
  and emigration/immigration, 141
  and the family, 145–6, 151, 214
  and gender, 141, 145, 151

justice – *continued*
  and disability, 145
  and race, 141, 146
  and the workplace, 214
  scope of, 148, 214–6
Justice as Fairness: A Restatement (Rawls), 142
justification, epistemic; *see* coherentism; foundationalism; theory selection

Kahneman, Daniel, 54
Kant, Immanuel, 6–7, 13, 33, 61–63, 70, 106–7, 130–5, 138, 143, 185–6, 221
Kant's four cases, *see* applied ethics
Kantian
  critique of Rawls, 144–5
  interpretation, 143, 144
Kantianism, 12, 130–8, 181, 184, 189, 221, 223–8; *see also* neo-Kantian
Kantian Model
  of first-personal deliberation, 61–64, 132
  not a causal theory, 62
Kavka, Gregory, 26
Kelvans, 69–70, 135, 224
kingdom of ends, *see* categorical imperative
Kingdom of Human and Sentient Ends Formulation, *see* Categorical-Instrumental Imperative
King Jr., Martin Luther, 105
knowledge, moral, 12
Korsgaard, Christine, 33, 131–1, 227
Kuhn, Thomas, 14

language analysis, moral, 2, 24, 32–3
Law of Peoples, The (Rawls), 142, 144, 214
Leviathan (Hobbes), 26
liberal-democratic, 144, 209–10
libertarianism
  about free will, 57, 64, 70,
  political, 2, 8, 111, 135, 137, 138, 144, 146, 149–51, 202–13, 216–7, 223, 225–6

Libertarian Egalitarian Communitarianism, *see* Rightness as Fairness
liberty, 8, 145, 203–7, 210–2
lying, *see* applied ethics

Mackie, J.L., 22
Madoff, Bernie, 105
Mandela, Nelson, 105, 114
Marx, Karl, 40
'Mecha', *see* A.I.: *Artificial Intelligence*
mental time travel
  absence of in nonhuman animals, 46
  in children and adolescents, 46–47, 222
  in normal human subjects, 44, 222
  and psychopaths, 46–47, 222
  relation to moral responsibility, 44–7, 79, 133–4, 219, 223–7
mind-independent moral facts, 1, 22
Moore, G.E., 12
moral agents, *see* agents
moral dilemmas, *see* applied ethics
moral facts, *see* facts; mind-independent moral facts; realism
moralism, 195
morality as its own reward, 76, 78, 102–9, 114; *see also* Categorical-Instrumental Imperative
moral language analysis, *see* language
Moral Original Position, the
  derivation of, 146–149
  differences from Rawls' original position, 6, 141, 146–51
  interests in, 147–9, 155–78
  reasons for risk-avoidance in, 155–6
  specification of, 6, 129, 155–8
  see veil of ignorance, Absolute
moral psychology, *see* psychology
morally relevant actions, *see* relevance
motivational consistency
  costs involved in achieving, 72–74
  interests against, 73–74
  interests in, 159

Nagel, Thomas, 33
neo-Kantianism, 130–8
negative fairness, *see* Rightness as Fairness

negativity bias, 104
neglecting others, 52, 55, 73, 105, 108, 112, 187
negotiation
  of costs, 173–4, 178, 180–3, 186–7, 196, 207–8
  as a moral requirement, 183, 186–7
  of political issues, 183, 212–17
  of moral relevance, 174, 178, 180
  principled fair, 2, 6–7, 138, 155, 178–9, 182–5, 187, 189–92, 194, 196, 200, 208–9, 212, 217, 223, 224, 227, 229
  with animals; actual, 165–6; by proxy, 175, 199
  with nonhuman sentient beings, 6–7
  with other people, 6–8, 163–5, 174, 177–8, 186–7, 189, 191–4, 196, 198–200, 203, 207
  see also applied ethics; Four Principles of Fairness; Rightness as Fairness
Newtonian mechanics, 11, 17–19, 23, 38, 219
Nietzsche, Friedrich, 68
noncognitivism, 1, 12
nonhuman sentient beings, see animals; beings
nonideal
  self, 73–4
  theory, 145, 146, 216–7
noninstrumental requirements of rationality, see rationality
nonnaturalism, 1, 22, 219–20, 225–6
normativity
  categorical, 27, 36, 38, 68, 136
  instrumental, see instrumentalism
  teleological, 27
  see also Humean reduction; categorical imperative

observation
  common human
    as standard in everyday life and modern science, 11–17, 19
    definition of, 3, 9, 11, 14, 16
    not respected in moral philosophy, 12–13, 30–35, 218–20

  see also theory selection, Firm Foundations
  nature of, 16
omniscient evil being, 68–70
'one thought too many', 135, 179
organ transplantation, see applied ethics
original position
  critiques of, 144–6; verified by Rightness as Fairness, 149–51
  Rawls', 6, 140–44
  see also veil of ignorance, Moral Original Position
ought-statements, See normativity
outcomes
  desirable, 26, 108
  expected, 65, 77, 94, 98–114, 118–20
  improbable, 43, 50–2, 71, 78, 79, 83, 95, 97–100, 112–3, 118, 121–2, 126–7, 156, 175
  possible, 52, 97–8, 101, 108, 111, 121–2
  probable, 43, 48–52, 66, 71, 74, 77, 79, 95–101, 103–4, 108, 113, 118–9, 121–2, 155–6
  relevant, in problem cases, 97–8
  see also infinite; utility
overdemandingness, see demandingness

Parfit, Derek, 219–21, 223, 225–6, 228–9
parsimony, see theory selection
particle physics, 1, 17, 19–21; see also Standard Model
particularism, moral, 2, 185, 220
Paul, L.A., 54–55
personal identity, 45–6
Planet Earth (BBC), 119
Plato, 12, 26, 30, 32, 37, 40, 68, 216, 220
pluralism, moral, 2, 220, 226
Pogge, Thomas, 229
political
  debate, 8, 210–212
  divisiveness, 212–14, 228
  morality, 203, 205–7, 209–11, 223, 225–6

Political Liberalism (Rawls), 142
positive fairness, *see* Rightness as Fairness
possible
  events, 43, 44, 46, 51–3, 56, 64, 83
  psychologies, 43, 53–6
  choices, 43, 56–64
poverty, world
  Singer on, 179, 194
  see applied ethics
practical deliberation, *see* deliberation
practical identity, unified, 132; *see also* Korsgaard
practical reason pure, 13, 133, 137; *see also* deliberation.
preference reversals, 54–6
Prichard, H.A., 36–7, 39
principled fair negotiation, *see* negotiation; Rightness as Fairness
principles, *see* Four Principles of Fairness; justice; Rightness as Fairness; theory selection
prima facie duties, 30, 185, 189, 200, 220
probable futures, see outcomes
problem of possible future selves
  basis of, 42–74
  cases, 78, 82, 93, 97, 100–2, 118, 122, 124, 156, 159
  contingency of, 43–44, 67–70
  solution to, 75–115
problem-solving, moral
  in Rightness as Fairness, 155, 179–84
  traditional approaches, 154, 228–9
progressivism, 210
prohibitions, in Kantian ethics, 131
proxy, representing nonhuman animals' interests by, *see* animals
prudence
  empirical relationships to moral behavior, 56, 65–67, 69–74, 75, 134
  typically distinguished from morality, 29, 31, 70, 136, 220–22, 225–6
  unified with morality, in Rightness as Fairness, 137, 220–22, 225–6

see instrumental rationality; instrumentalism
pseudoscience, 14–15
psychology
  early-to-mid-20th century, 1, 11, 15
  see also capacities; empirical studies; mental time travel
psychopaths
  and instrumentalism, 24–7, 31, 218
  deficient in mental time travel, 44, 46–7, 134, 22
  deliberation in, 58–9, 63, 171
  empirical psychology, 44, 46–7, 63
  failure to appreciate morality's normative force in, 30, 32, 34, 68, 95, 134, 222
  focus on the present, 46–7, 48, 95, 222, 224
  impulsivity, 46, 68
  lack of empathy, guilt or remorse, 35, 55, 122
  moral responsibility, 44, 46, 69, 70
  quotations of, 59
public reason, 142, 144, 145–6, 148, 149, 151–2
punishment, fear of, in deliberation, 53, 69, 76, 78, 120–1
purchasing a home, *see* home

QALYs (Quality Adjusted Life Years), 196–8
quantum mechanics, 17–21, 70
quasi-
  categorical, 39, 136
  libertarian, 203, 207, 209–11
  egalitarian, 203, 210–11
  realism, 12
queerness, Mackie's argument, 22, 28

rationalism, moral, 1, 13, 130–133, 137; *see* reason, pure practical; Kantianism; neo-Kantian
rationality
  ideal, 72–3
  non-instrumental requirements of, 4, 72–74
  see instrumentalism; instrumental rationality

Rawls, John, 6, 140–156, 173, 214, 216
reactive attitudes, 34
'reactive beings', *see* interests, involuntary; and interests, semivoluntary
realism, moral, 1, 22, 31, 32, 226
reasons
  altruistic, 34–5, 126
  fundamentalism, 24, 219–20
  moral, 33–4, 220
  motivational, 36, 39, 72, 225
  normative, 36, 38–40, 72, 107
  self-interested, 34–5, 120–1
  'wrong kinds of', 36–40
  see also Humean reduction
reasonable rejectability, 2, 221, 223, 229
reconciliation
  of different moral frameworks, 7, 184
  of different political frameworks, 8, 202–3, 206–12
recursive nature of morality, *see relevance*
reflective equilibrium, *see* equilibrium
relativism, moral, 1, 144
relativity, Einstein's theory of, 11, 14–15, 17–21, 23, 38
relevance, moral, 4–6, 95–6, 100, 108–9, 121, 169, 173, 176–80, 184
Republic, The (Plato), 26, 30, 17, 40, 68
responsibility, moral, 34, 46, 78, 138, 219, 223, 225
revealed preference theory, 164
Roosevelt, Franklin Delano, 210
Roskies, Adina, 78
Ross, W.D., 185, 189, 220
Rightness as Fairness
  analysis of moral rightness, 7, 154, 178
  analyses of other deontic notions, 178–9
  Four Principles of, 6–7, 153–4
  Libertarian Egalitarian Communitarianism, 8, 202–3, 206–17
  Moral Original Position, The, 6, 129, 137, 140–1, 146–52, 153, 155–200, 221

Principle of Negative Fairness, 6, 153–5, 163–6, 170, 175, 184, 186, 189, 192–3, 199–200, 206–10, 215, 223
Principle of Positive Fairness, 6–7, 153–4, 166–71, 173–6, 179–80, 182–5, 187, 189–92, 196, 200, 207–11, 213–17, 223, 228–9
Principle of Fair Negotiation, 2, 6–7, 138, 155, 178–9, 182–5, 187, 189–92, 194, 196, 200, 208–9, 212, 217, 223, 224, 227, 229
Principle of Virtues of Fairness, 6–7, 109, 154, 175, 176–77, 184, 190–3, 200, 208, 223, 226, 229
principled fair negotiation, *see* negotiation
reconciliation of opposing moral frameworks in, 7, 184
reconciliation of opposing political frameworks in, 8, 202–3, 206–17
see also Categorical-Instrumental Imperative
risk
  changing levels of tolerance for, 48–51, 54
  interests in avoiding, 66–67, 79, 92–111

sainthood, moral, 104, 136, 179–81, 223
Scanlon, T.M., 219–20, 229; *see also* reasonable rejectability
scarce medical resources, 7, 196–198
Schwitzgebel, Eric, 180
second-personal perspective, 33
seeming-truth, *see* truth
self-evidence, *see* beliefs
self-interest, *see* egoism; instrumentalism
selves
  backward-looking, 54
  cooperation between present and future, 75–85, 91–3
  forward-looking, 54
  future, 4–6, 43–74, 75–8, 80–7, 92, 93, 105–6, 109, 111–14

selves – *continued*
  past, 4–6, 43–44, 45–74, 77, 82, 84, 113–4
  present, 4–6, 43–74, 50, 76–7, 79–80, 82–5, 91–3, 113, 116–8, 128–9, 148
  possible future, 4–5, 42–4, 47–74, 76–87, 91–129, 134–5, 137, 139, 147–8, 156–9, 169, 172, 184; identified in terms of the interests of all possible human and sentient beings, 118–27; infinite in number, 159
  see also problem of possible future selves; personal identity
sentimentalism, moral, 1, 24
shared interests, *see* interests
simplicity, *see* theory-selection
Singer, Peter, 179, 194–5
skepticism
  Cartesian, 14, 16
  moral, 2, 12, 22, 31–32
  science, 17
Smith, Michael, 44–45, 72–74, 157
Standard Model, of particle physics, 20–21
standpoint
  first-person, 34, 56–64, 77, 82, 88, 90, 132, 155, 171, 227
  second-person, 33
  third-person, 33, 58
Star Trek: The Original Series, 69; *see also* Kelvans
Sterba, James, 34–35
Stocker, Michael, 84, 169, 179
Strawson, P.F. 34
strict compliance, *see* compliance
suicide, *see* applied ethics
Sumner, L.W., 40–41
supererogation, 178

teenagers, *see* adolescents
theory
  decision, 4, 26, 71–2, 93, 97–103, 164,
  ideal, 141, 145, 203, 216–7
  nonideal, 145, 146, 216–7
theory of everything, physics, 20
Theory of Justice, A (Rawls)141–2, 216

theory selection, principles of
  all listed, 3, 9–10
  Explanatory Power, 3–4, 9, 20–21, 27–35, 40–41, 47, 137, 224–6
  External Coherence, 3, 9, 18–20, 47, 133–7, 222–3
  Firm Foundations, 3–4, 9, 14–27, 30–38, 40–41, 42–3, 58, 68, 75, 78–9, 117, 131–3, 147, 150–1, 218–20, 222
  Fruitfulness, 3, 10, 23, 27–35, 40–41, 47, 117, 137–8, 184–200, 227–9
  Internal Coherence, 3, 9, 17–18, 20, 133–7, 220–2
  Parsimony, 3–4, 10, 21–22, 27–35, 137, 226–7
  Unity, 3–4, 10, 21–22, 27–35, 40–41, 47, 137, 226
third-personal perspective, 33, 58
Thomson, Judith, 32, 36–37, 40
torture, *see* applied ethics
transcendental freedom, 62, 70, 133, 137–8
transformative
  empathy, 55
  experience, 54–56
triple-theory, *See* Parfit
trolley cases, *see* applied ethics
truth
  as compared to 'seeming-truth', 2–3, 9–22; *see* theoryselection
  nature of, 14
  normative, 25

unconditional value, 12, 33, 132, 136, 138, 142
United Nations, 194, 215
unified practical identity, 33
unity
  of morality and prudence, 21, 27–31, 137, 220–22, 225–6
  see categorical imperative; Categorical-Instrumental Imperative; Rightness as Fairness; theory-selection; virtues
universalizability, 2, 134, 136, 142, 185, 223

utilitarianism, 12, 82, 179, 181, 184–5, 189, 220, 223–4, 226–9

vegetarianism, moral, 125, 199–200
veil of ignorance
  Absolute, 6, 147, 155–60
  Rawls', 141–2, 145
virtue ethics, 2, 7, 37, 40–41, 184–5, 222–4, 227–8
Virtues of Fairness, *see* Rightness as Fairness
virtues, unity of the, 221
virtuous agent, 2, 184, 228
voluntary action, *see* choice; interests; free will

Walzer, Michael, 206
weighing, ideals and costs, 104, 169–74, 181–2, 185, 189, 207, 209–11, 217, 220
wellbeing, *see* flourishing
Williams, Bernard, 72, 179
wisdom, 66, 69–70, 94–5, 104, 185
Wolf, Susan, 135, 179
worrying, about the future
  in everyday life, 47–53, 65–7, 75, 78–9, 84, 95–7
  role in argument for the Categorical-Instrumental Imperative, 103–11

Once judged wrong
& do it, or plan to
do it anyways, then
deterrents come into
play — will not get
          caught
        — will not have (or feel)
          any guilt or shame
        — etc — joy
          or euphoria

The consensus of the RSI
is that A's IP is the (SAG), NOT
       ~~kind that Acts~~ for (in published literature)
The RSI does not ~~allow~~ take
~~a lasting position~~ the fact
~~why~~ position ~~in the literature~~
The 7-Mry position (proposition)

only to the   grounds claims
eyes of the   by scholarly
RSI are   to the Dr. ants
relevant.

ONE should:
  IN EVERY relevant XN
  voluntarily AIM to
    – AVOID the interests (ends)
      of any particular SENTIENT
      b'g (human or inhuman);
    AND instead Act on
      INTERESTS (or ends)
      it is INSTRUMENTALLY
      rATIONAL for all
      SENTIENT b'g's to
      ∪ley agree to share
        (given their D't
         interests, be they, volty,
         morally, or Semi-Jolty)

  Where relevant XNS
      are determined recursively
      as those w/ which it is
        instrumentally rational
        for 1's present +
        future self to Agree

    AND where
      1's present self wants to
      know and to advance
      1's future is
        (which, in the future,
         when such is
         present themselves,
         1 can voluntarily choose)

Code
Number
 879
 3368

Settling whether an opinion to determine
has filed reliability proof
when it has any support.